Dear Sahay,

So glad our paths
have crossed again,
& Gods willing perhaps
there is something
we can still do
together.

In the meanwhile
I hope you enjoy
this book.

All the Best,

[illegible]

9/17/2015

Advance Praise

We live in a world of constant change and there seems to be a new book out every day. Unfortunately, many of the latest books could be categorized as "fads" or rehashing similar ideas. *The Fractal Organization: Creating Enterprises of Tomorrow* is quite different. It builds on the previous work of the author, *Connecting Inner Power with Global Change: The Fractal Ladder* (Malik, 2009), and is based on a solid theoretical foundation from the fields of psychology, economics, anthropology, and behavioral science. It offers a unique view of change and system patterns. This book reviews the theory behind the fractal ladder, provides exercises at an individual or group level for reflection and learning, and provides reflections and analysis for individual, group, and organizational levels. (I enjoyed the Dark Knight and the Fractal for Progress section as a great example behind the theory.) The book is not intended to be an "easy read." One needs to spend time understanding the theory and the "fractal architecture" of physical orientation, vital orientation, and mental orientation. However, if you spend the time and study carefully the flow of ideas, you can gain a new perspective of systems and change.

—**Dr Dale Spartz**, Organization Development Executive

[This book] provides an empowering approach and set of tools for leaders to grasp how we can impact the systems in which we operate. It is easy to be discouraged by the layers of complexity within organizations and, indeed, national and global economies. Understanding fractals and the power of "being the change you wish to see" is equally liberating and as it is daunting. Malik provides a strong theoretical basis for the fractal approach and guides willing readers through to understanding by doing. Thorough, deep work.

—**Dr Diane Osgood**, Director, Business Innovation,
Virgin Management Limited

[This book] is a wonderfully creative, practical, and effective approach to enabling the sustainable and high-performing enterprise. It is the most comprehensive and clearest approach in the field for implementing the fascinating concept of fractal organizations. Business leaders who are looking for creative new ways to transform their companies would do well to take this field guide seriously.

—**Dr Ram Nidumolu**, CEO, InnovaStrat; HBR Author

The Fractal Organization Field Guide provides a unique perspective on how each of us can have a meaningful impact on the world and help move business society and the economy toward flourishing. In Part I, the book provides original theory and terminology. The exercises in Part II and the reflections in Part III help bring the theory to life and make it relevant for you and your life. It is likely that you will find some of the concepts challenging to understand (unless you are familiar with the context from Pravir's previous books) and some difficult to agree with. But if you suspend judgment, engage with the book with an open mind, and look for those ideas that resonate with you will be justly rewarded. Many of the propositions parallel those advanced by complexity theory, integral theory, and systems theory. And those related to the power of emotional resonance, authentic intention, and multi-level intervention are consistent with new scientific findings in neuroscience, positive psychology, and positive organization science.

—**Dr David Sherman**, Co-author, *Flourishing Enterprise: The New Spirit of Business*

I've been impressed with Pravir's work using fractal thinking specifically as it relates to managing change. The methodology in [this book] opens up perspectives not normally considered, that can lead to highly accelerated adoption of the change process.

—**Greg Souza**, Chief Human Resources Office, Stanford Children's Health

[This book] provides an insightful framework for building sustainable organizations. It is particularly valuable as it enables critical thinking in a world where we are fast hitting limits on several fronts. As a bonus, the book provides exciting practical exercises for individuals and organizations to ground the theory in real practice.

—**Dr Kailash Joshi**, Co-founder, The Indus Entrepreneurs; Former General Manager, IBM

Pravir Malik uncovers the mysteries of complex systems through definition of the underlying patterns of progress and their interplay in [this book]. He provides an elegant model that defines how one can see and make the change within the complex compartments of the world. He defines a framework for analyzing and thinking through the change of large scale connected systems and the wicked problems associated with them. This book is a game changing set of lenses with which to view life, business, growth, and progress. A powerful read.

—**Michael P. Hruska**, President/CEO, Problem Solutions, LLC

By calling attention to the fractal patterns that reside within and all around us, Pravir Malik has given us a set of keys to unlock our inner potential, enabling us to more fully partner with "progress" and ascend the fractal ladder. This concept is both evolutionary and revolutionary and has been proposed by some of our greatest thinkers, including Mahatma Gandhi who once said, "You must be the change you wish to see in the world." With great depth and heart, Malik goes beyond merely referencing this powerful quote, he offers readers a simple formula (via the physical, vital, and mental fractals) to "be" the change. This book makes the connection between the individual and the world we each helped create, while at the same time elevating readers' consciousness to envision and co-create an even brighter future.

—**Laura Gottlieb**, Director, Enterprise Learning and Development, Lucile Packard Children's Hospital at Stanford

There's a quote by Proust: "The real voyage of discovery consists not in seeking new landscapes but in having new eyes." [This book] can give one a new set of eyes, with which to see (and seek) the tiny kernels of progress within larger patterns of activity. I will tell you this book is not to be taken casually. This is a book to be discussed with peers, friends, and colleagues who, like you, are actively interested in becoming the change you wish to see in the world. The ideas presented in this book are bold and challenging. If you are looking for an easy read, I would advise you to look elsewhere. I recommend this book because the ideas within are worth the struggle.

—**Aaron E. Silvers**, Partner, MakingBetter

I had the pleasure of collaborating with Pravir last year. I love the way he has created a simple, organic system to encompass and systemize the complex world of us human beings, and extends it to businesses and economy in [this book]. This fractal system is not about jamming a few personal patterns; it is infinite in its very nature, and yet conforms to an elegant theory. Definitely a model for today's and tomorrow's companies and economies.

—**Ritu Raj**, Founder of Avasta, OrchestratorMail, Objectiveli, and Wag Hotels

Creating Enterprises of Tomorrow incisively portrays the class of fractals that are of critical importance in creating sustainable and dynamic organizations. This carefully researched and well written book takes the reader on a journey of insight from the "theory" of the fractal organization, "exercises" which seek to translate key elements of the fractal based world view into practical activities and "reflections" which apply logic to our daily challenges and problems, whilst offering ways to address them. A thought provoking read!

—**Roque De Souza**, General Manager–Global Sales, Telstra

The Fractal Organization

The Fractal Organization

Creating Enterprises of Tomorrow

Pravir Malik

SAGE | Response Business Books
www.sagepublications.com
Los Angeles • London • New Delhi • Singapore • Washington DC • Boston

First published in 2015 by

SAGE Response
B1/I-1 Mohan Cooperative Industrial Area
Mathura Road, New Delhi 110 044, India

SAGE Publications Inc
2455 Teller Road
Thousand Oaks, California 91320, USA

SAGE Publications Ltd
1 Oliver's Yard, 55 City Road
London EC1Y 1SP, United Kingdom

SAGE Publications Asia-Pacific Pte Ltd
3 Church Street
#10-04 Samsung Hub
Singapore 049483

Published by Vivek Mehra for SAGE Publications India Pvt Ltd, typeset in 10.5/13 pt Adobe Caslon Pro by Diligent Typesetter and printed at Chaman Enterprises, New Delhi.

Library of Congress Cataloging-in-Publication Data
Malik, Pravir.
The fractal organization : creating enterprises of tomorrow / Pravir Malik.
pages cm
Includes bibliographical references.
1. Organizational Change—Philosophy. 2. Organization—Philosophy. 3. Organizational sociology. I. Title.
HM796.M35 302.3'5—dc23 2015 2015013819

ISBN: 978-93-515-0244-9 (HB)

The SAGE Team: Sachin Sharma, Sandhya Gola, Anju Saxena, and Vinitha Nair

This book is dedicated to the Great Designer
who reflects His fullness in every part

Contents

List of Figures

Foreword

This is a different kind of business leadership book.

It is, in some sense, a book about archeology and architecture on a cosmic and commercial scale. It is informed by the author's extensive experience as a global consultant, but it is equally inspired by his profound desire to examine the metaphysical subtleties of the world and, indeed, the universe. This is a book that explores what might be called *the wholeness of the parts* in an effort to demonstrate the significance of patterns, specifically, fractal patterns, in our lives.

Pravir Malik adopts a fresh and daring perspective in an attempt to bridge the science of fractals with the larger world comprised of these smaller pieces. "From individual to institution, there are profound connections," he says. Malik explores these relationships at the micro-level and endeavors to highlight their accumulated power at the macro-level too.

By helping us become more aware of this elegant latticework that runs through nature and human life, from physics and biotechnology to business, Malik hopes to point out the way to a dramatically new kind of leader and organization. He aspires to share a model that encourages the growth of progressive, sustainable organizations.

Like the ancient Greeks and their notion of the atom—then considered the smallest particle of matter—Malik invites the reader on a journey into the fractal realm to show how patterns at this level are reproduced and reverberated throughout our social and cultural institutions, including our organizations. He is a firm believer in cultivating greater awareness of these patterns so that individuals can best contribute to human progress at all levels in the organization, community, nation, region, and world.

By combining theory with examples from his professional life as well as with exercises designed to enhance understanding of his model—one with roots in his previous book, *Connecting Inner Power with Global Change: The Fractal Ladder*—Malik provides readers with an ambitious and intriguing framework unlike any other.

Open-minded practitioners from all walks of life should find plenty of food for thought and reflection in these pages.

Dipak Jain
Director, Sasin Graduate Institute
of Business Administration and former Dean, INSEAD

Acknowledgments

Over the last two decades, I have read a magnificent poem, Sri Aurobindo's *Savitri*, many times. In the first book of this poem, *The Book of Beginnings*, a great yogi, Aswapati, overcomes all terrestrial and cosmic bonds after which, being free, he is able to travel anywhere in the creation. The second book, *The Book of the Traveler of the Worlds*, describes Aswapati's travels, which begins with his perceiving "The World Stair." This particular canto had a deep impact on me. I do not know for sure what the author intends with that canto, but my interpretation of it created a seed with which I began to view many different events around me and which has resulted in this book.

This canto consists of the following lines:

Amid the many systems of the One
Made by an interpreting creative joy
Alone it points us to our journey back
Out of our long self-loss in Nature's deeps;
Planted on earth it holds in it all realms:
It is a brief compendium of the Vast.
This was the single stair to being's goal.
A summary of the stages of the spirit,
Its copy of the cosmic hierarchies
Refashioned in our secret air of self
A subtle pattern of the universe.
It is within, below, without, above.
Acting upon this visible Nature's scheme
It wakens our earth-matter's heavy doze
To think and feel and to react to joy;
It models in us our diviner parts,
Lifts mortal mind into a greater air,
Makes yearn this life of flesh to intangible aims,
Links the body's death with immortality's call:
Out of the swoon of the Inconscience
It labours towards a superconscient Light.
If earth were all and this were not in her,
Thought could not be nor life-delight's response:
Only material forms could then be her guests

Driven by an inanimate world-force.
Earth by this golden superfluity
Bore thinking man and more than man shall bear;
This higher scheme of being is our cause
And holds the key to our ascending fate;
It calls out of our dense mortality
The conscious spirit nursed in Matter's house.
The living symbol of these conscious planes,
Its influences and godheads of the unseen,
Its unthought logic of Reality's acts
Arisen from the unspoken truth in things,
Have fixed our inner life's slow-scaled degrees.
Its steps are paces of the soul's return
From the deep adventure of material birth,
A ladder of delivering ascent
And rungs that Nature climbs to deity.

Particularly the lines—"A subtle pattern of the universe. It is within, below, without, above."—meant to me that being within, below, without, and above, in effect everywhere and perforce on a different scale, could be same as being a fractal. In this interpretation, the fractal consists of physical worlds, vital worlds, and mental worlds stacked one on the top of the other and forms part of the blueprint for all existence. While this canto has been written from a Seer's perspective and, therefore, perhaps cannot be rightly and clearly understood, unless one enters into the consciousness of the Seer, this book by contrast has been constructed primarily through observation and logic using reasoning applied across time. Hence, the book represents a very different perspective to try to arrive at through logic what is evident to a Seer.

"The World Stair" and other cantos in *Savitri* have been the central inspiration for this book, and to the author I remain ever grateful.

Other life experiences, particularly while working as a consultant to many global corporations, have provided insight into business operations and to the self-imposed shackles of mediocrity that bind so many of us to a life of compromise. In particular, through my work at ZS Associates, Ernst & Young, EDS, A.T. Kearney, The Concours Group, Conner Partners, Business for Social Responsibility, and last but not the least Stanford University Medical Center, each of which has a different value proposition and quite different operating cultures, I have been able to intersect with a large business on different fronts and in different ways through the years. To this set of life experiences and to the consulting organizations that allowed me to experience these, I remain thankful.

There have also been several individuals who—knowingly through direct help or unknowingly through extremely confrontational relationships—have helped me to learn a lot about myself. To the hand of progress behind both these groups of people and to these people themselves, I remain thankful.

There are also several groups of people who have helped make this book a reality.

First, I mention Vivek Mehra, Managing Director and CEO of SAGE Publications India, without whose support this book would perhaps have taken much longer to come to fruition. I am also thankful to Dr Sugata Ghosh, Former VP–Commissioning at SAGE Publications, who encouraged me to write this third book in a series, on fractals and organizations. I am grateful to Sachin Sharma, Commissioning Editor, and R. Chandra Shekar, Associate Vice President Commissioning at SAGE Publications, for working with me through several iterations of this book. Sachin, in particular, has helped shape the present incarnation of this book. I am grateful to Sandhya Gola, the Production Editor, for her work in leading the editorial processes that have shaped this book, and to Vinitha Nair for designing the cover. There are others at SAGE Publications, who have worked behind the scenes, and I am also grateful to them.

Part II of this book, Exercises, was developed entirely while I was at Stanford University Medical Center. I worked closely with Todd Prigge, the Director of Organizational Development, and we created Part II together. Todd has a wealth of experience in translating concepts into practical exercises and with his help we crafted a number of practical exercises so that the concepts in Part I, Theory, could be more viscerally felt by practitioners, consultants, and decision-makers alike. I am grateful to Stanford University Medical Center for allowing this collaboration to happen, and especially grateful to Todd for agreeing to collaborate with me on this.

I am grateful to Dean Dipak Jain, who so graciously agreed to author the Foreword for this book. Dean Jain taught me marketing when I was a student at Kellogg two decades ago. We have remained in touch through the years and have recently embarked on a separate book project together. This has afforded us a close interaction in the last couple of years. He is one of the wisest and yet most humble human beings I have met, and it filled me with joy to have him as a part of this project as well.

I am also grateful to Dale Spartz, Diane Osgood, Dave Sherman, Ram Nidumolu, Greg Souza, Kailash Joshi, Michael Hruska, Laura Gottlieb, Aaron Silvers, Ritu Raj, and Roque De Souza, who have endorsed this book. Each of them has been involved in or has followed my work on fractals closely.

At one point, I thought that *theory* was enough and that people needed to take time to understand it. This stance was clearly reflected in my third book, *Connecting Inner Power with Global Change: The Fractal Ladder*. Fortunately, this stance has shifted and through the last few years, the books I have written have had a greater practical aspect to them. This urge to a greater integration involving more parts of the complex human being has surfaced through the travail of time, and to the great Protagonist behind, I am eternally grateful for continuing to allow these shifts to happen.

To this Protagonist, this Great Designer, to whom this book is decicated, I remain ever grateful.

Introduction

In 2009, Malik proposed a metatheory for progressive organizational design and dynamics.[1] In this theory, all instances of an organization, from the smallest, like an idea or a person, to the largest, such as global markets and the planet Earth herself, are fractals: the essence of their way of being is repeated on both smaller and larger scales than themselves. There is, however, a particular class of fractals, that of progress, of which the fractal ladder is an ever-present manifestation, which spawns organizations that are truly progressive and sustainable in nature. In the scheme of things, this class of fractals is of critical importance, and to master its replication and to fully understand the impact it will have in creating sustainable and dynamic organizations is a practical necessity. This book will precisely perform this task.

The book will first review the theory of the fractal organization. In this theory, it becomes apparent as to how the largest and most strategic plays have to be architected from the smallest, assumption, perception, and behavior-based plays. Further, it becomes apparent that only a high degree of personal awareness such that these smallest plays can shift as per the fractal for progress will create sustainable enterprises. These insights are weaved together in Part I. In Part II, the individual and the organization have a chance to practice the important shifts and reinforce the concepts that will lead to the enterprise of tomorrow. In Part III, some practical analytics, using the framework presented in Part I, have been used to reinterpret many practical organizational and system problems, hence giving a further practical aspect to building the enterprises of tomorrow.

Part I, Theory, of this book will present the theory behind the *fractal organization*. Hence, Chapter 1, The Pattern, will introduce the building blocks and the pattern that is the basis of the *ubiquitous fractal*. The notion that life is a vast, interconnected, fractal system

[1] Pravir Malik, *Connecting Inner Power with Global Change: The Fractal Ladder* (New Delhi: SAGE Publications, 2009).

will be elaborated upon, and the key components of the fractal will be presented. Chapter 2, The Person Pattern, will look at the building blocks and pattern that manifests at the level of the person. Hence, fractal architecture will be leveraged in coming up with a definition of a person and further the necessity and importance of living one's uniqueness will be focused upon. In Chapter 3, The Business Pattern, we will look at the building blocks and a pattern that manifests in business. Hence, we will consider what it may mean to be a physically-led, a vitally-led, or a mentally-led business. In Chapter 4, The Economy Pattern, we will look at as to how this pattern has almost automatically appeared at the level of the economy and how certain parts of the pattern are associated with higher degrees of freedom. Furthermore, we will hypothesize that the global economy fractal is an expression of the individual way of being. In Chapter 5, The System Pattern, we will further explore as to how this pattern has spontaneously emerged across several different disciplines—physics, management thought and biotechnology, among others. Chapter 6, The Evolution Pattern, will look at the evolution of life on the Earth, and how the patterns that are emerging in different fields of life parallel this overarching or the base pattern. Some insights on the Internet economy and the energy industry will be brought to bear.

Chapter 7, The Fractal Ladder, introduces a synthesis of all the observations to link together the similar patterns appearing across different fields and systems, and in reality different *scales*, to illustrate a fantastic ubiquitous fractal, perhaps part of a signature of a conscious design or implicit aspiration behind things. In Chapter 8, Fractal Properties, we will examine properties in a fractal world. These become tools, devices by which one maneuvers through a very different world. In Chapter 9, The Nature of Progress—the way it interacts with and ultimately shapes the fractal ladder—will be examined.

Now armed with a basic framework, we arrive at the culmination of creating the enterprise of tomorrow. In Chapter 10, Remaking the Business World, we will look at what a business and a corporation may become as the fractal ladder continues to progress. Chapter 11, Creating the Enterprises of Tomorrow, will look at the shift in the required leadership, the need to recognize the path one is on, and the imperative recontextualization to shift this path.

Part II, Exercises, will translate key elements of the fractal-based world view into practical activities and exercises at the personal and workplace levels. These activities and exercises will be focused on shifting the root pattern at the base of complex organizational fractals to shift the organizational reality being experienced by corporations. These exercises will in effect provide a basis for a practical, new, unique, and powerful approach to positively altering organizational dynamics through the leveraging of fractal dynamics in the workplace.

The range of practical activities and exercises will consist of the following:

1. Recognition of fractal building blocks—physical, vital, and mental—in oneself and in circumstances around oneself.
2. Recognition of fractals in oneself and in circumstances around oneself, including those fractals that drive organizational operation.
3. Recognition of stalled or counter-fractals.
4. Shifting of fractals in oneself, and in circumstances around oneself.
5. Creation of the Sun-marked physical–vital–mental fractal.
6. Practical exercises to build physical-level fractal ladder capability, such as universality, influence, recursion, completion, evolution, matrixing, step-wise development, and feedback.
7. Practical exercises to build vital-level fractal ladder capability, such as intersection, flow, facilitation, and upscaling.
8. Practical exercises to build mental-level fractal ladder capability, such as world-wiseliness, mirroring, affirmation, integration, and uniqueness.
9. Practical exercises to build capability with other fractal ladder properties, such as alignment, aspiration, surrender, rejection, and love.
10. Practical exercises to recognize and align with deeper and formative drivers: knowledge and wisdom, mutuality and harmony, service and perfection, and courage and adventure.
11. Practical exercises to develop element and holistic leadership.
12. Practical exercises to recognize emergence of alternative futures.
13. Practical model for driving organizational change based on Sun-marked physical–vital–mental fractal.

Part III, Reflections, will apply the basic logic of the Sun-marked physical–vital–mental fractal to many practical problems and situations we are faced with daily to suggest ways to address them. While I will start the reflections with a personal experience of fractals, we will quickly move into reflections at more complex levels of organization. Hence, beginning with the individual level, we will move into the realm of organizational development and design, and then onto industry development, financial crises, and the general world of politics.

As Albert Einstein has said, we cannot solve a problem with the same consciousness with which it was created. This "Field Guide" helps us to viscerally experience another level of consciousness and to interpret and apply this consciousness to solve many of the problems we are currently faced with.

My invitation to each of the readers is to make the materials in this book the basis for a living relationship, and to this effect, I offer some of the contents on my website http://www.deepordertechnologies.com as a continual resource that further explores these concepts in practical ways. Any reader can also always contact me with questions and to engage in deeper dialog through leaving me a message at http://www.deepordertechnologies.com/contact/ or through emailing me directly at Pravir.Malik@deepordertechnologies.com.

PART I

Theory

PART

Theory

The Pattern 1

Focus: An introduction to the building blocks and the pattern that is the basis of the "ubiquitous fractal."

Key Concepts: Dichotomies of life | Life as a vast, interconnected system | Problems caused by lack of system's view | The fractal nature of the system | Why problems can persist | Effort required to alter the base pattern | Pattern should be self-evident and pervasive | Beyond geography and history: Earth–Sun dance | Phases of a day | Physical | Vital | Mental | DNA of the Earth | Building blocks | Formation of kernel | Nature of kernels | Isolated development of kernels | The base or ubiquitous pattern | Complete journey and emergence of identity | Incomplete journey | Triplicity and its bias | Fractal opposition | Rite of passage | Mentality and identity | Evolution of the Earth

A Single Human–Earth System

It has been said that we are all authors of our own lives, and depending on the attitude, perceptions, and thoughts that form the kernel of our being, we create realities that resonate with that kernel. As we look at the contemporary unfolding of life around us, we cannot at first sight but be struck by the juxtaposition of vast contraries. On the one hand, there is the beauty of nature, reflected in star and sun, tree, bird, and cloud, among her many constructs. On the other, man's progressive despoliation of it, apparent in the thoughtless extraction of nature's resources, and the often equally thoughtless constructs whether of steel, cement, or the myriad other compositions, ranging from cosmetics to elaborate electronics, resulting from incompletely conceived designs. On the one hand, there is the glint in the eye that hints at the implicit creativity, power, love, and possibility resident in each living being, and on the other, the continued exploitation, compression, slavery, and killing of all that possibility through senseless acts of inhumanity.

What is at the kernel of these contraries? How is it that such vast contraries sit side-by-side? If we are each authors of our lives, then what do we use as material to author such lives? This book seeks to make sense of these questions by theorizing a vast and interconnected system in which each person is the key to the system. For various reasons that will become apparent, this system is conceived as a fractal system, a fractal being a pattern that repeats itself on a different scale, and the power to alter it is theorized to reside with each person. It has been said, "Become the change you wish to see in the world." But how on earth can anything one does have an impact on the whole Earth, unless that is the implicit nature of the Human–Earth system. This book will explore the real power that each of us has, by examining the incredible fractal that connects the smallest entities in the system, with progressively larger constructs, finally culminating in the canvas of evolution itself.

If we are implicitly connected with the play of larger, more complex movements – whether of weather or markets or geopolitical stability – then it must be that who we are, what we say, and what we do are ultimately creating the problems that seem so far removed, and conversely, that who we are, what we say, and what we do can concretely and effectively solve these problems. It must also mean that the vast numbers of problems we find ourselves in, whether globally, nationally, regionally, or locally, are due to the continued misapplication or perhaps even lack of application of the power resident within us. Being a key part of the Human–Earth system, each of us influences it by our small acts and words daily – however, we do not realize this. We do not realize the extent of the power we are invested with.

Acting in the system, without knowledge of our actions on the system, creates the dichotomies we are faced with today.

The first step, hence, is to gain clarity into the nature of the system. If we are a central part of a single Human–Earth system, then by definition, realization of this will necessitate a significant shift in our conception of the system, since currently we do not consider the system to be of such a nature. Such a reconception may, as Einstein has suggested, allow us to solve life's problems, since as he observed, we cannot solve life's problems with the same consciousness that we have created them with. The consciousness that has created it is a lack of knowledge of what the system that we are an implicit part of is. The change in consciousness is the awakening to knowledge of what the system is, and consequently to a more guided play of what the result of our actions on the system is.

An Integrated Fractal System

How is it that a shift in thought or attitude can have an impact on the whole world? It is fine to talk of a ripple effect or a viral effect. It is my sense, however, that the only way that a shift at a small level – bounded by finite space and time – can have a profound effect on levels removed from it, is if the bounded space and time is intricately connected with all around it and, further, is connected in such a manner that the nature of the shift is replicated in larger and larger spaces progressively removed from it. A system of this nature, where a self-similar pattern repeats itself on a different scale, is none other than a fractal. It is my contention, thus, that we are all connected by a ubiquitous fractal system, and it is by this nature of the system that profound shifts in ourselves can cause profound shifts in the world.

A variation of this idea has been amply explored by Mandelbrot and others at the material or physical level. Apparently nature employs fractals in building many of her constructs. Thus, clouds, snowflakes, crystals, mountain ranges, lightning, river networks, blood vessels, coastlines, and broccoli, among many other constructs, have been created as fractals. There is an inherent simplicity and efficiency in this approach, since a small amount of information contained as a seed pattern can be replicated on a larger scale to build far more complex structures.[1] This idea is also highly consistent with Buckminster Fuller's work, who explored the notion of nature as a highly efficient designer,[2] employing techniques to minimize the use of energy. In this book, there is a radical extension to the idea of employing fractal systems to physical systems only, to apply it to complex behavioral systems such as persons, corporations, markets, and other complex systems. There has been some attempt by both Mandelbrot[3] and Elliott[4] to interpret financial markets in terms of fractals. It is worth noting that both their approaches focus on change in numbers or physical patterns, and are a special or limited case of the fractal model presented in this book. We will briefly review some of their key findings in light of the model presented later in the book.

By this very logic, it also becomes apparent why the systems we live in can remain so obstinately the same. Unless there is a profound shift in the pattern that lies at the base of the fractal, the fractal will remain the same. In fact, the base pattern of the fractal, reinforced through a whole system or society that has grown from it, provides an easy mold within which to continue to live out the base pattern. It requires substantial effort to shift the base pattern, but once that is done, the effects inevitably impact the rest of the system.

We should also note that at the leading edge of science, fractals are being recognized as the patterns of chaos.[5] When we consider the vast contradictions abound in our world at first sight, these come across as chaotic. On deeper examination though, as will become apparent through the course of this book, a deeper and in

[1] Benoît B. Mandelbrot, *The Fractal Geometry of Nature* (New York: W. H. Freeman and Co., 1982).

[2] Buckminster Fuller, *Synergetics: Explorations in the Geometry of Thinking* (New York: Macmillan Pub. Co., 1982).

[3] Benoît B. Mandelbrot and Richard L. Hudson, *The (Mis)Behavior of Markets: A Fractal View of Risk, Ruin, and Reward* (New York: Basic Books, 2004).

[4] A.J. Frost and Robert R. Prechter Jr, *Elliott Wave Principle: Key to Market Behavior* (Hoboken, New Jersey: Wiley, 2001).

[5] Please refer to: John Brigg, *Fractals: The Patterns of Chaos* (New York: Simon & Schuster, 1992); James Gleick *Chaos: Making a New Science* (New York: Penguin, 1988), as starters in this subject.

fact the causative order will be observed in the fractals that peep through the veils of apparent chaos.

In Search of the Base Pattern

If indeed we are part of a fractal system, then the critical observation is one of realizing what the pattern at the base of the fractal is. If this is not identified, then the fractal will never be known. If it is identified, then effective insight and power are potentially unlocked. One may look at a broccoli for hours, but unless one sees the self-similar broccolette repeating itself at progressively larger scales, the simplicity of the overall structure and the corresponding power to effectively alter it will remain a mystery. Further, if indeed we are part of a fractal system, then the *base pattern* of the system must be apparent in plain sight, else it cannot be a fractal system. Hence, regardless of the scale we choose to focus on, the self-repeating pattern should be evident.

It follows that the pattern must exist in many facets of our history and geography. While we could examine instances through history and across geography, we will leave such analyses to be discussed later in the book. For now and as the most fundamental of starting points possible, let us examine the deepest of our histories and among the vastest of our geographies, in the relationship between the Earth and the Sun. By definition, such a starting point would then be present as the play of history and geography unrolls. Imagine then the interaction between these defining entities through the ages. For eons, the Earth has revolved around the Sun. In that revolution, it has continually rotated around its own axis, thereby creating a rhythm of night and day, repeated endlessly. But look more deeply at that rhythm, and the three distinct phases seem to characterize the day.

As the Sun first breaks across the horizon, light is shed upon the constructs on the Earth, and in that light, there is an awareness of the boundary that defines each construct. Having awoken from slumber, each form, as it were, becomes aware of what it is—there is an awakening to the *physical* structure that defines it. As the Sun rises, the form becomes active, and in that activity as to what it is and what it stands for becomes clearer. The activity expresses its *vitality*, and in that vitality, there is interaction and experimentation and the vast play of one life-form with another. As the sun descends, so as to speak, and countless stars emerge in the sky, it is as though the myopia that had bounded our focused actions through the day is removed, and we begin to see the stage of our day from many more perspectives. The phase of vitality has yielded to a phase of *mentality*, where a relative increase in introspection, reflection, and consideration of many more points of view comes into focus.

These three phases – physicality, vitality, and mentality[6] – have repeated themselves day after day since the Earth and the Sun first began their mutual dance with each other. In this manner of seeing, just as the constant exposure to the Sun has filled up life forms with solar energy, so too the play of the mutual Earth–Sun movement has embedded these three phases into the very fibers of life. Perhaps it is fair to say that the DNA of the Earth, of circumstances on the Earth, is imbued with the physical, vital, and mental phases.

Physicality, Vitality, and Mentality

But what really does it mean to exist in a physical phase, in practical terms? The emphasis in this phase is on the structure, on what is made visible by the first play of light on things, by what the eye first sees, when it sees the object. It is not necessarily seeing what the object is doing or what the object is expressing, but it is seeing what the object is physically. The defining characteristic, the mantra of the phase can perhaps be thought of as "reality that is experienced by what one sees with the physical eye." The form is the focus, and the form tends to be synonymous with the established order of things. It exists. It has a high measure of stability or even rigidity to it. Once established, it takes a substantial passage of time to alter it. In other words, change is marginal and can only occur in bounds or limits

[6] The terms physical, vital, and mental were coined by Sri Aurobindo. Please refer to *Sri Aurobindo's Collected Works* (Pondicherry: Sri Aurobindo Ashram, 1950).

established by the structure. The structure has to be the basis of the change, and even when change does occur, it is incremental.

In the larger play of life, hence, the basis is seen as the physical form. It is the interaction of form with the form that creates other possibilities. This is the basis of creativity. Bring two gases together, for instance, and they will react in a particular way because it is the nature of the form of one gas to react in that precise manner with the form of another. Bring two children together, and it is the nature of the form that will cause them to play with each other. Bring two animals together, and depending on what type they are, they will play with, threaten, or devour the other. The system is a function of physical form, and just as there are fixed forms, so too, there are fixed laws that accompany the individual behavior of each form, and the interaction when one form is brought into proximity with another. In this view, nothing can change, because what is, is already determined by the form and the laws that accompany that form and the law that accompanies the interaction of form. In this play of life, if there is creativity, it is confined to the boundaries of the myriad laws already in place. Hence, it is marginal.

In the vital phase, the emphasis is on assertion of energy. In this phase, the life constructions are absorbed in a dynamic activity. They are now exercising their faculties in the play of life. Life constructions seek to assert themselves and grow through experimentation. It is as though the energy of the Sun is translated into an abundance of different kinds of energies. Each form, relatively dormant at the break of day, now finds its innate energies being released and exercised. This phase is about the interaction of energies. Some energies overpower others. Some express themselves in harmony with others. Some combine with others to create new forms of energies. The searching and humming of bees interacts with the attractiveness of flowers. People and markets seek to grow in whatever ways they can. All is alive with activity, and in this activity, the character and characteristics of each gets expressed and in one way or another, refined. The mantra of this phase is more likely "reality as experienced by assertiveness and the myriad play of energies."

In the larger play of life, hence, it is assertiveness and energy that dominates. The energy of each seeks to assert itself at any cost. It seeks to gather more energy by any means, and to establish its rule over other forms, that it may have a base by which to continue to increase its energy and exercise its assertiveness. There is vast experimentation in this phase, but it is not driven by thought or by order. There is a devouring to devour, a conquering to conquer, and it is perhaps the strongest and longest lasting energy that triumphs in the end. There is constant change of form in this configuration, but the essential drive remains self-assertion and conquest. Change will continue to occur so long as some forms' assertiveness is accomplished in the bargain.

The phase of mentality is characterized by an increase of introspection, reflection, and assimilation. It is as though with the dawning of the stars, the focus has shifted from here and now to the mysteries of the unknown. What does one stand for? What will happen tomorrow? Who is the one in the play of life? Why did today unroll the way it did? Such questioning leads to the meaning and perhaps even the trajectory of one's activities becoming clearer, and that which one is secretly or even overtly working toward, comes more to the surface. Such questioning leads to a progressive understanding of the meaning of not only oneself, but also of others in the vast play of life. And that questioning, to a deeper recognition that all forms exist for a reason, and just as the self exists for a purpose, so do all other selves. In such thought, the purpose of form and the purpose of energy can also become clearer. The mantra of this phase is perhaps best characterized as "life as experienced by thought and the idea."

Permutations of the Pattern's Building Blocks

The three fundamental building blocks of the all-present pattern are hypothesized to be this physicality, vitality, and mentality. These building blocks can occur separately or in different configurations, and depending on the explicit permutation forms one of the several seed-states that becomes the active kernel within us. That kernel then, through its implicit fractal power, gives birth to the reality that settles around each living being. When we talk of the contradictions of life around us, we will see, as the book develops, that it is the play of different fractal realities emanating from different seed-states that creates this condition. It is also, perhaps, the contradiction between the one implicit ubiquitous fractal, that we are yet to discover, and the myriad fractals so created from many different seed-states that also create the vast contraries juxtaposed among each other.

A kernel formed from the pure physical state would see the world as fixed and the notion of change beyond marginal limits as impossible. A kernel formed from a pure vital state would see the world as a constant flux of random energies, with domination by a particular energy determined by strength of energy. A kernel formed from a pure mental state would see the world as a changing and progressive play of ideas and ideals. But there could also be a combination of states that forms the kernels. Hence, it could be that a state dominates, and others, in a manner of speaking, serve it. It could be that the vital and mental states serve the physical state. In this permutation, the energies of the vital, and the thought power of the mental, would be subservient to the status quo embodied by the physical. Then all would be a play of prolonging yesterday's laws and yesterday's glories, through enforcement of energy and power and through rationalization of thought. Or, it could be that the physical and mental powers are subservient to the vital. Then, always it would be the strongest energy that would lead in the play of life, with physical structures being created to support this, and the power of mind being used to rationalize why a dominant energy needs to lead and being used to advance the play of that energy. Or it could be that the mental stance leads, with the physical and vital powers supporting its play. In this case, it would be the idea that leads, and physical structure and vital energy that offer themselves in advancement of the leading idea or ideal.

Each of these combinations could live as kernels in individuals and collectivities and, by fractal pressure, create the practical reality that those individuals and collectivities are embedded in. Then, when these different practical realities meet or intersect, vast contraries could come into existence. So long as individuals and collectivities are separate, the corresponding practical realities work themselves out according to the seed-state resident in them. Until quite recently, for example, much of our world functioned in isolated blocks, which also perhaps gave these seed-states a chance to express the possibilities resident within them more completely. Hence, we may find that some countries such as USA developed along more physical or material lines, as compared to other countries such as India, that relatively speaking have developed along more mental lines. Now, however, through rapid advancement of technology, increasing globalization, and increasing cosmopolitanism, the world has become more of a melting pot, and different practical realities are pressed against one another to create a number of vast contraries. But it may even be that some overarching fractal reality is using seeming contraries to more effectively work out its own reality. This process will be examined in more detail later.

The Base Physical–Vital–Mental Pattern

One can see that the fundamental building blocks either in isolation or in specific combination with one another can be the basis of a seed-state that then creates a reality consistent with its seed. At first sight, one could make the case for any of these combinations being the fundamental base pattern we had started our exploration of the fractal with. That is, physical, vital, and mental combining in any order whatsoever. If, however, we revisit the Earth–Sun dance in which the physical, vital, and mental states had arisen, and if we use the movement of the Sun as the key to discovering the potential order of the three fundamental states, we will see that the fractal pattern must be the progressive movement through the physical, vital, and mental states, in order. As the Sun interacts with the Earth, it does so in such a manner that it is the physical state that yields to the vital state that yields to the mental state. Hence, it is a progression through these three states in that order that becomes the base fractal pattern. And remember, we are saying that this is important because this is what is embedded in the DNA of life.

In another way of seeing, it is as though each of the phases feeds into the other and is a fundamental part of the whole that defines how each form comes into its own. It does not make sense to speak of one phase without reference to the others. Consider the example of a seed becoming a flower. One may think of the seed as being the physical beginning. It appears dormant and has precise boundaries observable with the eye. The phase of vitality is characterized by movement. Tendrils reach out. The play of energies is accelerated. The tendrils move toward the Sun, and the roots from the seed move deeper into the Earth. There is more give and take—gases, water and nutrients enter into the seed-tendril structure, and other compounds are simultaneously released. At the culmination of this, a flower emerges and then the meaning of the seed becomes clear. This is its identity, what it has stood for secretly in the play of things. This is its expression in the play of things. And yet, it required a passage through the three phases – physical, vital, and mental – to express that identity.

But imagine if the movement did not culminate in the reality of the flower. That is, the journey through the three states had been forestalled. Then, the possibility inherent in that creation would not be fully realized. Certainly, something would have been created, for that appears to be the implicit characteristic of life, but it would have been only a shadow of what was possible. Now imagine that the many movements across the Earth are not necessarily unfolding along the physical–vital–mental path, and further, that there are many movements that are in fact headed in the opposite or in lateral directions. What kind of Earth would this create? Likely one filled with many, many contradictions.

In the Earth–Sun dance, it is the interaction of the Sun with the Earth that creates a fundamental triplicity that forms have to journey through. This triplicity has started from the physical state, and if we objectively view the relative timing when humans, the potential mental beings, appeared on the Earth scene, it is recent. Hence, it is as though the existing triplicity itself is biased toward the physical state. That is, the vitality and mentality seen more in service of the physicality than the other way round. The fractal so created has taken on more of a characteristic of obstinately fortified structures prolonging the law of yesteryear. Hence, as strong as the natural physical–vital–mental path defined by the movement of the Sun in the Earth–Sun system is, it appears to be constantly held back by a long-standing fractal pointed in the other direction that seeks to maintain the rule of yesteryear. It is as though this opposition of fractals has created a rite of passage that we humans, potential mental beings, must pass through, in order to arrive at a realization of our identity. It is as though in order to cross through this rite of passage, the power of mentality and, hence, individuality must begin to shine in us, and the physical and vital powers must gladly offer themselves in service of the growing mentality, or emergence of our individuality. When this happens, the new-born power causes old orders to crumble, and the meaning of individuality and its inevitable impact on creating progressive change in the world becomes apparent. Note that we are not saying that the mentality is the secret of our identity. We are saying that with the expression of mentality that identity becomes clearer.

In the dance of the Earth with the Sun, the physical–vital–mental triplicity is reinforced daily. And yet, at the end of each day, there is a period of night that precedes the journey of the next day. Perhaps it is a deeper rest and assimilation that occurs in that time, and when the new dawn emerges, each construct is approaching the journey from a slightly new vantage point. Thus, not only is there a movement through three phases in a particular order, but there is a general intention of progress that seems to accompany it. In the vaster scheme of things, it is almost as though the Earth itself uses the passage defined by the triplicity to arrive at a reality in which the triplicity is itself transformed by the increasing light of the Sun, to thereby become another Earth entirely. What is the notion of identity in this? Is it that some implicit identity uses circumstance to define itself? This is a notion that will have to be explored further.

Summary

We have so far focused on identifying the fundamental pattern of a potentially ubiquitous fractal. We identified fundamental building blocks of the pattern, and further suggested that there is a meaningful order to the building blocks that when so arranged becomes the fundamental pattern that should be evident in any field of life. Such observations will need to be borne out in further chapters. We have also suggested that it is possible to create fractals through a different combination of the fundamental building blocks, and that when fractals emanating from these building blocks play themselves out, they result in vast contradictions in the play of life. In fact, the mental stage being relatively recent implies that even the ubiquitous fractal has a bias toward physicality in its natural expression. This creates an inherent opposition to progress. We have suggested that the opposition of these contrary fractals to the one ubiquitous and Sun-marked fractal forms a rite of passage, and in actively engaging this passage, true and progressive individualities are born. It is with the birth of such individualities that the real and progressive change happens and that the power resident in oneself can be seen to have a real effect on positive changes in the world. Though figuratively, we have suggested that the *Earth* and the *Sun* are real actors in the unfolding of life, and perhaps somehow give context and meaning to a ubiquitous fractal that may emerge or stand behind things, the role of *Earth* and *Sun* and individuality, and the purpose of the ubiquitous fractal have yet to be explored. This too will occur in subsequent chapters.

While these suggestions are hypotheses at this point, they will need to be borne out by further observations as we progress through the materials in this book. Nonetheless, we will use this pattern and possibility as our starting point.

The Person Pattern 2

Focus: A look at the building blocks and pattern as it manifests at the level of a person.

Key Concepts: Application of fractal architecture in the definition of a person | Kernel reality through fractal pressure | Creation of tendencies | Perpetuating the nature of the world | Countering of world's natural commerce with its creatures | Progression through Sun-marked fractal and identity | Tendency vs identity | Tendency fractal contrary to ubiquitous fractal | Progressive organization and mentality | Importance of questioning | Uniqueness working itself out through play of tendencies | Living one's uniqueness | Life pattern and Maslow's psychology | Expression of Earth through physical, vital, and mental masks | Earth becoming an Earth–Sun | Uniqueness as a creative force

Concept Recap and Introduction

In the previous chapter, we hypothesized that there is a ubiquitous fractal that connects an individual with the entire Earth system. It is by virtue of this fractal that an individual has the power of making a meaningful change in the world. While the notion of *meaningful* will be further developed as we read through the book, we already know from the discussion in the last chapter that at least this could mean the overcoming of contrary fractals emanating from potentially discordant kernels or base patterns in oneself. It could also mean the awakening or mobilization of the Sun-marked physical–vital–mental base pattern within oneself, by virtue of which the deeply embedded yesteryear-oriented Earth fractal can be overcome progressively. This is no trivial task and marks a rite of passage that will likely awaken something significant in the being.

We will begin this chapter with an examination of what the potential fractal building blocks—physical, vital, and mental—mean at the level of a person. We will then examine how these building blocks might combine with one another to create different *personalities*, *tendencies*, or *habits* that define who one is, consequently also blocking other possibilities in the being. In the context of these tendencies, we will examine what the Sun-marked physical–vital–mental movement might signify, and what might get released if this were to become a person's modus operandi. We will also look at what kind of pattern tends to emerge as one moves through his life.

The Architecture of a Person

In the Earth–Sun dance, the structure of a day is marked by three phases. Applying a similar architecture to each of the three fundamental building blocks, thereby also beginning to test if the easily evident fractal can indeed be used to arrive at a more complete conception of things, would mean that there are perhaps three ways to interpret the terms physical, vital, and mental in the context of a person. In the previous chapter, we had suggested that *physical* referred to structures that the eye can see, *vital* referred to energy flows of various kinds, and *mental* referred to thoughts and ideas. Let us, hence, use each of these orientations to hopefully gain more insight into each of the three terms as they apply to a person. That is, starting with the *physical* or structure-based orientation, let us focus on the terms physical, vital, and mental. Then, let us use the *vital* and *mental* orientations to revisit each of the three terms.

Under the physical orientation, *physical* would refer to the body itself. *Vital* would refer to the energy or flows in the body, whether of blood, nerve impulses, passage and digestion of foods, and flow of air, among other vital flows. *Mental* would refer to the intelligence embedded in the body by which each subsystem integrates holistically with the body system.

In the vital or energy-based orientation, we are broadly focusing on self-referencing flows of energy. Hence, at the *physical* level, such states of being would be the ones that focused attention on the body, such as: fatigue or inertia on the negative side, and flexibility, strength, or dexterity on the positive side. At the *vital* level, states of being would be ones that though primarily self-referencing, yet tended to be sparked by or to engender interaction with others. On the negative side, such states of being might be anger, depression, doubt, fear, jealousy, and pride, among others. On the positive side, such states of being might be courage, determination, humility, joy, and gratitude, among others. At the *mental* level, states of being would be related to the thought. Hence, on the negative side, these may be anxiety, mental noise, perturbing thoughts, and short-sightedness, among others. On the positive side, states of being might be more systematic thinking, increase of imagination, and ability to synthesize, with the caveat that this would take place with a bias around self-positioning or self-referencing, rather than for the sake of pure knowledge itself.

Mental or thought-based orientation would refer to the basic perceptions about oneself and the world. Hence, the *physical* level would refer to the notion that life and its possibilities are a function of physical structures. Life and thought emerge from physical reality and all possibilities are a function of form. Change must be dictated by what is possible at the level of form. The *vital* level would refer to the notion that life and its possibilities are a function of energies and interaction of energies. Assertiveness of energy, conquest of one energy by another, and possible combination of energies would be the rule of the game, and change would be driven by whatever energy was on the rise at the moment. The *mental* level would refer to the notion that life and its possibilities are a function of thoughts, ideas, and ideals. Possibility would be dictated by what thought can conceive. Physical form and play of energy cannot restrain thought. Thought is the master and change can occur at the speed of thought.

Figure 2.1 The Architecture of a Person

Building Block \ Orientation	Physical	Vital	Mental
Physical	Body	Physical states of being	Structure-based outlook
Vital	Bodily flows	Emotional states of being	Energy-based outlook
Mental	Body intelligence	Mental states of being	Thought-based outlook

Hence, having applied the three building blocks of the ubiquitous fractal to each of the building blocks themselves results in a more robust and elaborate definition of each of the elements in the context of a person. If, when randomly asked, a person were to define herself, she might suggest that she was an accumulation or conglomeration of the body, feelings and emotions, and thoughts. Applying the building blocks to each of these, however, results in a more complete sense of what each of these is, as we have just seen. This should not be surprising, given that we are hypothesizing that the three elements are embedded in the fiber of life, and hence application of them in elaborating or thinking about any construct must result in a more complete definition of what the construct stands for. The physical, vital, and mental building blocks, hence, have provided a basis of definition or at least partial definition of a person. This definition is summarized in Figure 2.1.

Creation of Tendencies

A more elaborate range of possibility resident in each of these blocks or states has been fleshed out through application of the physical, vital, and mental lenses. Yet, there will be peculiar and particular projections based on what is active or what leads in these states. In other words, particular kernels or base patterns in the person will, through force of fractal pressure, create a reality consistent with that kernel or kernels. We know that the kernels will be comprised of one of or some combination of each of the three fundamental building blocks. Depending on what part leads, the kernel will either be in alignment with the ubiquitous fractal or will be in opposition to it. In a person, however, the situation is made more complex because of the many combinatorial variations in the vital and mental beings. Hence, there are two levels that need to be looked at. Let us consider a few examples to illustrate this potential complexity.

Imagine someone who has a great love for food. At some point in the person's development, there may have been an association of satisfaction through consuming food. In terms of the interaction of the basic building blocks, it is entirely possible that there is a physical element in the being that feels its reality from continuing to imbibe various foods. There is then a vital element attached to it, say a feeling of happiness or joy that is associated with the eating. There may be a mental element attached to it where the person is planning as to what their next meal could be or even what they need to do in order to earn money to buy food. It seems these basic building blocks then join together, either through habit or perhaps some other process, to create a tendency of some sort. This tendency becomes a kernel in the person, and through virtue of the creativity embedded in each of the building blocks and, therefore, in the tendency itself, imposes its own reality that emanates out like a fractal. That tendency exists to fulfill its reality. The person who houses this tendency will, thus, likely spend a fair amount of their time planning for food because they know that eating gives him pleasure.

Or, consider, that when a child was growing up, they see displays of anger in their house. They also see how the person who exercises anger seems to get their way in the end. So, in this instance, anger, a vital element, takes the lead. There is a mental element attached to it – the thought that if one needs to accomplish something, they need to exercise anger in order to change circumstances. This vital–mental combination settles into a habit and, in doing so, attracts some kind of physical structure or sheath around it to give it permanence. This anger-based vital–mental–physical tendency now also exists and, like other creations, seeks to fulfill the meaning of its reality through exercising its raison d'être at every possible opportunity.

Consider another example of someone who loves to read philosophy. Perhaps it was the love for ideas that dawned on this person. This was the mental element. The joy that this activity provided drew energy to support the act of reading. This joy–energy vital conglomerate then became the vital element supporting the mental element. Force of habit drew some kind of physical structure to it, to give it permanence. This mental–vital–physical tendency, hence, came into existence and, like any other tendency, seeks to continue to perpetuate itself.

There are hundreds and hundreds of opportunities for tendencies of this nature to come into existence within any one person. The passage of life is a continual exchange between a person and his environment, and in that exchange, it will perhaps be the norm that the substance and norms of life will incarnate in the substance of the person. Another way of putting this is: there are many fractals that exist in the world, and as one enters into proximity with them, it is highly likely that materials or tendencies, or kernels, pass from those fractals into one's person. This is perhaps how the nature of the world is perpetuated. It cannot be any other way if there is reality to the fractal nature. For a kernel in some being somewhere exists to propagate itself—that is its nature. It is also the nature of constructs of Nature to receive these influences and often to imbibe them.

The Alteration of Tendencies

It is only when the Sun-marked physical–vital–mental fractal becomes active in one, that there is a counter-force that can alter the balance of the world's natural commerce with its creatures. It requires something of a different nature than the existing nature to alter the existing nature. And we have hypothesized that the existing nature is through eons of habit—a fractal that is led by the physical component more than anything else—and is therefore effectively pointed in the opposite direction to the ubiquitous Sun-marked physical–vital–mental fractal. Hence, it is only when the Sun-marked fractal can become active in oneself, that there is the possibility of the normal flow of interchange to change. The normal flow is one of the circumstances, environments, norms in society, or exercises of other personalities imparting something of their substance into the person. It is only when the person becomes an individual, a truly creative entity in the scheme of things, that this flow is reversed. It is then that something unique from within the person can begin to flow from within and alter external circumstances.

When one considers who they are, they see that really, practically speaking, they are beings of many habits. And these habits, as we have just seen, are emanations or the nature of tendencies that exist within oneself. One wakes up in the morning, and depending on the nature of sleep they had and the perceived demands of the day, there may be some of the several tendencies that exercise themselves: one calling to attention the disturbed sleep they just had—a tendency whose core element is vital, that is frustration, and whose mental element is the play of theories as to why this was and what could be done to promote a better sleep. Another, surfacing the fear with a presentation to be given later in the day. Next, exhibiting haste because one is already 10 minutes late, and so on. Later in the day, one walks into a room, and even if they felt quite grounded prior to that, the active vibrations of the other fractals swirling in that space and emanating from other people there, pull them into one or more different orbits or surfaces, matching tendencies from the host of *guests* they house within themselves.

Who is one, in all this? In the mutual Earth–Sun dance, the progression of the Sun through the day marked a movement through three phases: the physical, the vital, and the mental. This in itself is not the identity, but the identity is revealed through this progression. The myriad tendencies in ourselves clamber for their own expression, often at any cost. "So long as my desire is fulfilled right now," says one tendency, "I do not care for any consequences to myself or to another." And this is repeated by so many of these small voices, so many times a day, that even if one had a unique identity, it seems to recede into or to be left in the background. But what if the same pattern of progression as embodied by the Sun-marked physical–vital–mental pattern is similarly applied to each of the tendencies? Would this allow the identity to reveal itself? Let us look at this more closely.

Let us pick up one of the tendencies already considered. Say, the one of anger. This tendency is led by the vital element of anger. This is the nexus of its being. It is organized around this. Even though it has a mental element, one that believed that the exercise of anger is necessary to achieve things, it is not the same thing as altering the nature of the nexus in accordance with the progression exhibited by the Sun-marked physical–vital–mental fractal. Hence, each time this tendency exercised itself, if one could in a manner of speaking detach themselves from the active experience or the lure of its reality, they might be able to impose upon it another way of being. Perhaps progressive thought can be imposed upon the tendency to persuade it that more complete reason must be used each time that anger arises. Hence, through rationality, the accompanying mental element can perhaps be persuaded that anger in itself is not the way by which one's plans can be fulfilled. That tendency can be given a stronger and truly more rational mental element, by which the raison d'être of the tendency is altered.

The main point is that the fractal that this tendency is exhibiting is pointed in a direction contrary to what we are hypothesizing to be the ubiquitous fractal. So organized, it perpetuates its own reality, and it, by definition, cannot progress. In fact, it will likely strengthen its tendency to assert itself, always allocating or drawing more mental, vital, and physical elements to strengthen its central nexus of anger. By contrast, if a willingness to alter its components by yielding control to more progressive mental elements is admitted, its fundamental milieu is altered and progress becomes possible.

When such tendencies admit of the paradigm of progress, a whole different dynamic is set up in a person. We are not implying that progress is synonymous with being in a mental state all the time. In fact, as we have hinted at, and will hopefully make more concrete as the materials in this book develop, is that the physical, the vital, and the mental are all crucial components of a full existence, and each in fact needs the other not only for its own completeness, but also for the completeness of the whole. It is the nature of the organization that is of importance. And what we are suggesting as a paradigm of progressive and currently needed organization is embodied by what we are terming as the Sun-marked physical–vital–mental fractal.

This marks a progression of one stage to another in the order of physical to vital to mental, because as each of these powers of organization currently stands, a mental orientation allows the notion of progressive questioning and an idea-driven life, and at its limits, perhaps even movements such as intuition, inspiration, and revelation, that hint at or always show more clearly the limits of current constructs, and the possibilities that may exist if one were to truly continue a paradigm of progress.

When thus, we have myriad tendencies within ourselves, which in reality are expressions of a stagnated way of being, then how is it possible to enter into a phase of true questioning? The questions can be so many, and their power is in opening up the being to possibilities. But if we do not even reach that level of human possibility where established structures, established contraries, and established tendencies are questioned, how can we possibly move beyond them. If there is something else that life can offer us, how would we know that unless we are willing to ask the question? If the way that we are living is incomplete and if there are hidden powers and potentialities that are waiting to manifest, how would we know that unless we were willing to ask the question. But the question itself is not what is important, it is the attitude and the meaning of asking the question that is important. Do we ask because we truly do not know? Or do we ask because of some intellectual curiosity. In our progress, we must reach the stage of realizing that there are mysteries, perhaps pointed to by such a thing as a ubiquitous Sun-marked physical–vital–mental fractal that opens us from the inside out to a new level of possibilities.

In its essence the *physical* seems to indicate that which has already manifested. The mantra of the physical, let us remind ourselves, being "that which the eye can see." This marks the stability or the foundation on which future edifices may be constructed. This is the established order of things and is the result of all the efforts of the past. The *vital*, on the other hand, seems to indicate the present. There are plays of energies and forces tussling with one another to establish their respective rules of law. Recall that the mantra of the vital is "reality as experienced by the myriad play of energies." But what do these energies represent. In many instances, possibly yesterday's structures seeking to prolong their rule into tomorrow. In many instances, tomorrow's possibilities seeking to establish their forms today. That energy which wins today will establish tomorrow. The *mental*, by contrast, indicates the future. The mantra of this level, recall, is *life as driven by ideas*. And this hints at myriad possibilities. Seek refuge in the mind and this is where one can find release from the constriction of today. This is where one can soar on flights of fancy and imagine what is possible tomorrow. This is the great force that can analyze and be critical and open passageway into dreams and visions that ultimately becomes the stuff of life. Tomorrow's realities are today's ideas.

Hence, we are saying that at the level of a person, a general paradigm of the physical orientation yielding to the vital orientation yielding to the mental orientation is what is required to avoid stagnation. Avoiding stagnation implies that the myriad voices and habits emanating from yesteryear-pointed tendencies lose their hold over one's reality, thereby allowing other deeper possibilities to surface. If there is something one stands for, if there is uniqueness in one's self, it can never come to the surface unless all the easily surfacing movements lose their hold. The easily surfacing movements are those that live in established reality, either in one's self or in larger environments, and often represent a backward-pointing orientation rather than a progressive one. In allowing these to progress, thereby changing or dissolving them, something other than the common reality of yesterday has a chance of manifesting.

Depending on how far one is able to penetrate within oneself, it seems plausible that radically different possibilities could emerge. If one, for instance, were able to change or dissolve a small number of tendencies, then potentially a small number of new tendencies would manifest. Perhaps these new tendencies get their birth from new thoughts and attitudes, that one would prefer to exercise. If, on the other hand, one were able to do a deeper level of work and change or dissolve a much larger number of tendencies, then one might find that one's effective personality, who one is, has drastically changed. Something that one is deep within oneself, inherently, may manifest. Not ideas and attitudes adopted from some bestseller or popular new-age movement, but something that one inherently is within oneself, with powerful innate feelings, thoughts, and a unique way of being. This then could become the active kernel or base pattern of one's life and emanate out as a truly creative fractal, one that potentially altered life in the world. That is the point of this book.

The Emergence of Identity

As one considers the vast number of tendencies that exist within each person, a general question that arises is why the manifestation of these tendencies varies by person, especially if, as we are hypothesizing, birth of tendencies is generally a function of commerce with life. While there may be general tendencies that exist in all people, yet one person exhibits an almost unique combination of tendencies when compared with any other. Why is this so? It could be that in fact there is a certain uniqueness embedded in each person that works itself out through the play of tendencies resident in that person. By overcoming, causing progress of, or opening out these tendencies to the possibility of a general physical–vital–mental progression, it could be that as to what one stands for in one's self, gradually has a chance to manifest itself. Each person's rite of passage, though constituted of a general opposition comprised a number of self-born and backward-pointing fractals to the general physical–vital–mental fractal, is yet unique in the precise constituents of the opposing fractals. Overcoming the unique combination of contraries requires manifestation of a unique combination of inherent strengths or powers, which once manifested forms the basis of a new being, in general alignment with the ubiquitous Sun-marked physical–vital–mental fractal.

It follows that the sign of not living from one's uniqueness or core identity would mean that a person is continually afflicted by yesteryear-pointed tendencies that generate a mediocre living involved with trifle emotions, small wants and deeds, and habitual thoughts that one cannot really call one's own. Living one's uniqueness, on the other hand, would be marked by the absence of such trivialities and would potentially be accompanied by such dynamics as are the stuff of identity. This will require a separate and deeper examination and shall occur later in the book. It is also worthwhile reflecting on what ideal identities or kernels would be, if say, one were at the helm of a corporation, or a country, or even if were an artist, a musician, a writer, or an engineer, among other professions.

In the previous chapter, we had indicated that the physical–vital–mental pattern, if it is truly the base pattern of a ubiquitous fractal, must be evident in all aspects of life almost automatically. If we were to observe the general tendency of a person's life, we would see that, in fact, such a pattern does emerge of itself. Hence, in one's younger days, one is more concerned with establishing a secure base for life—ensuring that one has money and food and security for one's self and family. This is the physical phase. Later, perhaps more in the middle age, the general tendency is to experiment more. Once one has secured the basis of life, one is freer to assert one's self and engage other energies, knowing that there is a basis of security on which to act. Hence, there is a wider interaction with people, and more of a coming into one's own rhythm of life. This is the vital phase. Finally, after one has played in life, there is more of an introspective phase that dawns: a questioning of what really it is all about, an opening to deeper mysteries and possible realities, and perhaps even a reinterpretation of self in context to the larger picture. This is the mental phase.

Not surprisingly, this passage through life is consistent with Maslow's psychology[1] of the human being, embodied in his Hierarchy of Needs, that puts needs in a ladder-like or more precisely a pyramid structure, with physiological and safety needs at the bottom, the *physical* phase, belonging and esteem in the middle, the *vital* phase, and what he referred to as self-actualization, the *mental* phase, at the top. It was not that all human beings stepped through all phases of the pyramid. Rather, once one had taken care of the *lower* needs, then one was free to climb to higher needs. In fact, the lower needs once fulfilled provided the foundation by which the higher needs could exercise themselves. Whether he realized it or not, his model is a manifestation of the base pattern in our hypothesized ubiquitous Sun-marked physical–vital–mental fractal, and also an expression of how truer identity emerges.

In our Earth–Sun metaphor, it is as though Earth stood for a progressive being that grows through overcoming various obstacles that themselves have their basis in the physical, vital, and mental building blocks. It is as though in going through passages defined by the interaction of various physical, vital, and mental elements that the combination and general orientation of these building blocks can

[1] A.H. Maslow, A Theory of Human Motivation, *Psychological Review* 50, no.4 (1943):370–96.

alter, giving rise to an enhanced physical, vital, and mental combination. In a certain sense, it is as though the Earth were expressing itself through continually and progressively changing physical, vital, and mental masks. The changing masks themselves seem to be changing to imbibe more of the nature of the Sun. What started off as self-centered, small, and myopic seems through the action of the Earth–Sun dance to be assuming more of the nature of the Sun. That is, to become more timeless, vast, and self-radiating. But this should not be surprising. In this metaphor or model, the Sun has assumed a central place. Physicality, vitality, and mentality assume meaning because of it, and perhaps even are manifestations, on Earth, of basic principles of its being. Perhaps through the mutual Earth–Sun dance, the Earth becomes an Earth–Sun. Perhaps that is the meaning of identity and of uniqueness, and perhaps all obstacles are shadow states that when opened out to the natural progression marked by the Sun's movement across a day on Earth reveal that identity which is the unique play of the Sun in each formation of the Earth.

The manifestation of uniqueness or identity by definition becomes a creative force in the world. That is the notion of creation. By fractal pressure, anything that is created has its impact on the world. When the tendencies we had referred to earlier are created, they are just reinforcing what already has existed, and therefore their impact may not necessarily be felt because what they reinforce is what we are already used to. When something new is created, however, its effects are felt immediately. It becomes a force for change in the world. Hence, the true act of creativity is to be able to create something new in oneself. And life offers us hundreds of opportunities in a day to work toward this. Each time the action of a yesteryear-pointing tendency is felt, if we were able to recognize this and allow a movement of progress to infuse it, something of the innate uniqueness resident in each may be able to reveal a little more of itself.

Summary

In this chapter, we began by considering what physical, vital, and mental may mean in the context of a person. We found that application of the physical, vital, and mental building blocks to each of these orientations in fact resulted in a more elaborate definition of a person. We found that self-organizing combinations of these basic building blocks also resulted in myriad tendencies that through fractal pressure created the reality that a person may experience. We hypothesized that each of these self-organized fractals, drawn from the existing order of things, acts in general opposition to the Sun-marked physical–vital–mental fractal, and *addressing* these self-organizing fractals or tendencies becomes a rite of passage by which truer identity can manifest. We hypothesized that *addressing* each of these tendencies is synonymous to opening them out to the Sun-marked physical–vital–mental pattern that allows the tendency to partake of progress. Such progress, we hypothesized, is like imbibing more of the characteristic of the Sun into each formation on Earth. By virtue of its creation and the fractal reality that accompanies it, this truer identity becomes a force for change in the world.

How this change works out in the world will be the matter of further chapters.

The Business Pattern 3

Focus: A look at the building blocks and pattern as it manifests in business.

Key Concepts: Application of fractal architecture in definition of business | Three types of assets in physical orientation | Three types of flows in vital orientation | Three types of outlooks in mental orientation | Physically-led organization | Vitally-led organization | Mentally-led organization | Combinations and governance | Kernels or seed states and fractal pressure | Alignment of kernels with Sun-marked physical–vital–mental fractal | Opportunities for *rite of passage* multiplied | Stepping into a particular kernel at will | Fractal link between personal and business levels | Relationship of identity with Sun-like properties | Stringing of states and milieu of progress | Strengths and shortcomings of physical, vital, mental orientations | Business logic of integrating three orientations | Automaticity of Sun-marked physical–vital–mental fractal at business level | Shift in feeling and thought orientations in bringing about change | Validation of fractal model

Introduction

As in the previous chapter, we will begin our explorations of the ubiquitous fractal in the business world with clarification on the meaning of the terms physical, vital, and mental in the business world. We will look at as to how the different building blocks can combine in different ways to create a differently run business. We will also examine the necessity of the integration of all the building blocks in thinking about the running of a corporation. Finally, we will examine the link between the fractal at the personal and business levels, thereby beginning to make a logical case for the existence of the hypothesized fractal model.

Architecture of Business

When we began to interpret the meaning of physical, vital, and mental at the level of a person, we applied the components of the Sun-marked physical–vital–mental fractal pattern to each building block independently to arrive at a more robust sense for what each building block could mean at the level of the person. Remembering the physical mantra—"what the eye can see"—let us extrapolate what such an application could mean for the *physical* aspect or component of a business.

Under the physical umbrella, the *physical* state would refer to tangible, material assets possessed by a corporation. To elaborate, this may mean equipment, buildings, land, inventories, and product. The *vital* state under a physical umbrella or orientation would refer to assets that represented tangible, touchable energy, such as money or available cash of a company. The *mental* state would represent assets of an intangible nature, such as the brand, the goodwill, and the intellectual property of the company. We had suggested earlier that the physical represents the past, the result of all the ideas and energies that had played out to create the foundation of tomorrow's world. Assets are such a representation of the past results of organizational action and, therefore, belong to the physical realm.

Remembering the vital mantra—"the play of energies"—let us extrapolate what that could mean for a business. Under a vital umbrella or orientation, the *physical* state would refer to the flow of goods, transportation networks, telecommunication networks, and other tangible networks that a corporation may possess. The *vital* state would refer to the flows of energies, comprising such energies as financial assets—cash flows, costs, sales, profits, return on investments—and the flow of emotion at the employee, customer, and other stakeholder levels.

Flow of emotion captures an important part of the intangible experience that any party interacting within or with the company may experience. As at the level of the person, all these flows are primarily self-referencing: that is, they exist to aggrandize the conception of self or in this case of corporation. In the case of financial flows, the emphasis is on what the corporation must do in order to ensure that these continue to aggrandize the corporation. Similarly, in the case of experience, the emphasis is on what must be done so that the employee or the customer affirms or reinforces the dynamics of the corporation. The *mental* state would refer to flows at the level of thought or concept. Hence, what are the processes or the flows by which intellectual property, brand value, or goodwill are created? Who is involved and how does this type of value get created by the interactions between those involved.

Remembering the mental mantra—"reality as shaped by thought"—let us explore its implications for the business. Under such an umbrella or orientation, the *physical* would refer to the notion of a fixed world. Key ideas about what is possible in the marketplace would be dictated by the notion that "what the eye can see" is what is possible. Hence, corporate strategy, or corporate possibility, would be a function of the fixed nature of things. Whatever had made the corporation successful in the past is what will make it successful in the future. If a corporation has failed in the past, it simply would need to emulate another plan that had been successful in the fixed world, to itself become successful. *Vital*, on the under hand, would refer to the notion of a variable world, in which assertion of energy is going to determine a successful outcome. Nothing is fixed in this orientation: success is a function of asserting the corporation through financial means. The boundaries of the world, in this kind of orientation, are much more fluid. Processes, strategies, and products do not need to remain essentially the same as in the physical orientation. Anything can change so long as financial and stakeholder success, defined in terms of financial impact, is upheld. It will be possible to go into new markets, new geographies, and new products, with new people and new processes, if need be, in order to ensure that the all-important financial return is assured. *Mental* would refer to a world driven by thoughts and ideas. The primary impetus for driving a corporation would not be financial

Figure 3.1 The Architecture of a Business

Building Block \ Orientation	Physical	Vital	Mental
Physical	Tangible asset such as land	Tangible networks such as transportation	Fixed world, processes, approach
Vital	Tangible energy such as cash	Flows of energy such as financial assets and customer experience	Variable world; assertion through financial means
Mental	Intangible asset such as goodwill	Flow facilitating creation of intangible assets	Idea-driven and higher fluidity

returns, under this outlook, but the idea and the ideal. Needless to say, this kind of world would potentially be the most variable. Not even the constraint on ensuring financial returns would necessarily impede it. Hence, such a corporation would potentially much more easily change product, process, market, and geography, if the idea that drove it demanded that kind of action in return.

The *architecture* of a business is summarized in Figure 3.1.

Hence, as in fully defining the architecture of a day in the initial Earth–Sun analogy and in fully defining even the *architecture* of a person, the physical, vital, and mental building blocks can quite completely define the architecture of a business. There must, as such, be some validity to applying them to an organization in the business world.

Permutations of the Physical, Vital, Mental Building Blocks

As in the case of a person, different combinations of building blocks will yield different kernels that, through fractal pressure, will tend to create different guiding and operating realities for businesses.

Stringing corresponding components of each orientation together, for example, yields a *purer* physical, vital, and mental state, respectively. The purer state can be thought of as the repetition of the corresponding state from each orientation. Hence, the physical at the physical state, the physical at the vital state, and the physical at the mental state would combine to form the purer physical. Necessarily in the purer physical state, it is the physical that would lead. The overarching guiding ethos of such a business may be, "in fixed markets, and with fixed products, we combine and manipulate hard, physical assets to arrive at value for the organization." The primary orientation would be one of ensuring the preservation and maintenance of physical assets above everything else. In a particular situation, this kind of orientation would no doubt be very valuable. For instance, in the case of warfare, the protection of a country's physical assets such as boundaries and resources would be paramount. At the same time, one can see that this orientation is going to provide actors of this view with a limited set of actions when confronted with change. It is not unlikely that such actors will be at a substantial disadvantage when one considers the competitive play and the very changing nature of markets. But if it were the mental part of the physical or the vital part of the physical, as opposed to the physical part of the physical that leads, one can see how this would vary the practical orientation of governance. If it were the mental–physical that leads, for instance, it would be the preservation of the accumulated goodwill or brand that would be the most important. This orientation would likely be most important in a situation where a corporation could uphold the brand by the right tweaks, as opposed to major market plays.

In practical reality, it will unlikely be the purer state that would lead—for humans and corporations are complex entities with many different potential combinations that will interact to determine the overall practical orientation of a company. To illustrate, the three states within three orientations yield nine seed states that can lead. Assuming many parts to an organization, the general kernel or state of each of these parts of an organization combined with kernels or states of each of the others, yields many different kinds of possible cultures.

No doubt that from time to time, it will be useful for a business organization to purposefully step into a certain state of being at will. In other words, given a particular challenge, is it possible to assume a mental–mental or a vital–physical or a vital–vital approach, for instance, to best respond to it? This would require that – that part of being or way of being becomes active in that part of the organization which is responsible for a particular response to a particular situation. In other words, the functions of marketing or finance, research and development, or engineering, among others, would each require a certain kind of seed orientation in order to do justice to the nature of their required roles. But that kind of self-awareness, defined by both clarity of the seed orientation one may be holding at a particular time and the ability to change it to another seed orientation depending on the demand of a particular situation, is rare even at the level of a person, let alone a collectivity of multiple personalities that together comprise a larger suborganization.

There is an important point to draw out here. One can perhaps see that a particular orientation, that is physical-leading, vital-leading, or mental-leading, applied at a particular time, would yield the best outcome possible. But unless one were first able to become aware of these potential states of being, within oneself to begin with, there is likely no way that a suborganization responsible for a particular response will ever be able to create a particular way of being first. This hints at the link between the consciousness at the level of person and the corresponding organizational response. We will come back to this a little later, since this link is at the crux of the fractal model.

For our analysis, the fundamental question is whether these seed states are potentially in alignment with the Sun-marked physical–vital–mental fractal. This becomes important, because if not, then we are potentially looking at many more sources of contrary and opposing fractals that ultimately lead to stagnation as opposed to progress. On the positive side, there are now so may more opportunities for individuals to exercise or prepare for traversing the rite of passage into a fuller and more creative individuality. Only, these have to be recognized as so.

The Best-run Organization

In the Sun-marked physical–vital–mental fractal, that we are hypothesizing is embedded in the DNA of life, there is an inherent logic to the stringing together of the states in a particular sequence that culminates in a general milieu of progress. The stringing together, so that it is the mental that leads or so that a particular process culminates in the mental state, defines progress, as we have already proposed. This notion of progress is at the crux of life, and those entities or organizations that are able to replicate a similar dynamic in their behavior are able to break loose of a general physical-oriented opposing fractal and arrive at an increasing expression of their identity. When this identity expresses itself, less of the opposing fractal remains, and by virtue of the fractal nature of creation, even when that creation is contained in a small space, the effect is that Earth itself moves closer to becoming an Earth–Sun.

Like the sun, all then tends to become a little more timeless, solid, vast, and self-lit. In the context of current activity at the individual or business level, surely this is a desirable outcome. The hurriedness of life and the orientation of decisions biased toward the short term could certainly do with an elongation of time and a more practical sense of the existence of eternity. The self-deprecating tendencies of people and the easy compromise to opportunities that waste one's energies and resources could do with a sense of solidity. The narrow frameworks and perceptions, whether at the individual or the organizational level, could do with a sense of vastness. The easy flitting from idea to idea or trend to trend, or where the voice and call is the loudest, could do with guidance from the truth of one's self or from a state of being self-lit.

This puts into context the potential play of myriad seed states that can be experienced by complex organizational constructs like business organizations. It is good to have subcultures and responses of different kinds. The point is: as we mentioned in the previous subsection, are they self-organizing to align with or even replicate in some way the Sun-marked physical–vital–mental fractal? If it is many different unaligned or misaligned or even random ways of being and responses that animate an organization, this will likely take on the characteristic of noise and will at best allow a stepwise, labored, and perhaps very circuitous movement that may or may not move away from the general and seductive gravitation of the age-old physical-oriented opposing fractal. Let us, hence, examine the logic of integrating the three states for optimal running of an organization.

An organization that is primarily physical-oriented, we have said, will view the world and markets as fixed, and through leveraging, the existing assets will seek to maintain its position in such a playing field. In a fixed world, this orientation will no doubt be very valuable. The world, however, is anything but fixed. Sometimes when we forget this, the circumstance will itself remind us so. Today, hence, when we consider the number of different changes underway simultaneously—from climate change to resource shortage, globalization and technological innovation among many others—we are again reminded that even this world which so many are proud of now, and have marked as developmentally sound, is only a temporary step in a continuous journey. To remain solely fixed in a physical-orientation would yield to circumstances that themselves will likely shake the very foundations of all that is wrongly considered fixed. Myriad examples exist, even in the business world, of the entire industries disappearing: typewriters, railroads, and mainframes, to mention a few. For survival, it therefore becomes necessary to combine the physical orientation with at least another. Such an orientation could be the vital. In the vital-orientation, the world and markets are viewed as constantly changing. Change is dictated by application of energy. Such an orientation already allows a much higher degree of adaptability. When the goals of a business organization, hence, are sales growth, market growth, or other financially led goals, the means become less important. Extrapolated out, we have a situation, therefore, like the one we are faced with today, where other business responsibilities to society, such as stewardship of resources and corporate citizenship are foregone in the interest of a narrowly defined self-interest. Hence, while this orientation provides energy and adaptability, it too requires another orientation to be combined with it. This would be the mental orientation. Mental orientation allows deeper questioning and rationalization to enter into the picture. Hence, narrowly defined, self-interest can be expanded out to include larger responsibilities to society and future generations. Fundamental raison d'être can also be clarified and such an examination and clarification is invaluable.

From the point of view of completeness of action, it, therefore, seems necessary that the three orientations combine with one another. We have arrived at this conclusion through examination of sole orientations and the lack they would be faced with when operating in their soleness. Let us re-look at the situation from the point of view of positives. The physical orientation is secure and based on actions that have culminated in an organizations success to date. Current assets are a result of past success and provide a stable foundation on which future action can take place. For completeness of action, even if an organization is primarily idea-driven, and there were plenty of these toward the late 1990s with the birth of the Internet era, they would need to backward integrate so as to ensure they had a secure physical foundation. The vital orientation is driven by energy and assertiveness and allows an organization through these very devices to take most advantage of its time in the present to create its future. The mental orientation allows reason, questioning, identity, idealism to drive organizational creation, and action. One way of being complemented with another allows for a more integral, meaningful, effective, and stable action to manifest. This is summarized in Figure 3.2.

Without reference to the Sun-marked physical–vital–mental fractal, and without reference to the effect of the fractal resident in people on business organizations, even if one were to consider business logic alone, one would still arrive at the conclusion that the most well-run organization would be mentally-led, with physical and vital orientations being subservient to it. A physical-led organization would seek to maintain the boundaries of yesterday's actions and way of being by subsuming vital and mental capacities and capabilities, such as finances and energies of various kinds and ideas and know-how,

Figure 3.2 Logic for Integration

Building Block

Drivers of Integration	Physical	Vital	Mental
Capacity	Stable foundation	Energy and adaptability	Identity, idealism, deeper questioning
	←→	*Assimilating capacities*	←→
Incapacity	Stagnation	Myopic development	Castles in the air
	←→	*Overcoming incapacities*	←→

respectively, to it. This could very well lead to suboptimal operation and likely demise in periods of rapid change. A vitally led organization would seek to grow itself at any cost, by commandeering any and all assets, and by gross rationalization of its purposes, to ensure it had the foundation and support necessary for what would very well turn out to be irrational growth. A mentally-led organization would, on the other hand, more than any other, likely be led by idea or idealism, and mobilize the necessary funds and infrastructure to support that. Through leveraging higher purpose, relatively speaking, and through broader and more comprehensive questioning when it came to times of change or matters of societal context, such an organization would likely be the best run.

The Causal Link

Let us remind ourselves that what we are trying to establish is a fractal model that ultimately illustrates quite concretely how global change is connected and in fact driven by change at the individual level. For this to be true, the fractal for progress at the individual level that has been established to be a manifestation of the ubiquitous Sun-marked physical–vital–mental fractal, must similarly have its counterpart at the next significant level of organization, the business, which we have just illustrated, and further, the fundamental physical, vital, and mental building blocks at the personal or individual level must have causal connection with the physical, vital, and mental building blocks at the business level. Let us focus on exploring this causal connection.

If an organization is run with a physical orientation, we can predict that it will run into particular kinds of problems, and even advise it to adopt more of a vital or a mental orientation depending on the circumstances it is faced with. To briefly illustrate, in times of rapid market change, physical orientation would only allow stepwise and closed-box thinking. To be able to arrive at a creative new play that can move an organization to a new level of operation, it will be necessary to either forcibly look at expansion into new and unrelated products and markets—the vital play, or rethink raison d'être, to arrive at something completely different even if it is in its existing market—the mental play. To be able to successfully execute on either of these, it will, however, become necessary to dislodge or shift the current thinking and possible feelings of key leaders in an organization.

This means that at the personal level, there has to be a shift from a physical orientation to a vital or a mental orientation. Who a person is being, therefore, has to go through a change. This will have to occur at the level of both feeling and thought. If market conditions and one's historical orientation in the market has been of a particular kind, the entire thinking and feeling associated with ways of operating in that situation has to change. On the side of thought, if one believes that everything is fixed, then the likelihood of engaging in any kind of change is very low. This fundamental orientation in thought will need to go through a shift so that markets and the world can be viewed as flexible and changing, either randomly, the vital orientation, or purposefully, the mental orientation. Similarly, the fundamental orientation in feeling will need to go through a shift – for without the right kind of feeling driving action, the action is unlikely to occur, or suboptimal action is likely to occur. It may be the case that in the face of change one is experiencing continued inertia or complacency—primarily *physical* emotions. Then, to expect meaningful action is unlikely. Even if the emotional response changes to negative, *vital* emotions such as anger or fear, action is possible, and the organization may shift out its current situation. The quality of the action, however, will be questionable.

But taking the linkage even further, if there is a fundamental response of feeling at the individual leader level, then corporate action will also have the texture of or tend to emanate from that level. To illustrate, if one is experiencing inertia, then what impetus to change the way things already are, even if repulsive? Hence, the feeling being at the physical level will tend to reinforce corporate action at that level. If there is a response of fear or anger at the individual leader level, essentially negative self-referencing flows of energy characteristic of the vital level, the corresponding corporate action will also tend to be of a similar characteristic: myopic self-referencing flows of energy at the vital level. This may manifest as lay-offs or cutting of corners so that financial results appear positive, for instance.

Stepping back from this, the question is as to what kind of response is being created by leadership in the face of change? If it is a response that is driven by a belief that the world is fixed and no substantial change is possible, a physical orientation at the level of thought, and is accompanied by a mixture of inertia and fear, a physical–vital component at the level of emotion, then sure enough that is the reality, through timely and pervasive influence, that is going to assert itself in the world of that organization. Corrective action has to start at the root, and in this case, the fundamental underlying response at the level of thought and of feeling that is going to determine future action in the face of the change will need to be changed. But, this individual response and its resultant effect on organizational action reinforce the strong link between an individual's orientation and resultant action in an organization. It reinforces the notion of a fractal—of a pattern repeating itself on different scales. If from the response of a *fixed world* accompanied by feelings of inertia in the face of that, the response is changed to one of *variable and purposeful world* accompanied by feelings of enthusiasm, the organization will be much better positioned for success. If the seed fractal is changed, then the organization has a chance to go through a corresponding positive change. This notion is summarized in Figure 3.3.

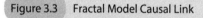

Figure 3.3 Fractal Model Causal Link

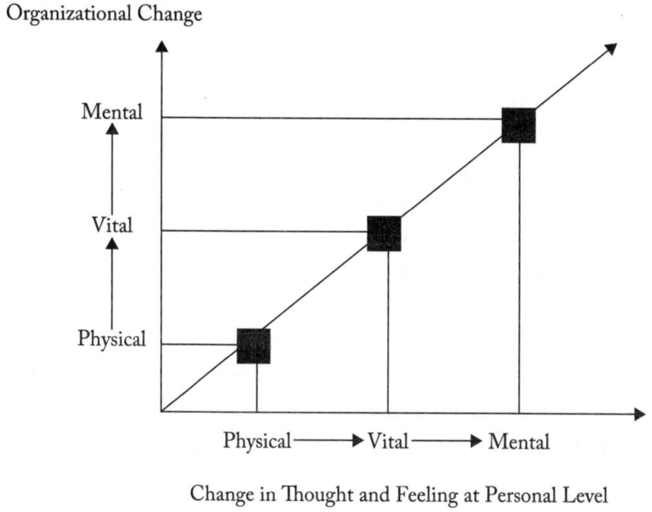

While it is the general thrust of the book to establish the case for a ubiquitous fractal by establishing the naturalness or automaticity or self-emergence of that pattern at each progressively more complex level of organization, at the same time to show the link between one level and the next more complex level as we step from rung-to-rung in the fractal ladder, is useful. This is what we have done here and will return to a more complete examination later in the book.

Summary

In this chapter, we began with an examination of what the terms physical, vital, and mental could mean in the context of the business world. We applied the physical, vital, mental lenses to each of the three terms iteratively in order to arrive at a fuller comprehension of the architecture of these terms. In some sense, this reinforces the inherent advantage of an approach of this nature. We then examined some of the complexities of combination of these individual states in the context of organizations. We considered that a large number of potential seed states was possible and asked the question if it is possible to step into a particular seed state at will. This highlighted the potential link between the individual and the organization in terms of states at the level of individual influencing or even determining states at the level of organization, thus *independently* hinting at the validity of such a fractal model. Note, as stated above, that while our overall approach to validating a fractal model is to examine each *level* of complexity—individual, organization, system, evolution—independently, it is still of value to ensure that from a point of view of practical logic that link makes sense as we step through the sequence of levels. We then reminded ourselves of the desirable outcome of seeing or replicating the Sun-marked physical–vital–mental fractal in the business world and went on to a separate examination of the logic of combining these states together, with the mental leading, to arrive at the optimal running of organization. The logic itself suggested that these states need to occur in the same sequence as the Sun-marked fractal for the most optimum outcome, thus establishing the automaticity of the fractal at the business level. We then revisited with a more concrete example the link between the individual and organizational states of being and suggested that for organizational change to come about, the action must take place first at the root—that is at the individual level, thereby further validating the hypothetical fractal model.

While we have focused on business at the level of individual or distinct organizations, we now need to turn our attention to the cumulative effect of business, or the next layer in the fractal model—that of economy. This is the focus of the next chapter.

The Economy Pattern 4

Focus: A look at how this pattern has almost as if automatically appeared at the level of the economy, and how certain parts of the pattern are associated with higher degrees of freedom.

Key Concepts: Bottom-up fractal analysis | Top-down fractal analysis | Global economy fractal | Multiplication of mediocrity | Agriculture and physical phase | Industrial economy and vital phase | Digital economy and mental phase | Automaticity of traversing physical, vital, and mental phases | DNA of life and Sun-marked physical–vital–mental fractal | Assessment of progress from physical, vital, and mental points of view | Fractal within a fractal | Approaching limits of the vital phase | Global indicators of a breakdown | Birth of the corporation and fractal pressure | Corporation as a quintessential vital animal | Necessity of completion of Sun-marked physical–vital–mental journey for corporation | Subphase within a phase | Rite of passage at the economy level | Degrees of freedom | Primary actors of a phase | The vital milieu | Pushing instant gratification to its limits | DNA of life and push to transcend limits | Kernels of chief actors | Tendencies and fractal pressure | Aura of impersonality | Difficulty of change at impersonal levels of organization | Encountering and surpassing demons of creation | Global economy fractal as expression of individual way of being | Key to global economy shift lies in shift at the individual level

Introduction

So far we have hypothesized the existence of a Sun-marked physical–vital–mental fractal that animates progressive life. We examined the meaning and possibility of this fractal at the level of the individual and the level of the business organization. The individual and the business organization are, in a manner of speaking, more *manageable* organizations as they are less complicated than an entire economy, the trajectory of development of the economy, or of a similar large system. Hence, our approach to the examination of the Sun-marked fractal at these simpler levels was from the bottom-up. At the level of economy, however, we shift approaches and we begin to look at the existence of the fractal from the *top-down*. In other words, we will initially focus on the evidence or existence of the same fractal at the level of economy and, then, begin to dissect it to make further sense of it.

In this chapter, hence, we will begin with the examination of a global economy fractal. We will then step back and ask as to how did it happen? That is, how did this very same fractal, running through the physical, vital, and mental phases, appear at the level of the economy? We will examine the nature of this fractal in greater detail, which will reveal some interesting practical characteristics. We will then begin to dissect the nature more closely to look at implications of what we are seeing. Specifically, the notion of multiplicity will be examined, and in this particular case, the multiplication of *mediocrity*. We will then examine the cumulative effects on the person, drawing back to our notion of a yesteryear-pointing physical-oriented fractal. Finally, we will conclude with a beginning examination of where it is that business and the economy need to go, in light of the hypothesized fractal model that we continue to develop.

The Global Economy Fractal

Broadly speaking, the global economy has traversed three stages. These are the agricultural economy, the industrial economy, and more recently, the digital economy. Let us examine this more closely.

The agricultural economy is primarily focused on a more physical asset—the land. Its very modus operandi has tended to be physical in nature. That is, it is all about working physically, with physical implements, to rearrange or exploit Earth-based physical assets. It is all about operating with "what the eye can see." Hence, we may conclude that the focus on agriculture is really a focus on the physical phase of the global economy fractal.

More recently, over the last century, focus has shifted on industry. This focus is all about working with large flows. Its very purpose is to create large flows. Hence, there is the flow of cash leveraged to bring about flow of product. In the bargain telecommunication flows, people flows, and resource flows—and this also includes energy and metal extraction, energy and metal processing and distribution—other flows of trading, flows of financial instruments of all kinds to further bring about the essential flow of product have been accelerated. In other words, the focus has been all about the "play of energies," which is characteristic of the vital phase. We can conclude, then, that the industrial phase is synonymous with the vital phase, and that by engaging in this kind of industry, the global economy has essentially traversed a vital phase.

Currently, we have entered into the digital economy. The late 1990s saw the birth of the Internet era. It was idealism of sharing information, of transcending traditional silos that gave birth to the Internet. Subsequently, there were a number of radical ideas, relatively speaking, that gave birth to entire new companies. Bring a virtual library and bookshop with millions of titles into one's living room, for instance. Conduct all financial transactions on your computer, for instance. The focus of this phase of the economy was much more on ideas. In other words, the focus has been on the mental phase.

The global economy, hence, appears to have gone through the physical, vital, and mental phases automatically. It is not that someone decided that now a majority of business activities will transition from one emphasis to another. There is a level of self-organization here that, as the term suggests, happened itself. It is not that the mental phase appeared first, followed by the physical, and the vital. The phases appeared in the same sequence as the

Sun-marked physical–vital–mental fractal. The automaticity of this is important. For it suggests that if progress is to happen, the logic of the Sun-marked physical–vital–mental fractal that we are suggesting is imprinted in the very DNA of life, must be followed.

The Global Economy Fractal and Progress

The question is "Has progress happened?" To answer this, we will need to refer to the elements of the ubiquitous fractal itself. Many will say that progress is going to depend upon the base orientation that actors within a system have. Let us follow this line of thought. If the general orientation is *physical,* then the most important element for actors is going to be preservation of yesterday's world. In this case, the dynamics of past markets, past communities, and past roles is what will be viewed as the standard. Change that breaks these boundaries will be threatening and, in the final analysis, will not be viewed as progress but more likely as chaos.

If the general orientation is *vital,* the most important element for actors in the system is going to be constant change marked by the aggrandizement of one's own individuality or organization. So long as the chief actors of that system are benefiting—and in a vital world this will necessarily be the few who are strong or energetic enough to impose their world views—it will be deemed that progress is happening. These are perhaps the captains of industry, the autocrats or self-proclaiming elite of government, and those few others, who support the enriching of the few by themselves pocketing riches in the bargain.

If the general orientation is *mental,* then progress is going to be determined by acceptance of some commonly accepted or vied for utopia. The notion of utopia may compete with the notion of utopia. But so long as the spirit of true questioning remains alive and more of an attempt is made to arrive at a universal sense of utopia, this will be deemed as progress.

Using these notions of progress, in whose context may we have progressed? Certainly not for any who have the physical orientation. For the world as we know it seems to change its basic bearings from day to day. And reality of yesterday continues to be further shattered as day leads to new day. For those who have the vital orientation, we have certainly progressed. For the few are getting richer at the expense of the Earth and many communities and people around the world, and what is more, the commonly accepted notion of progress is generally synonymous with the notion of business development. That is, so long as business is developing and so long as all are playing their parts to progress world business in general, constituents or actors are considered useful. For those who have the mental orientation, there has likely never, in the last few decades, and even perhaps centuries, been any generalized and deep enough questioning as to the purpose of it all. On the contrary, there has been acceptance of a way of being that has been successfully imposed by those in power. Hence, even from a mental orientation, progress has not really happened.

If progress is only true as defined by a vital orientation, is it true progress? This question necessarily leads us into the idea of a fractal within a fractal. By definition, a fractal is a pattern that repeats itself on different scales. Hence, this kind of dissection should be natural when fractals are used as a lens to study any phenomena. When we assess that the global economy has gone through the pattern as depicted by the Sun-marked physical–vital–mental fractal, and if our hypothesis about progress being synonymous with this proposed ubiquitous fractal is true, then we must conclude that any movement through the physical, vital, and mental phases in that particular order must necessarily result in progress. How can this be true though when the Earth, communities, and many individuals have paid an unfair price for that progression? The progress can be seen as progress if we consider that the current movement is happening within a single, larger physical, vital, or mental phase, and is in fact the ubiquitous fractal applied to that overarching phase that is thereby pushing the boundaries of that phase. In other words, the current global economy fractal that has progressed through the agricultural–industrial–digital phases is a manifestation of the Sun-marked physical–vital–mental fractal applied to, or within the limits of a larger, overarching vital phase of the economy. This idea of a fractal within a fractal is captured in Figure 4.1.

The true nature of the current global economy is vital. Within that our increasing digital focus, the indication of the culmination of

Figure 4.1 The Global Economy Fractal

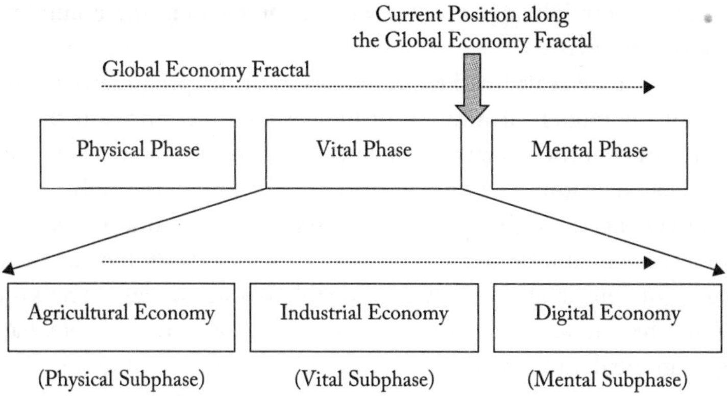

a physical–vital–mental movement, suggests that we are approaching the limit of the vital economy. Let us probe this further. Approaching the limit would suggest that there is going to be a general breakdown of the accepted order or way of doing things. Without going into a detailed analysis at this point, are we in fact approaching a general possible breakdown? Several global indicators would seem to suggest this. Witness the recent financial crises with the utter breakdown of the global financial system. Banks and numerous other prestigious financial institutions the world over have declared bankruptcy. National economies have declared recessions and some even suggest they are on the verge of depression. Witness further, in the decades preceding these recent events that even though monetary wealth had been increasing for regional and the global economy as a whole, the happiness of people was reported to be deteriorating. Further, climate change has become a major issue and if not adequately addressed within a prescribed time frame, it will reportedly lead to major catastrophes on many different fronts. Finally, the Earth is in general in a reality termed as *overshoot*. That is, Earth's ability to sustainably generate natural resources is short of demand for these resources and this gap appears to be growing daily. Analysis suggests that these major trends are a result of human action, and further, a result of business, as usual. This phenomenon will be explored in further detail in subsequent chapters. The point is, our business mindset and actions seem to be pushing us to the limit of the *business* way of being. Hence, it certainly appears that we are approaching the boundaries of a certain phase.

This can be reaffirmed by examination of the progressive formation of the modern institution of the corporation. Through the last couple of centuries, the modern corporation has been accorded with many of the rights of a human being; for example, the right to buy property and the right to protection under the law, but not perhaps equal accountability and responsibility to society. A human being has rights but is also strictly accountable before the law. The same cannot be said about corporations.[1] Corporations, for example, have been granted limited liability. Couple this with the rapidity with which financial assets can be transferred to parts of the world where a corporation does not operate, or which are tax havens, and many large corporations exist in a reality where they can become centers of incredible flows of various kinds, without equal responsibility for the impact of those flows.[2]

This is unlike the situation of a person who under most circumstances is under scrutiny of the law where they live. In other words, the modern-day global corporation is the quintessential vital animal. Its birth is vital in nature, and therefore the reality and the world it has reinforced around itself, by dint of fractal pressure, is necessarily vital. It is not surprising that the economy is bumping into limits, as evidenced by some of the trends we just reviewed. If its birth has been of a vital kind, we know by applying the logic of the Sun-marked physical–vital–mental fractal, that if it does not complete the movement to incorporate and in fact be led by the mental component, it will stagnate. In other words, given the possible overarching reality of a ubiquitous Sun-marked physical–vital–mental fractal and the necessity of progress embedded in this fundamental movement, and the fact that as per our analysis the global economy fractal is already at the limit of the vital phase, it is a foregone conclusion that the

[1] For a more detailed examination of this subject, please refer to: Joe Balkan, *The Corporation: The Pathological Pursuit of Profit and Power* (New York: Free Press, 2005).
[2] For a more detailed treatment of this subject, please refer to William Brittain-Catlin, *Offshore: the Dark Side of the Global Economy* (New York: Picador, 2006).

modern-day institution of business must either radically transform or will be replaced by something of an entirely different nature. We will have more to say about this in subsequent chapters.

Let us return to further examination of the modern-day global economy fractal. We have suggested that the global economy is fundamentally in the vital phase, and within that, has traversed the physical and vital subphases, and has recently entered into the mental subphase. We asserted that this movement, even though of a primarily vital nature is still progressive because it is pushing us against limits of the vital phase. In fact, the general issue can be restated in terms of an initiation rite. The general obstacles we see around us now can be thought of as the manifestation of a contrary fractal, and in that its nature is not to yield to the mental control but to likely continue forever with the untransformed vital dynamics, and has therefore resulted in the construction of a passageway through which we must pass to break-through to the other side. This becomes our rite of passage – for it means that a very different way of being has to emerge in order to overcome the challenges of today.

Degrees of Freedom

Let us also pause here and examine the notion of the degrees of freedom afforded to the primary actors in the vital phase. From a vital standpoint, the physical or agricultural economy allowed some fulfillment of the characteristic vital goals of self-assertion, conquest, self-aggrandizement, and flows of energy even if of a random nature, often at any cost. But this was not enough. To create slave labor or even slave traffic from one region of the world to another, so that requisite amounts of sugar or cocoa or spices could be cultivated and feed a global industry that in turn fed the taste buds of some target populations, that in turn enriched the captains of commerce and other favored elite, simply did not afford enough vital satisfaction. In fact, all it had done from the vital point of view was perhaps what the appetite of the chief actors of this system was. This focus on the agricultural or physical phase allows its actors only a limited amount of *degrees of freedom*. They were bound by "what the eye can see"—by current markets, current products, existing target customers, and existing strategies. There was a need to push the limit into another way of increasing vital satisfaction. This way was provided with the birth of the more complex machine.

It is not that the birth of the complex machine was a bad thing. It was just that the general milieu of the time controlled by opportunistic vital actors was such that its appropriation to drive the engines of industry and the consequent birth of the industrial economy was perhaps inevitable. This entrance into the vital phase of the vital economy provided many more degrees of freedom to its actors; it became a "play of energies." Product, market, and customer were no longer bound. Thought was appropriated to dream up new strategies, processes, and devices to continue to feed the vital kernels of these actors. The general populace had clearly not developed enough of the sense of identity and uniqueness to even challenge what was happening. If this had happened, perhaps now there would be no need for a more formidable rite of passage. Unfortunately, this was not to be the case. For, by now, the general sense that all exists for business and that business is the only way for the world to progress had been embedded into just about any and every institution. The vital phase of the vital economy fully fulfilled its purpose in this regard, and the sense that reality is nothing other than a vital play in a vital world became as though deeply ingrained.

And now this general belief was so formidable that even when the Internet was born, mainly due to entirely non-commercial reasons, its possibilities were like the emergence of the complex machine before it quickly appropriated to push the global economy into the digital or mental phase. In other words, the general vital milieu had now a new set of channels and methods to continue to push its basic vital agenda. Barriers to trading and facilitating flows of all kinds broke down. More and more products were easily put in the hands of consumers. Instant gratification was being pushed to its limits. Demand for resources and intensification of production processes of course expedited the push against limits. While there is no doubt great promise and many good things that have simultaneously emerged with the birth of the Internet, and these will be put into context in a subsequent chapter, the point is that it has also provided the chief actors of a vital phase

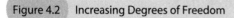

Figure 4.2 Increasing Degrees of Freedom

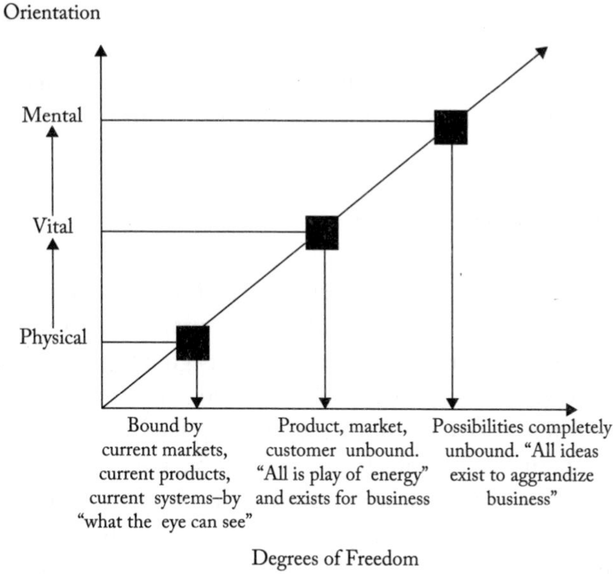
Orientation
Mental
Vital
Physical
Bound by current markets, current products, current systems–by "what the eye can see"
Product, market, customer unbound. "All is play of energy" and exists for business
Possibilities completely unbound. "All ideas exist to aggrandize business"
Degrees of Freedom

the icing on the cake so as to speak, that pushes their degrees of freedom to a new level. Figure 4.2 summarizes the notion of increasing degrees of freedom as orientation shifts.

This notion of increasing degrees of freedom also sheds light on why, logically, it would make sense for an economy to move from a primarily physical to a vital and then on to a mental orientation. For such movement accords the chief actors added capabilities – in the form of increased physical, vital, and mental powers—to more fully achieve what they want to. At the same time, and this is no doubt not in the active consciousness of the chief actors, it expedites the movement toward the limits of a particular system, increases the need for potentially heroic efforts to address the resulting challenges, to thereby facilitate the birth of the next phase in the ubiquitous fractal.

In our hypothetical model, the DNA of life is embedded with the implicit need of progress as charted out by the Sun-marked physical–vital–mental fractal. This means that all nature's constructs, whether the individual, the organization, the economy, or any other construct that we may not have considered yet, are pushed to transcend their limits so that they reach that mental stage of sincere questioning. While that may seem like the end point of the journey given where we are at present, in itself it is likely only a starting point to a whole set of new possibilities. This will have to be explored in greater detail later.

The Multiplier Effect

We have stated that it makes sense if chief actors have a vital orientation that the economy would have developed the way it has—through the agricultural, industrial, and beginnings of the digital phase—because this movement brings into the hands of the chief actors greater satisfaction of the overarching vital goals. There are a few important observations to be made at this point. First, the chief actors are still individual personalities. The whole development of levels or organization removed from them—in this case the level of corporation, and then further, the level of the economy—takes on the characteristics and hue of the seed patterns or kernels resident in these chief actors. Certain vital tendencies, as it were, exist to fulfill their realities, as we hypothesized earlier. These tendencies determine the nature and characteristic of the business organization created. Through fractal pressure, this nature and characteristic reinforces itself by influencing and drawing other entities into its orbit. An entire business organization with this fundamental characteristic in turn becomes a multiplier of the same effect: a more complex dynamo in a manner of speaking, to both broadcast and receive, and thereby further imprint or reinforce this general vital tendency on the nature of life. When a whole host or business organizations exist for the same purpose—vital self-aggrandizement—the resultant fractal is formidable. Mental components will easily find themselves subdued to this general atmosphere, and the reinforcement of cycle upon cycle creates an economy that in itself is like its actors, chiefly vital in nature.

As discussed in Chapter 2, at the individual level, tendencies compete with tendencies, and through careful observation and effort, it is more easily possible to bring certain tendencies that are arrested in their fractal movement into the light, so as to speak, to make them progress or somehow even to dissolve them. When, however, a business organization of a certain nature is created, it has already taken on an aura of impersonality. That is, its characteristic and culture now to seem to exist on their own, and do not lend themselves to the opportunity of being changed or transformed or dissolved so easily. Push out another level of general organization to the level of the economy now, and the essential character by the same logic will be far more difficult to change. Media, personalities, and larger societal norms will have been imbued by the general character of the economy, and if another way of being is suggested, it will be viewed as non-traditional, non-conforming, or generally destructive to the established goals of life, or even perhaps as heresy, depending upon how deeply embedded other actors in the system are to the now established way of things.

In this general development of layer of organizational complexity laid upon the layer of organizational complexity, it is as though veil has been placed upon veil, and as citizens we have forgotten that the root of what exists *out there* – with the problems of decreasing happiness, widening inequality, systemic resource shortage, climate change, or whatever else may manifest – exists within ourselves as tendencies or kernels or seed patterns that through force of creativity and fractal pressure must create what they have been brought into existence to create. These levels of increasing impersonality in effect imbibe the removed levels of organization with all the strength of a yesteryear-pointing and contrary fractals that in effect act to prolong its reign and its incomplete way of being. Our own biases, traumas, inconsistencies, and ignorance create kernels within ourselves that do the very work they were created to do, result in massive and progressively removed levels of organization, culminating in the general tendency and thought of cultures and society, and become formidable obstacles or challenges that in the final analysis are the very material against which we have to battle in order to assert our nascent and truer individuality. For recall that the general habits and ignorance are not truly us, but tendencies that have manifested in us because they exist in the environment and are part of the ubiquitous yesteryear-pointing fractal that seeks to prolong its own reign. That individuality, in fact, as we have already stated finds expression and its right to be when it has successfully encountered the demons of its own creation, and surpassed them with new creations, and a deeper reality of being that becomes a creative force in its own right.

We know that the global economy fractal, that as we have stated, is at the boundary of the vital level tending toward the mental, is none other, therefore, than the expression of who we are in the way of our being. When we speak of the business world and the economy needing to move to the next level in the Sun-marked physical–vital–mental fractal, it is therefore we as individuals who first need to complete that same journey. The organizations we create and the society we have created are indices of our own personalities. If we are bumping into global limits, by this logic, it must be the reality that we are in fact bumping against limits of who we are being in the first place. If we have to reinterpret or reform business organization and the global economy, the nature of that will have to find its key in the shift in nature that we ourselves have to go through. Figure 4.3 captures this idea.

Figure 4.3 The Multiplier Effect

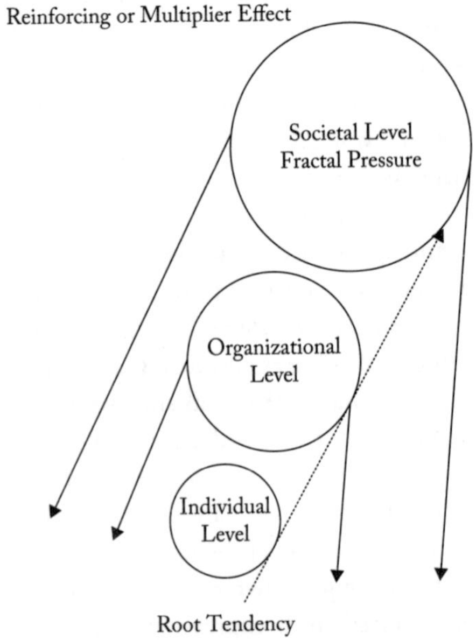

Summary

We began this chapter with an examination of the manifestation of the ubiquitous fractal at the level of the economy. We then questioned whether this manifestation spelt progress and discovered as to what in fact we were seeing at the level of the global economy was a fractal within a fractal. The birth of the digital economy was the mental subphase in an overarching vital phase. We concluded that indeed progress was happening, and in fact it was the nature of the progress to push to limits even the depravity of a certain way of being. We examined the notion of degrees of freedom and suggested that logically even without considering a possible fractal model that in any case would lead us to reinterpret our entire way of looking at things, it made complete sense for an organization to want and need to traverse the physical, vital, and mental phases for its own fulfillment. In doing so, however, along with the apparent progress, the shortcoming of the approach would come more into relief, and if noticed and acted upon, would potentially lead to an entire new way of functioning, that it can be predicted, would be in line with the movement of the Sun-marked physical–vital–mental fractal. Finally, as we had done in the previous chapter, we examined the causality linking different levels of organization—that is, the individual level to the business organizational level to the level of economy—and suggested that even to successfully plan or envision where larger levels of organization—the economy—must go, one would have to go to the root, or the individual level. We further concluded that the economy as is, and the myriad organizations that comprise it, are means or rites of passage that individuals must go through in order to arrive at a deeper and truer possibility of what can be. What can be is hinted at in the possibilities of the Sun-marked physical–vital–mental fractal, that of course exists in the DNA of life.

The System Pattern 5

Focus: A look at how this pattern has spontaneously emerged across several different disciplines—physics, management thought, biotechnology, amongst others.

Key Concepts: Mental subphase of vital phase of global economy | Digital economy fractal | Brochure-ware and the physical phase | E-commerce and the vital phase | Reconceptualization and the mental phase | Increase in degrees of freedom | Energy industry fractal | Oil and gas extraction and physical phase | Maximizing energy flow and vital phase | Alternative energy and mental phase | Global politics fractal | Fractal within a fractal | World War I and II and physical phase | Cold war and vital phase | Globalization and mental phase | Exchange rate fractal | Gold standard and physical phase | Balance of power and vital phase | Real-time creativity and mental phase | Science-based systems of thought | Physics fractal | Atomic view and physical phase | Quantum view and vital phase | Unifying theme and mental phase | Biomimicry fractal | Form and function and physical phase | Imitation of process and vital phase | Whole system's view and mental phase | Organizational design fractal | Silo-mentality and physical phase | Process view and vital phase | Raison d'être and mental phase | Fractal for progress | Element focus and physical phase | Experimentation and vital phase | Mastery and mental phase | Leaders push the sequence | Sun-marked physical–vital–mental fractal in DNA of life as causal agent of progress

Introduction

Thus far our essential line of development has been to observe instances of the ubiquitous Sun-marked physical–vital–mental fractal at progressively more complex levels of organization. We started at the level of the person, progressed to the level of the business organization, and in the previous chapter studied the level of the economy. It was found that the fundamental building blocks of the ubiquitous fractal, which recall, we derived from observation of the phases of the day in the mutual Earth–Sun dance, shed insight into the structure and essential operations of those levels. When strung together or combined in the same sequence as the Sun-marked fractal, we have observed that the conditions for progress at that level logically and even automatically come into being, as would be predicted by the fractal model we are in process of developing. When strung together in different sequences, opposing fractals come into being. Through fractal pressure, the opposing fractals tend to reinforce their reality and, hence, the status quo. Opposing them, however, can become a rite of passage by which the Sun-marked sequence and, hence, truer identity can manifest in oneself, in the construct exhibiting the opposing fractal and through fractal pressure, in larger and larger levels of organization. We also observed, as we would expect in a fractal model of this nature, that there is a causal link between a building block or fractal at one level and the nature of the next level.

Earlier on we had stated that if there is validity to the ubiquitous fractal, that is, to the physical–vital–mental sequence, it must be evident regardless of where we look. So far we have looked at a person, a business organization, and the global economy as a whole. We have found that this sequence manifests when there is progress at that level of organization. We chose these instances because they are each manifestations of progressively more complex organizations. In other words, they represent different scales in organizational complexity. Recall that a fractal is a self-similar pattern that repeats itself on different scales. Now, however, we want to cast a wider net and begin to study instances of the same Sun-marked fractal in different areas of life. While there are no doubt more examples than we can possibly enumerate here, for illustrative purposes we will choose a few samples from diverse areas. These will illustrate how the ubiquitous fractal pattern is abroad in many areas of the *system*.

In particular, we look at a couple of system-wide economy-related fractals: the digital economy fractal and the energy industry fractal. We will then look at a couple of system-wide fractals related to global politics: the balance of global power fractal and the exchange rate fractal. Finally, we will look at two system-wide general fractals: the organizational design fractal and the fractal for progress.

System-wide Economy-related Fractals

Let us start the broader look by focusing attention on the mental subphase of the vital phase of the global economy fractal—the digital economy—to see whether the same pattern has manifested itself here. It is interesting to note that, broadly speaking, even the digital economy has been characterized by three distinct phases. When it first came into being, entities indulged in what we can in retrospect call brochure-ware. That is, they simply took what they had available in the existing media or brochures and replicated that onto webpages. In other words they took what *the eye could see* and put it onto the new *media* as is. Fundamentally, the business model remained the same, it continued with the status quo. In other words, brochure-ware exemplified the physical phase of our hypothesized ubiquitous physical–vital–mental fractal.

Some more adventurous entities then experimented with the second phase of the digital economy, which we can call e-commerce. In this phase, selected business processes were transferred onto the Internet. The most common being the customer-ordering and customer-fulfillment processes. That is, selected business flows, aimed at increasing selected financial results, were mapped onto the Internet. This is none other than a vital dynamic. Hence, e-commerce can be thought of as the vital phase of the digital economy.

Some entities went even a step further, and invented, reinvented, or reconfigured themselves to highlight fundamental Internet-based characteristics as the basis of their business models. Hence, such characteristics as global ubiquity, 24 × 7 presence, disaggregation whereby entities can focus on what they do best and partner with select entities that have core competencies in other areas, among other characteristics, became the basis for reinventing the business model. Such reconception is none other than a mental-level dynamic. The reconceptualization can be thought of as the mental phase of the digital economy.

We see that the physical–vital–mental phases have manifested in that very sequence in the digital economy. It is not that there was collusion or the stepping back of players to decide the time for the next phase in the sequence to happen. It happened of itself because it made sense to do so. It happened because the degrees of freedom of the players involved were increased when the physical tended to the vital and when the vital tended to the mental. Perhaps we can even say that it happened because of the pressure of the ubiquitous Sun-marked physical–vital–mental fractal that is embedded in the DNA of life, and that seeks for instruments to continue to push forward the dials of progress. We will return to the example of the digital economy and the notion of progress in more detail in the next chapter. This progression of the digital economy fractal depicting the relationship with increasing degrees of freedom is captured in Figure 5.1.

Let us also examine the appearance of the physical–vital–mental fractal in one of the most highlighted areas of today—that of energy. Here too, the energy industry is displaying movement through the same three phases. For decades, the focus of energy availability has been primarily through extraction. That is, the primary source of our energy has been carbon-based through oil and gas extracted from the Earth. Let us understand this orientation in a little more detail. In this orientation, the world is viewed as fixed: our source of energy is oil and gas, and these have always provided our energy needs, and will always provide our energy needs. Such notions as the imminence of peak oil, that states that petroleum production will decline at the point where the rate of global petroleum extraction reaches a maximum,[1] are imaginary or are no cause for worry because if it exists, it exists in

[1] For further discussion on this, please refer to: Campbell Colin, *The Coming Oil Crisis* (Essex, UK: Multi-Science Publishing, 2004).

Figure 5.1 The Digital Economy Fractal

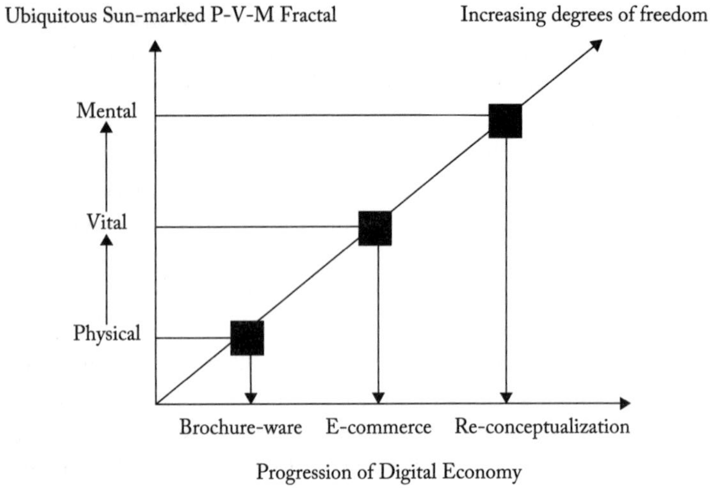

the indefinite future. Further, a carbon-based energy world is what our world is, and nothing can change that now or in the future. In the worst case, if we run out of points of extraction under our existing control, we will extend that control into other areas and regions of the world, or perhaps even into other worlds if need be. This is a purely physical orientation to life, in which the notion of what has been is what will continue to be.

In the face of an increasing acceptance of peak oil and the increasing reality of climate change—a direct result of our obstinate insistence on a way of being that has outlived its utility—there has been a growing shift to maximize the existing flows of extracted energy. That is, without fundamentally altering the source, we are gravitating toward a mindset of allowing the extracted energy to remain in existence for longer, through changing the way it flows and the way it is used. That is, we have begun altering devices and the way energy flow takes place through pipes, so as to prolong the existing flow. This orientation on prolonging or maximizing existing flows is none other than the vital orientation. Ideally, the vital orientation should have existed right from the beginning. But the apparent abundance of extracted energy has not necessitated the movement from the physical to the vital phase of the energy fractal. Actors have been satisfied in staying where they are, and it is only when the limits of a certain orientation are reached that the more progressive among the actors are willing to alter their orientation, thereby also increasing their own degrees of freedom and their ability to become instruments for the underlying Sun-marked physical–vital–mental fractal.

This fractal story does not end here, however. The most progressive among the actors have taken a leap into alternative non-carbon-based energies. There is out-of-the-box thinking on how energies from other sources can be made practically available and utilizable. There is out-of-the-box thinking on what a non-carbon-based economy may look like. This kind of out-of-the-box thinking is representative of the mental dynamic and marks the early transition into the mental phase of the energy industry fractal. A point to be made is that if the ubiquitous Sun-marked physical–vital–mental fractal is a reality, and it certainly seems like it may be, though we will discuss this in more detail in the next chapter, then we already know what shifts people need to make in themselves to facilitate and remain ahead of what seems like an inevitable path on the part of the larger energy fractal. The leaders, whether of this fractal or any other that is discussed, will be those who can make the physical–vital–mental journey in themselves.

The energy industry fractal and its relationship with increasing degrees of freedom is depicted in Figure 5.2.

System-wide Global Politics Fractals

Let us first consider the fractal of relatively recent global politics. Here too we see a shift from the physical to the vital to the mental phase. Note, however, that like the fractal for the global economy, the active and overarching phase is currently at the vital level, and within that we have traversed the fractal within a fractal, through the physical–vital–mental subphases. Hence, in the earlier 20th century, politics was marked by physical prowess and threat. World War I and World War II epitomized this physical orientation in which politics was

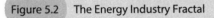

Figure 5.2 The Energy Industry Fractal

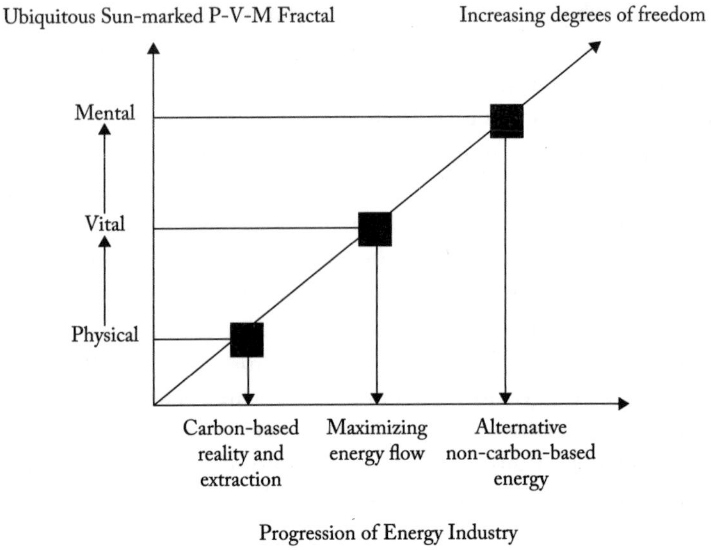

largely about a display of physical powers—armies, weapons—and involved threat to physical boundaries by virtue of physical armies. Balance between global powers was a result of such displays of physical powers. This was the physical phase of the global political fractal.

Post World War II, politics was not so much about the actual physical powers possessed by a country, but about the fear factor involved that the physical powers could be unleashed. Fear, hence, was the motivating lever. In the Cold War, it was the threat and fear of possible nuclear attack that maintained the balance between global powers. The confrontation was not physical, but it was based on emotion and, therefore, self-referencing flows. This is a vital dynamic. Hence, for practical purposes, politics shifted to a primarily vital phase. It is to be noted that for the actors involved, such dynamics offered higher degrees of freedom in which there was no actual loss of physical assets and no actual loss of life, to yet maintain actual power in global affairs.

In more recent times, the balance of global power has become far more complicated and has become dependent on the development of technology and other corporate prowess. Through products and services of different kinds, a country's culture and way of being can be implanted in another part of the world, and its influence can be tangibly felt, without even lifting a finger so as to speak. This is a far more mental orientation to global power. An insightful overview of this approach is provided by John Perkins in his book "Confessions of an Economic Hit Man."[2] Through a clever idea, a whole new way of being can exercise its influence in another part of the world. The promise of local or national business development can cause local governments to yield to other governments. In such a manner, global power is maintained. This orientation to maintaining global power allows its actors an even higher degree of freedom in which the development and the exercise of novel ideas, as opposed to physical assets or vital ploys and masquerades, can alter the global balance of power. This relationship is captured in Figure 5.3:

Figure 5.3 The Global Politics Fractal

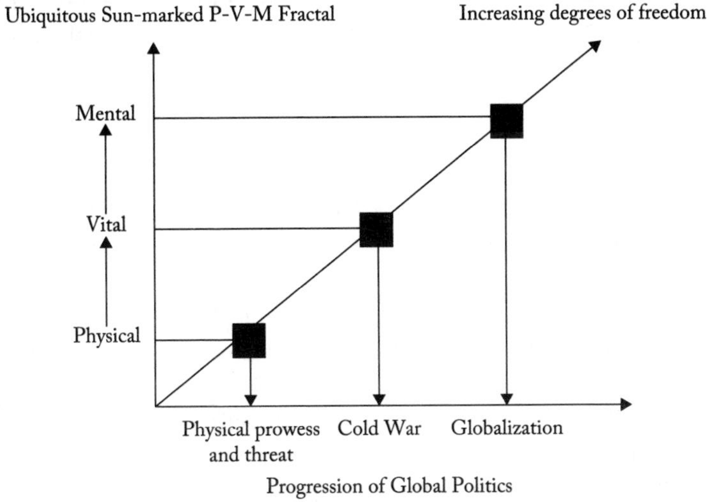

[2] John Perkins, *Confessions of an Economic Hit Man* (Berret -Koehler Publishers, 2005).

Let us look at another manifestation of global power and politics, in the setting of global exchange rates. At the start of this exchange rate fractal, the method for setting global currency rates was purely physical. The amount of gold—a concrete and practically timeless physical asset—a country had determined the strength of a country's currency. This is a purely physical orientation.

At some point, there was a more sophisticated strategic approach that was thought about. The relative vivacity and effective strength of a country's activities in the global arena, measured through demand and supply of a country's currency, being used to determine its currency rate. This is a mental orientation and of course offers actors involved much higher degrees of freedom in which creativity and unleashing of a country's powers can literally overnight alter the demand for its assets.

In reality, we are today at some kind of middle ground between the planned ideal and the gold standards of the past. Hence today, currency rates are for practical purposes set by the balance of power. This is the vital play. Even though it should really be the real-time creativity of a country that determines the demand for its assets, the negotiation between presidents with side deals of all sorts is much more effective in doing so at the moment. Nonetheless, the trajectory is the same. We have the physical-level gold standards of the past, the vital-level negotiations and side deals of the present, and the mental-level real-time creativity of a country of the future. This is summarized in Figure 5.4.

Fractals Related to Science-based Systems of Thought

We will begin by looking at the fractal for physics. For centuries, physics has had a primarily physical orientation. Atoms were thought of as being the indestructible building blocks of every existence. These building blocks were thought of as acting according to fixed laws. All matter was composed of these fundamental building blocks. Understand the nature of these laws and the nature of the atoms, and everything is known regardless of differences in time or space. That is, regardless of how short or long or how slow or fast the time

Figure 5.4 The Exchange Rate Fractal

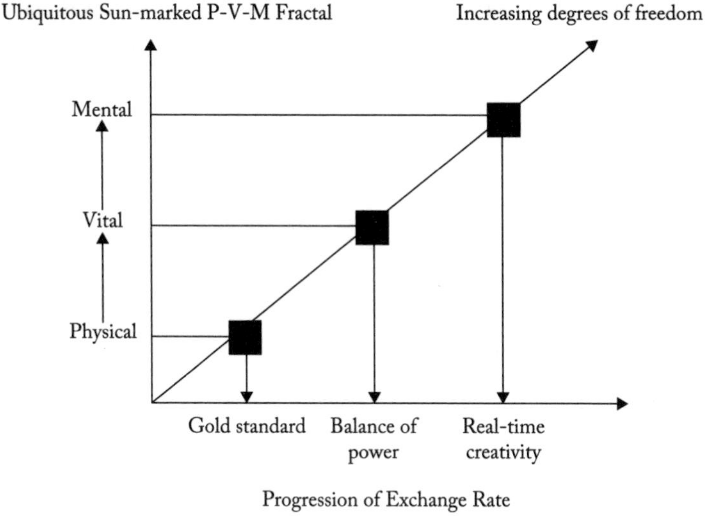

moves, or how minute or vast the space itself becomes, the laws even if understood within a certain time and space, would apply inevitably as the same laws in time and space. This orientation is physical in nature and perhaps is known as the atomic view of nature.

In time, it yielded to the quantum view of nature. This, as we will see, is more of a vital orientation. In the quantum view, the fundamental building block is no more a fixed and indestructible unit—the atom—but a dual-wave particle that changes its nature based on the observation of an actor. Waves become particles, and particles become other particles. There is a spontaneous flow that seems to accompany the fundamental notion of reality. This notion of flow is essentially vital in nature.

It is not that there is a grand purpose, a unifying theme or a teleological underpinning to reality, which would imply a mental orientation and is perhaps where physics is tending to move currently. Hence, the active trajectory has been physical to vital for the beginning of mental. The same physical–vital–mental fractal is revealing itself. This is captured in Figure 5.5.

Figure 5.5 The Physics Fractal

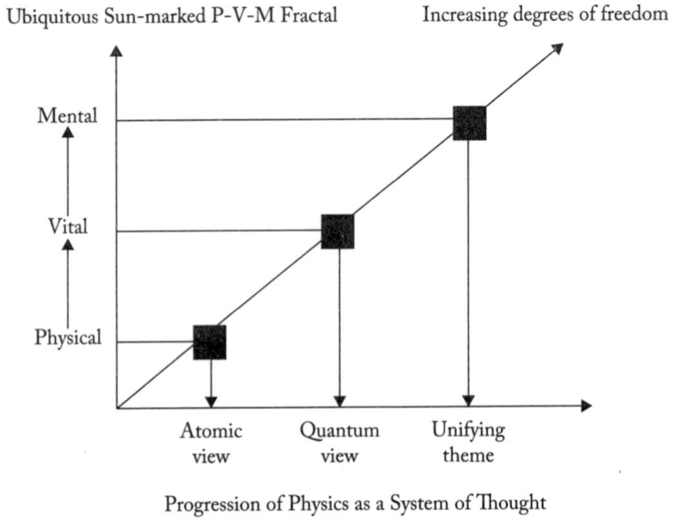

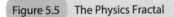

While the physics fractal spans a few centuries, let us turn our attention to an entire field that is only decades old—that is biomimicry. Biomimicry is concerned with design of product and process through emulating nature.[3] In some respects, this is centuries old and some of the wisest most sustainable man-made designs through the centuries have been a result of mimicking nature. In recent decades, however, it is interesting to note that this very field has itself gone through three active phases. In the first phase, there has been an imitation of the form and function of nature. That is, the outer physical aspect of nature has been mimicked in the form and function. An example is as in the Velcro strip which imitates the form and function of a plant in nature. This approach to product and process design is clearly at the physical phase.

Biomimicry then began to emulate process as opposed to form. That is, the focus shifted to the way nature manufactures a product. The emphasis is not on why, but more on what. Hence, for

[3] For a more elaborate treatment of this subject, please refer to: Janine Benyus, *Biomimicry: Innovation Inspired by Nature* (New York: Harper-Perennial, 2002).

example, nature's approach to manufacturing insulin was emulated by an understanding of the process by which this happens. The same agents and the same process as occur in nature were then emulated at manufacturing scale. This imitation of process, without getting into the how and why, without fully understanding the larger system question of how product manufactured in this fashion might interact with other cells in the body, or without a comprehensive understanding of what is really happening at the level of the cell, is a vital as opposed to a mental process. Hence, this phase of biomimicry can be thought of as the vital phase.

In the third phase, emphasis of biomimicry has shifted much more to a whole system's view. Hence, designs such as closed-loop life cycles, cradle-to-cradle design, and the notion that waste equals food, that are based on a far more holistic understanding of nature's operations, have begun to become archetypes for the creation of human product designs and manufacturing processes. McDonough and Braungart's book *Cradle to Cradle: Remaking the Way We Make Things*[4] is an insightful exploration into this approach. This is clearly at the mental level in which deeper and more elaborate system design is understood and, then becomes the basis for not just replicating, as in the physical and vital phases, but of the formulation of design principles that are then leveraged in the creation of product and process that have hitherto never appeared in nature. Hence, we find the same physical–vital–mental sequence repeated in the specialized field of biomimicry. This sequence is summarized in Figure 5.6.

Other General Fractals

In organization thought too, we see an instance of the ubiquitous fractal repeating itself. When an organization is first conceived, it is often done so as a conglomeration of distinct and isolated departments. There are perhaps many ways in which these distinct departments could in fact interact with one another and operate together. It is interesting

[4] William McDonough and Michael Braungart, *Cradle to Cradle: Remaking the Way We Make Things* (New York: North Point Press, 2002).

Figure 5.6 The Biomimicry Fractal

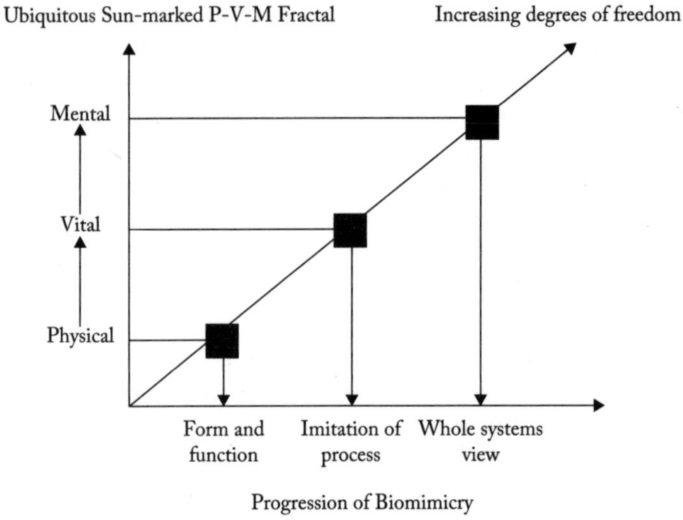

to note, however, that in most cases what emerges quite naturally is a silo mentality. Each department, unit, or function views itself as independent from the others. These attitudes or biases get hardened into fact, and what emerges is the physical view—the fixed view of a fixed world. This has its utility in which the different departments, functions, or units are able to specialize and incarnate something of the meaning of that silo more fully.

If an organization were to continue with this orientation, then increasing inefficiencies would result soon. Of necessity, the organization would need to morph into another conception of itself. As we look at the historical evolution of the modern-day organization, what we find is the function of department view morphing into the process view. The organization is often reconceived as a number of processes that exist to fulfill the stated goals of the organization. If it serves customers, then there may be a customer ordering and a customer fulfillment process. There may be a quality management process, a product design process, among others. These processes typically cut across established functions of departments and increase the *flow* in the organization. Established views are broken down, and increasing activity and connection are bought to the organization. Raw material sources are linked to subsequent value-adding activities that culminate in the final product or service that the organization provides. In this respect, this is a vital orientation to organizational design.

A mental orientation would necessitate the organization, reconfiguring itself in real time to best allow fulfillment of what needed to be accomplished at the moment. All moments would lead inevitably to fulfilling the raison d'être of the organization. The raison d'être, hence, would be the real driver of organizational design and, in the end analysis, would stand as the arbiter for how an organization needed to morph in order to fulfill its purpose. It may be the case in which processes become fully dynamic in nature. That is, the required process taking control as the need arises. Processes and focus become active as needed. Parts of the organization reconfigure themselves to dovetail into the needed focus areas. Note that such an organization can only come into existence once the physical and vital stages of organizational design have been mastered. For a real time, reconception of activities of an organization requires a high degree of skill and capability that the other phases allow it to develop. Hence, the organization design fractal too appears to display a sequential movement through the physical, vital, and mental phases. This is summarized in Figure 5.7.

We have of course stated through the length of this book that the Sun-marked physical–vital–mental fractal is the fractal embedded in the DNA of life and that pushes life to make progress. But let us independently examine the process of progress. Whether one is learning to play tennis or learning a new language, or whether a business is learning the ropes in a new market segment, there appears to be a common three-phased process of making progress. At the first stage, there is an introduction to the elements of the new field. One learns the alphabet if they have the basic elements which when practiced begin to bring mastery in the area. Each of these basic elements has a distinct reality and appears as an independent entity that has to be assimilated into one's way of being. This focus on learning the independent and distinct elements is like passing through the physical phase of progress. The reality of the ball and its motion, the racket and its motion, and the stroke combining the two have to be independently

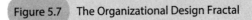

Figure 5.7 The Organizational Design Fractal

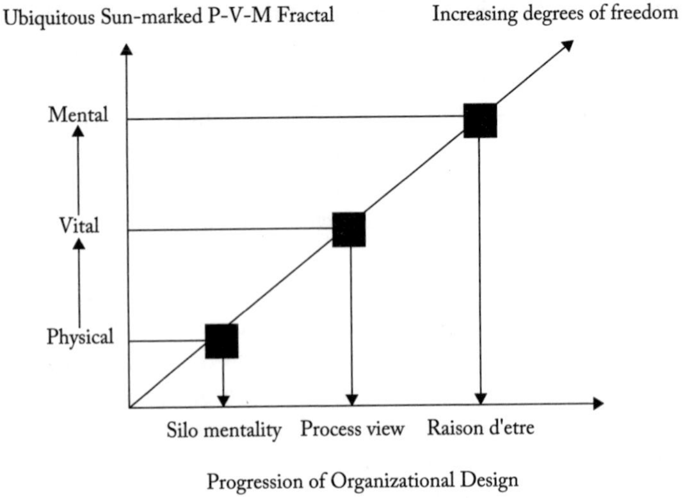

practiced again and again. Then, a phase of experimentation begins, the phase of vitality, where different combinations can be practiced. Finally, this culminates in a phase of mentality, where uniqueness and truer mastery can manifest. Without first passing through the physical and vital stages, however, the reason for playing and the reason for entering into a new segment can never be realized. The process for progress itself, therefore, seems to need to traverse the three stages. This is summarized in Figure 5.8.

Summary

In every system-related fractal discussed, the trajectory of progress is determined by the physical–vital–mental sequence of phases. It is not that the majority of actors move automatically from one to another. Rather, it is the leaders who make the move. We can hypothesize that they were able to make the move because within themselves, it is the mental orientation that is far more active than the vital or physical orientations, or they worked to make this the reality of who they were being. The rest of the actors followed as a natural

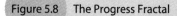

Figure 5.8 The Progress Fractal

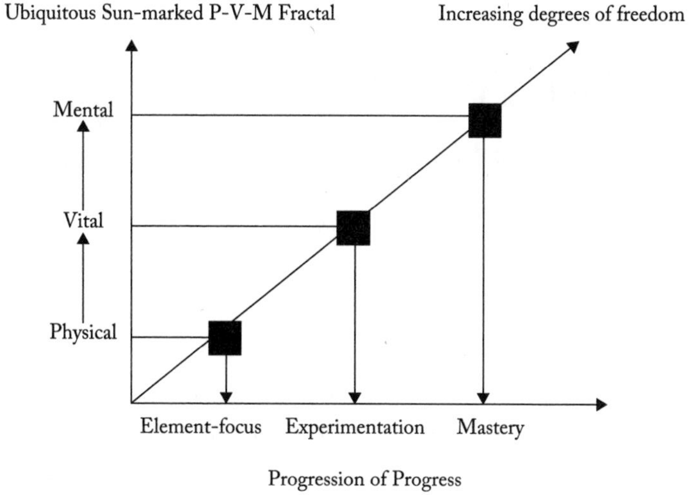

act of survival, precisely because it is the mental level that affords many more degrees of freedom. The natural tendencies, the traditions of the hour, are no doubt backward-pointing. Against this general milieu, it is our hypothesis that the break from the past to the future offered the various protagonists of the aforementioned fractals a chance to further strengthen their individualities. Their uniqueness and way of being was reflected in the general breakthroughs that manifested in the shifting of phases of the fractals themselves. It was the rush of this experience, of incarnating something of who they really are, that in itself becomes the draw for completing or pushing the respective fractal journeys. We can further hypothesize that this inherent draw, this urge to complete the fractal journeys originates from the reality of the ubiquitous Sun-marked physical–vital–mental fractal that has embedded itself in the DNA of life.

In this chapter, we have examined general fractals that occur at the level of the system. This examination completes our general examination at progressively larger and more complex levels of organization. In the next chapter, we will turn our attention to the process of evolution itself, and then step back to examine the fractal model and its validity.

The Evolution Pattern 6

Focus: A look at evolution of life on Earth, and how the patterns that are emerging in different fields of life parallels this overarching or base pattern.

Key Concepts: Nature of creation as a function of sequencing of building blocks | Single ladder | Blueprint of progress | The evolution fractal | Records of evolution and progressive manifestation | Physical subphase of physical phase of evolution fractal | Atomic particles and physical sub-subphase | Fusing together and vital sub-subphase | Identity of form and mental sub-subphase | Closed-system interaction and vital subphase of physical phase of evolution fractal | Yearning and mental subphase of physical phase | Autonomous cellular activity at physical subphase of vital phase of evolution fractal | Experimentation and vital subphase of vital phase of evolution fractal | Increased yearning for identity and mental subphase of vital phase of evolution fractal | Culmination of vital phase of evolution fractal and basis of mental phase of evolution fractal | Simple thought elements and physical subphase in mental phase of evolution fractal | Choice and experimentation and vital subphase in mental phase in evolution fractal | Advanced mind elements and mental subphase of mental phase of evolution fractal | "What the eye can see" and physical sub-subphase of mental subphase of mental phase of evolution fractal | Beginnings of history | Vital sub-subphase of mental subphase of mental phase of evolution fractal | Transition from vital sub-subphase to mental sub-subphase of mental phase of evolution fractal | Recorded history as journey through vital sub-subphase | Birth of the Internet as a water-shed event | Internet soft-voice fractal | Beginning of open communication and physical phase of Internet soft-voice fractal | Multiplication of voices and vital phase of soft-voice fractal | Shifting of power and mental phase of soft-voice fractal | Carbon-based economy as surfacing of embedded physical–vital patterns | Carbon-based economy as a rite of passage | Earth–Sun dance | Extending the Gaia hypothesis: Earth becomes an Earth–Sun | Fractal architecture applied to Earth–Sun dance | Astronomy and the physical view of the Earth–Sun dance | Astrology and vital view of Earth–Sun dance | Purpose and meaning and mental view of Earth–Sun dance | Sun-potential

Introduction

Thus far, we have focused on several rungs of a potentially single ladder consisting of progressively more complex and encompassing instances of an organization. Interpretation and clarity with respect to dynamics of these rungs was afforded by hypothesizing a seed pattern prevalent in the mutual Earth–Sun dance. This seed pattern revealed the building blocks for each rung on the ladder. Many different creations are possible, and we hypothesized that the stringing together of the building blocks in a particular sequence will determine the nature of the creation or creations at that particular rung. We also hypothesize that the rungs are part of a single ladder, if and only if the building blocks are sequenced to replicate the Sun-marked physical–vital–mental pattern at each subsequent rung all the way till the highest rung we can conceive – a level that transcends efforts by the human species. This has to be the case if we are talking about a single ladder that connects the person level to such a level. That is, this hypothesis has validity only if we see the physical–vital–mental pattern prevalent at a level where human beings have had no possible influence over the existence of this pattern. This would prove, from a logical point of view that indeed the hypothesized seed pattern that we started out with exists in the context of a larger, beyond-human creation, such as the mutual Earth–Sun dance.

If this were the case, this ladder, this fractal ladder, then conceivably forms part of a special imprint that is in a manner of speaking a ubiquitous blueprint for progress. We examined the person rung, the business rung, the economy rung, and several instances of the *system* rung. In other words, we have examined successive levels of human creativity and found that indeed progress at each of these levels is determined by the particular sequencing of building blocks as embedded in the Sun-marked physical–vital–mental fractal. That is, where this sequencing is not repeated, we do not see a progressive creation, but rather a status quo or even a destructive creation. Now we step beyond systems of human creativity to examine the canvass of nature herself. Does this same imprint of progress manifest itself in the DNA of nature? If so, as we have suggested, this opens us to a wholly different context and interpretation of the fractal ladder.

In this chapter, we will examine if the physical–vital–mental pattern similarly exists in nature. If so, we will further apply the same architecture of a day – the physical, vital, and mental phases that complete its sense, to gain further insight into the physical, vital, and mental phases that must have appeared in nature. We will examine the implications of this progressive imprint in nature. We will in particular examine the vast output of the last century in the context of this progressive imprint. This also leads to an interesting reinterpretation of history and geography. From the vantage point we have gained, we will also examine the meaning of the Earth–Sun dance in more detail. We will reserve the next chapter, however, for reexamining the rungs and context of a potential fractal ladder and for beginning to shed a different light on the established systems and other possibilities of human creativity.

The Physical Phase of the Evolution Fractal

Getting right to the key point, in a nutshell, records of evolution on Earth have indeed revealed a progressive manifestation. In very broad terms, a purely *physical* creation characterized by inanimate matter, yielded to a progressively more active *vital* creation characterized by many different life forms, that in turn yielded to a progressively more active *mental* creation characterized first by simple mental capability in animal form, and then by relatively more complex mental capability in human form.

Let us examine this journey in more detail. In the beginning, there were purely material elements of the likes of rock, minerals, and water. This perhaps can be thought of as the physical subphase of the physical phase of the evolution fractal. Figure 6.1 sheds light on this breakdown.

This subphase is characterized by the creation of visible material elements. There is no movement and no activity between the material elements. These base materials house many different atomic and molecular configurations that manifest in different color and texture and substance. These then become the basis for a more progressive creation. This initial state of stability can itself be thought of as being the result of the physical–vital–mental fractal and as the starting point for a new physical–vital–mental fractal. In a fractal model, such an analysis, leveraging recursion is natural.

In the case where the physical subphase of the physical level is the result of the application of a physical–vital–mental fractal, the starting point must have been a universe of atomic particles (see Figure 6.1). This initial state of atomic particle can be thought of as the physical sub-subphase in the physical subphase. These atomic particles then fused together, likely under intense temperatures that may have characterized the nature of existence eons ago. This fusing together can be thought of as the vital sub-subphase in the physical subphase. When all the flowing and fusing is done and when atomic particles have exercised their energies to form new and more elaborate structures, what results is a final physical identity of various forms of matter, the mental sub-subphase in the physical subphase.

This then is the new starting point, the physical subphase in the physical phase, where there are different base elements – the rocks, minerals, and water. In the vital subphase, the geographical placement of these base elements is rearranged, whether through earthquake, wind, storm, action or primeval fire, to create a landscape in which interaction of basic elements in a continual and closed system

Figure 6.1 The Physical Phase of the Evolution Fractal

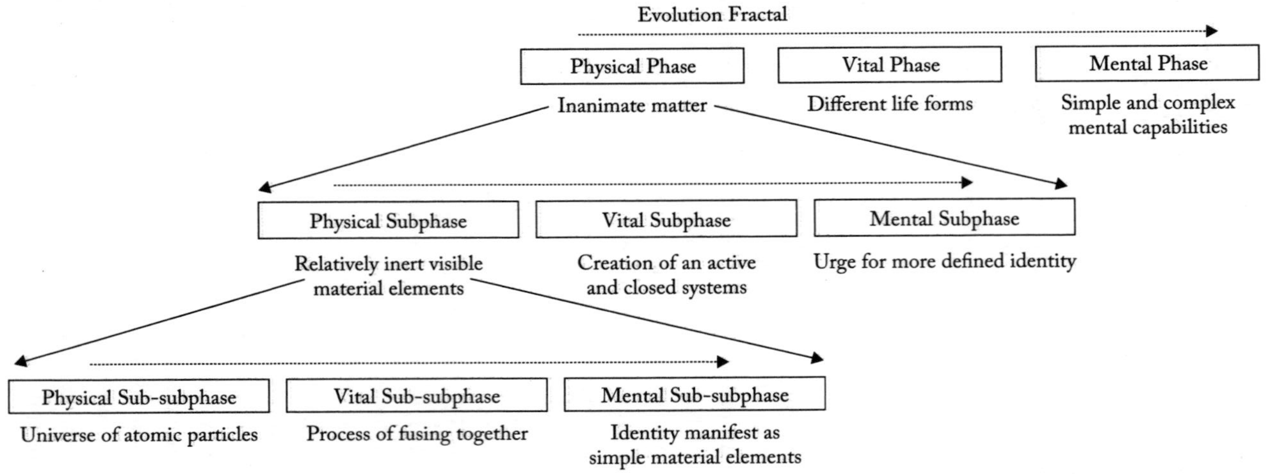

becomes the reality. In the mental subphase, the urge for a more defined identity surfaces, and a fundamental yearning to more fully express and to be amidst the possibility of the interaction of the elements also becomes alive as depicted in Figure 6.1.

The Vital Phase of the Evolution Fractal

This yearning, this need to be more fully alive expresses itself in simple single-celled organisms. This is the start of life, of a much vaster experimentation, of a play of myriad energies, and of the vital phase in nature's evolution. In other words, this basis of autonomous cellular activity represents the physical subphase of this vital phase of the evolution fractal. Figure 6.2 depicts this and other developments.

At the culmination of this subphase, cells have perhaps learned a number of important basic functions: assimilation of sunlight and other basic nutrients from their environments, processing of these nutrients to accommodate a more complex set of basic activities such as locomotion, elimination of unneeded byproducts, alteration of genetic material to accommodate new and valuable impulses, creation of different chemicals and substances that manifest in different physical features and functions, most optimal processes for sub-division and combination with other types of cells, among others.

The physical foundation of the vital phase has been laid. In the vital subphase, there is expression and experimentation and combination of these single and emerging multi-cellular organisms to create an abundance of plant life and even very simple animal life in the waters and on the land. The yearning in matter has now expressed itself in simple life forms that are pervasive across and within the initial material elements. In the mental subphase of the vital phase of the evolution fractal, this abundance of simple life yearns for even further definition of identity and expression of possibility. Collectivities and group-intelligence forms: Ants live in anthills, bees form beehives, and birds fly in packs and figure out what best to do prolong their collective lives. This is the culmination of the vital phase in the evolution fractal, and the basis of the mental level in the evolution fractal.

Figure 6.2 The Vital Phase of the Evolution Fractal

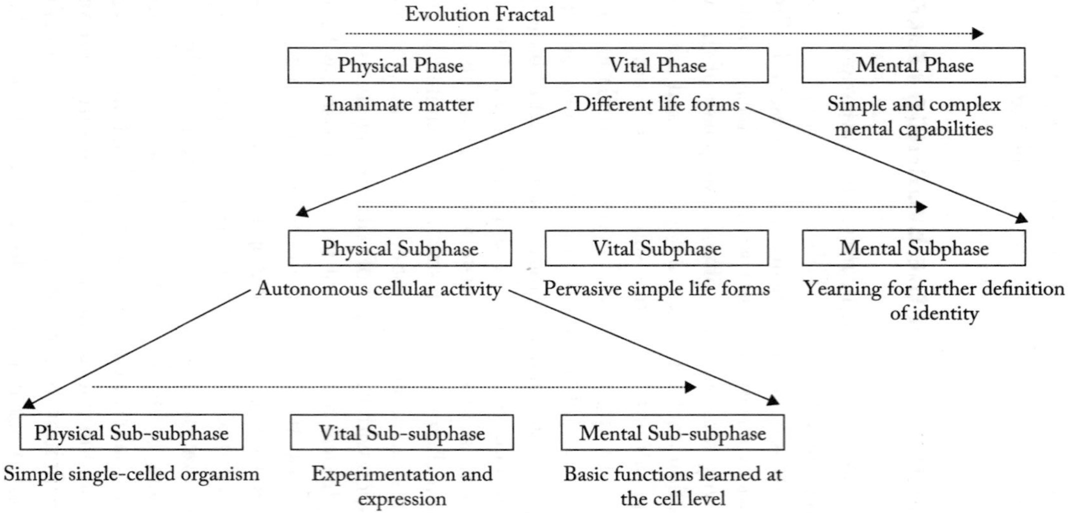
Evolution Fractal
Physical Phase
Inanimate matter
Vital Phase
Different life forms
Mental Phase
Simple and complex mental capabilities
Physical Subphase
Autonomous cellular activity
Vital Subphase
Pervasive simple life forms
Mental Subphase
Yearning for further definition of identity
Physical Sub-subphase
Simple single-celled organism
Vital Sub-subphase
Experimentation and expression
Mental Sub-subphase
Basic functions learned at the cell level

The Mental Phase in the Evolution Fractal[1]

Thought that is instinctive as opposed to reasoned is already manifesting. Grunts and whistles of animals and birds are forming the bases of language. Coordination of hand with eye to manipulate objects in the environment is becoming more of a reality. Simple cause and effect relationship and logic is beginning to manifest. This can be thought of as the physical subphase in the mental phase of the evolution fractal. Figure 6.3 depicts this and other developments at the mental level.

This development takes place using "what the eye can see" as the laboratory. All is applied simply to external objects. The physical subphase, thus, occurs in the physical context. Animal life applies simple physical orientation, mental-level dynamics to enhance basic life functions.

Ape now chooses to stand upright and seeks to explore the realms beyond forest and tree. Choice, or disengagement from the herd mentality, is beginning to surface more. Now begins the phase of more conscious manipulation of life and environment to further differentiate oneself. Experimentation more forcefully combines with basic mental-level capabilities, all in the pursuit of more complete expression of emerging identity. This is the vital subphase of the mental phase of the evolution fractal. Some walking apes go south, some go west. Some live in caves, some near the water. Some eat deer, others eat nuts. Some sing at the end of the day, and some dance at the end of the day. Some kill with rocks, some discover fire. At the end of this phase, ape, perhaps, has become a simple man. This marks the transition to the mental subphase of the mental phase of the evolution fractal.

Fundamental basics for mental level functioning – reason, logic, memory, and even imagination – are beginning to manifest. When we

[1] Please note that while the creation of these phases is only a thought experiment applying the emerging fractal model, Sri Aurobindo's *The Life Divine* (Pondicherry: Sri Aurobindo Ashram, 1950) has the most detailed and robust explanations of evolution I have been exposed to. This thought experiment is likely influenced by his thought.

Figure 6.3 The Mental Phase of the Evolution Fractal

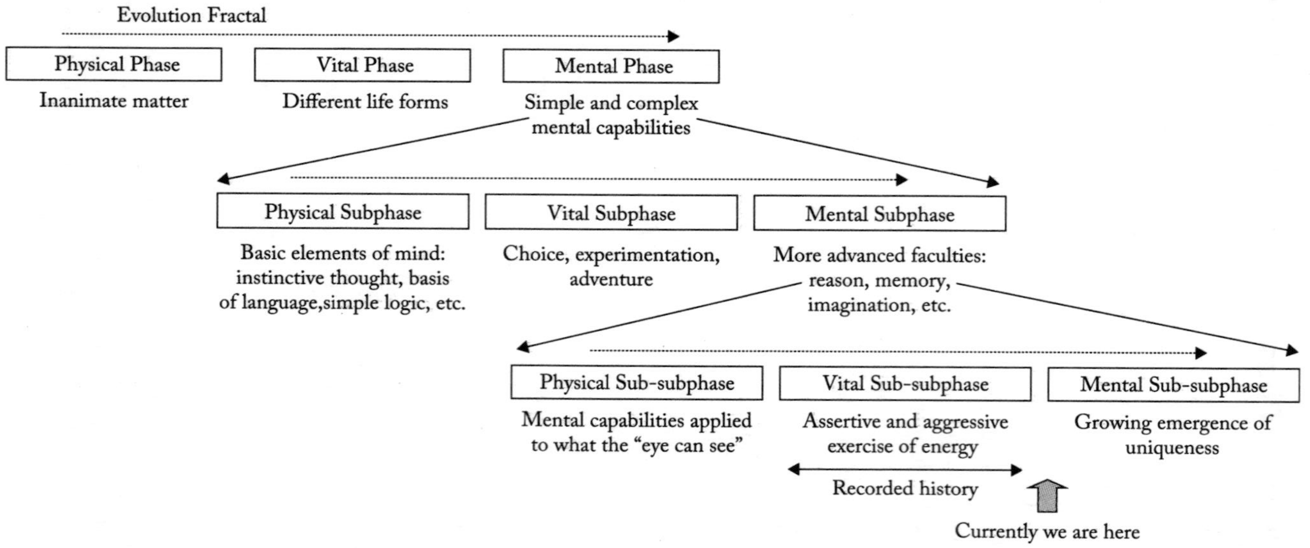

began exploration of the Sun-marked physical–vital–mental fractal at the level of person in Chapter 2, we had discussed the mental orientations that a person can have that would influence his outlook and lives. This is the stuff of the mental subphase of the mental phase of the evolution fractal drawn out over a much longer stretch of time. At first humans apply their growing mental capabilities to what the eye can see. This is the physical sub-subphase of the mental subphase of the mental phase of the evolution fractal. Possibility is an incremental function of what has already been achieved. And even that possibility cannot transcend certain limits inherent in what has already been created through eons of history. The past defines the future. Material reality is the basis, and material reality has established laws which when known, everything is known. The human is a material being. Expression and mentality have arisen as means to prolong this material basis and to protect and incrementally enhance possibility within reasonable limits. This physical sub-subphase of the mental subphase of the mental phase of the evolution fractal perhaps marks our very, very distant past and the beginnings of history that we have lost track of or have not even considered when we consider the progression of history. This is approximately speaking, for who knows what level of sub-fractals journeying through the respective physical–vital–mental realms had to be pursued to make the shifts that would endure and to be followed by the vital sub-subphase of the mental subphase of the mental-level fractal.

The vital sub-subphase was likely marked by the need for assertive and even aggressive exercise of growing energies, in the interest of further expression of identity. Identity, however, was synonymous with experiencing a range of emotions and narrower self-building thoughts and actions of various kinds. I would opine, given many of the global challenges that we are facing on a simultaneous basis, that we are now beginning to transition from the vital sub-subphase to the mental sub-subphase of the mental subphase of the mental phase of the evolution fractal. I would opine that all recorded history is only the imperfect recording of our journey through this vital sub-subphase. (Both these opinions are depicted in the lower right corner of Figure 6.3 by respective arrows.). Further light can likely be shed on this by considering the physical–vital–mental fractal that animated this sub-subphase. I would opine that the human species has yet to become the true mental being. Perhaps the next thousand years is all about this.

Transition from the Vital Sub-subphase to the Mental Sub-subphase

The point is that even when we consider the canvas of nature and her evolution, we see this progression through physical, vital, and mental phases. From carbon dating, we know that rocks have been around much longer even than any fossils, whether of plant or animal, and certainly much longer than human skeletons. We thus know for a fact that the physical preceded the vital that in turn preceded the mental. In the discussion here, we have hypothesized how each of these phases may have unrolled, using the physical–vital–mental sequence itself to shed light on each phase of the evolutionary fractal. We have an indication that history must be very, very old and that we are now undergoing a transition likely between the vital sub-subphase and the mental sub-subphase of the mental subphase of the mental phase of the evolution fractal. By some preliminary estimates, linked to initial European exploration by sea to Asia and the Americas, and the consequent vital-level exploitation that has proceeded in each of these regions, the transition has been in effect for perhaps 2,000 years or more, and is now reaching a head as is evident by major global problems we are facing on many different fronts. More will be said about this later. A potentially 2,000-year transition from one sub-subphase to another perhaps sheds light on the expansive timelines of history, especially if one considers that a physical phase is, by definition, obstinate and long, and must exist for a much, much longer time than a vital or a mental phase and the transition of 2,000 years we are talking about now is in the vital phase which by its nature is likely much more fluid than others that preceded it.

On a philosophical note, when we contrast what are potentially such expansive timelines with a day any one of us may be experiencing today, replete with its overwhelming issues, we must pause and ask, "but what will endure?" and "what would make sense were we to step into the silence in the eye of the storm?" We will come back to this later as we begin to consider some of the properties of a world that perhaps is animated by a fractal ladder of the type we seem to be uncovering now.

Ostensibly, a defining event that has signaled transition from a predominantly vital to a more mental phase, even if it be within an overarching vital phase, is the birth of the Internet and the ensuing digital economy. This event was initially the result of idealism, a decidedly mental-level dynamic. Researchers in different universities around the world were motivated to share files and research. An *open* architecture as opposed to the *closed* or *secretive* dynamics of a self-enhancing vitally centered organism was the basis of this creation.[2] This led to the rapid growth of local networks connecting together to form regional and finally a global network that soon came to be known as the Internet. A very different form of interaction and communication between peoples around the world had been facilitated. E-mail, webpages, file sharing, voice and audio sharing, and video sharing, though initially designed for asynchronous communication, through the increase in computing and network processing power is for all practical purposes rapidly approaching synchronous communication. This is facilitating the formation of the Internet-based communities, and the more cohesive organization of softer voices, in the face of the dominant and louder vital voices of the present that it can be argued, is expediting transcendence of existing barriers and threatening dominant corporate-based power structures.

But it should also be noted, as pointed out in a previous discussion on the digital economy fractal, that the birth of the Internet and the digital economy has also facilitated the more rapid development of vital-level tendencies and is in fact bringing the vital-level nature of the global economy to a head. For instance, facilitated by rapid digital-based asset transfer, corporations can now more easily disconnect their presence from their action, transferring their ownership, losses, and profits, from one place of the world to another, thereby becoming more elusive and much more vital in nature. Similarly, it is

[2] For a more detailed treatment of this subject, please refer to: Don Tapscott, *The Digital Economy* (New York: McGraw-Hill Book Company, 1996).

much easier for desire of all kinds, a decidedly vital-level dynamic, to be instantaneously fulfilled by virtue of the rapidity and immediacy of transaction offered by the Internet. In some sense, the Internet has become a magnifier of tendencies. Being that the general milieu in which the Internet has grown is already vital in nature, it is the softer voices, perhaps of the future, that relatively speaking, are magnified more and that stand out as a potential threat to deeply embedded power structures. It is this relative shift in power, from the past to the future that is of significance, and when seen in context of the overarching dynamics of a fractal model indicate the cusp or the potential beginnings of a more progressive dynamic in line with the overall evolutionary fractal we are presently considering.

But even these softer voices need to go through the physical–vital–mental fractal to reach a more progressive culmination of their possibilities. If they go through another pattern or simply remain at the physical level, we hypothesize that they will not reach the most progressive culmination of their possibilities. The facilitation of the softer voices through the opening up of communication can perhaps be thought of as the base materials, the physical phase in this fractal. In the vital phase, there will be many more soft voices that are heard. Different points of view will rise to the surface. Many different points of views, let us point out, are characteristic of the mental level and are no doubt good, especially given that at the cusp it has been a few loud voices, typically that of elitist vitally driven organizations, that some would say have been the occult rulers of society, and that seem to be driving things. However, in the vital phase of this soft-voice fractal, it will be difficult to judge as to who truly represents the future and who is just expressing because expression seems to be the thing of the day. Unless this fractal can migrate to the mental level, it will likely result in little action that truly moves the needle in shifting power away from the occult or overt and elitist rulers of society.

At the end of the day, this fractal model is about connecting inner power with global change. It is about the potential of this, where certain inner conditions to be fulfilled. These inner conditions have to do with making a fractal journey within oneself so that one may break the bounds that keep them anchored to the past. It is about a deep level of questioning in which who one stands for, at the core of their being, is allowed to come to the surface. This cannot happen unless the various tendencies that one is inundated with and constantly lives with, can begin to recede into the background, and the authenticity of one's being, that creative ability that finds effectiveness in the fractal dynamic of influence, can come to the surface. In the light of that inner authenticity, the violations that are constantly prolonged, even by many softer voices, will become clear, and then the soft-voice fractal that is even being facilitated by the Internet will find culmination in a truer mental phase. For what standard, except that of a greater and more comprehensively perceiving and guiding light, the substance of authenticity can possibly dissect the need of many voices and discover the thing to be done, among the many choices that seem to be continually flung into one's being from the possibilities of life. The progression of the soft-voice fractal is summarized in Figure 6.4.

It is significant to note that we are currently in the extraction or vital phase of the energy fractal, which we had discussed in the previous chapter. Symbolically, extraction of gas and oil is about unearthing deeply embedded physical and vital constructs in the form of

Figure 6.4 The Internet Soft-voice Fractal

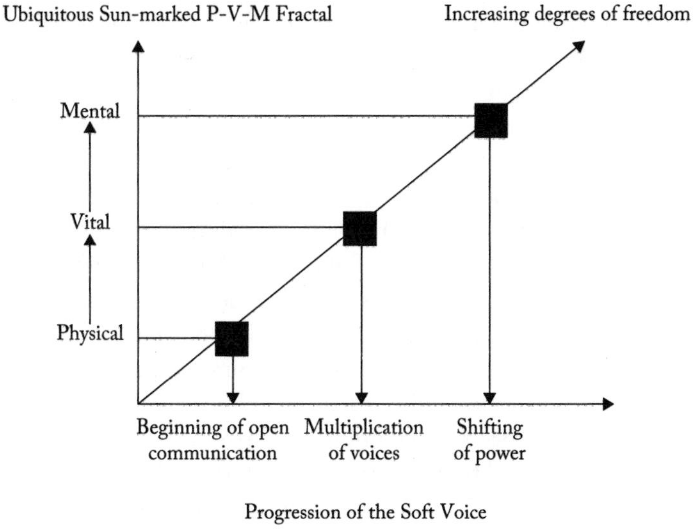

millennium-old plants and animals to fuel the present. These myopic albeit energetic constructs, and what they stand for in the consciousness and outlooks they represent, have in a sense resurfaced to fuel our present. It is not surprising, therefore, that we have blind dynamics abroad in all aspects of our global life that, of course being of a purely physical–vital nature, cannot see beyond its own nose and is swiftly and assuredly leading us toward the end of a phase. The carbon-based economy, in this view of things, is the unearthing of an outdated way of being that needs to be worked through and resolved, that becomes a massive rite of passage, in order that we can more completely grasp the glory of the future. In this passage though, repeated global crises of various kinds, ranging from social to environmental to financial, are inevitable. Culmination of a number of global fractals, including the global economy, global political, and energy fractals, that we have already discussed in previous parts, hint at the possibilities of the immediate future. These will be discussed in greater detail later in the book.

The Earth–Sun System

When we view this evolution fractal from its origins of atomic particles, through inanimate matter and animate life, through birth of man, and the push to greater collaboration and reason, as made possible through the surfacing of the Internet, one must ask, but who is it all for? When we viewed the fractals that were the result of human creativity, we could position the human at the center and say that the progress is all for the good of humankind. But what when we look at this vast evolution fractal that scans the development of nature? Where was the human in all of this? The human is just a recent addition in the scheme of things. What is the necessity of this same pattern developing over eons and eons, and who benefits from it all?

Let us go back to the original Earth–Sun dance for a possible answer to this question. The Earth and Sun have been locked in mutual embrace since the beginning of Earth time. Some have posited that it originated from the Sun, as most other planets in our solar system. It was flung off as a ball of fire into orbit around the Sun and gradually condensed into more solid and recognizable form. All its life, following that, has been an expression of the mutual Earth–Sun dance, in which its very dynamics have been determined by the nature of the dance. We had begun this book with the hypothesis that the constant spinning around its own axis, a primary movement of that dance, had embedded the three-part architecture of the day into its fibers and into its very meaning. Physical, vital, and mental phases, consequently determined the DNA of the progress of the Earth.

So when we come back to the question as to who has benefited from this progress, the comprehensive answer is much more than the human. It is certainly the entire Earth–Sun system that has benefited, of which the human is a recent surfacing. In considering the evolution of nature on Earth, it is clearly Earth that has progressed. Earth has expressed the possibilities at its core, in progressively more elaborate physical, vital, and now mental garbs. It is not the structures that have emerged in the physical, vital, and mental plays that have been the recipient of the progress—it is Earth—that seemingly stands behind all this. Lovelock's Gaia hypothesis[3] has posited a living Earth that regulates herself to ensure her own longevity. But in this fractal hypothesis, we are going even further to say that the physical–vital–mental journeys gradually imbue the constructs of Earth with more of the characteristics of the sun. Earth herself becomes an Earth–Sun. There is permanence, solidity, expansiveness, and self-light that emerge as a result of the successful physical–vital–mental fractal journeys. The nature of the Earth changes to embody the nature of the Sun in material form. The Earth–Sun system regulates itself to bring the energy and consciousness present in the Sun into very material form using the matter of the Earth. But why should this be surprising, given that Earth is herself a portion of the Sun?

Applying the fractal architecture to the Earth–Sun dance, we emerge with three interpretations of the Earth–Sun reality. In the physical interpretation, all is "what the eye can see." This view is consistent with the view of astronomy and is most concerned with the evolution, from a material point of view, the physics, chemistry, and

[3] For a detailed treatment of the Gaia hypothesis, please refer to James Lovelock, *The Revenge of Gaia* (New York: Basic Books, 2006).

interaction of the Earth with the Sun in its material aspects. In this view, the Earth is bound to the Sun by laws of physics and develops under the aegis of solar energy which becomes the basis of all chemistry on Earth. The interaction of the Earth and the Sun sets the rhythms of days, seasons, and years.

The vital interpretation tends more, perhaps, to the views of astrology in that the apparent relative positions of celestial objects, and in this case the relative positions of the Earth and Sun against the backdrop of the heavenly skies at certain times determine the nature of a vast array of earthly matters. This view is not so much about the meaning of things, as about the flows of earthly circumstance, determined by the position in relative trajectories or flows of celestial bodies. Hence, it appears to be more of a vital interpretation than anything else.

In the mental interpretation, there is an underlying and combined meaning and purpose in the interaction of the two entities. The meaning and purpose is greater and invisible and the Earth–Sun system is a symbol of this meaning and purpose. There is no part of this combined construct that is small or less important. In this interpretation, Earth is the starting point in this eon-long journey, and the Earth–Sun is the apparent end. The very fact that Earth evolves into an Earth–Sun indicates that it always had the Sun-potential inherent in it. In the mental interpretation of the Earth–Sun dance, there is also something behind the physical, vital, and mental plays and appearances, whether at the level of the person, the organization, the economy, or one of the many systems or of evolution on Earth, that seems to be the witness and benefactor of the progress. In fact the progress can only take place when there is a certain separation from the physical, the vital and the mental, and a realization that each of these is only a phase through which more of what exists *behind* is effectively expressing itself. We will come back to this in more detail when we consider what it means to operate in a world characterized by a fractal ladder of the type we are hopefully beginning to more concretely envision now.

The point to be noted is that as in the application of fractal architectures to various entities we have examined earlier, there is a fuller meaning and possibility inherent in the entity that surfaces and that can be grasped than in the absence of applying such fractal architecture analysis. The richness of the Earth–Sun construct and the possibility and meaning of it similarly comes to the surface on application of fractal architecture analysis.

Summary

In this chapter, we have examined the existence of the Sun-marked physical–vital–mental fractal in the progression of an eon-old nature. This brings to completion our examination of the observable rungs of existence, starting from the micro- and macro-fractal dynamics at the level of person, through the levels of organizations, corporation, and economy, through the various system-level instances, culminating in the very canvas of nature. These observations have surfaced an extension to the Gaia hypothesis, to view our vaster system as a manifestation of a living Earth–Sun system, and left us with the question as to who is the real benefactor of such progress as made possible by the physical–vital–mental journeys. It has also left us with the question as to how fundamental dynamics of life may be reconceived in light of a possible fractal ladder. These are questions we will begin to turn our attention to now.

The Fractal Ladder 7

Focus: The linking together of the similar patterns appearing across different fields and systems, in reality different *scales*, to illustrate a fantastic ubiquitous fractal – perhaps part of a signature of a conscious design or implicit aspiration behind things.

Key Concepts: Pathways | Common building blocks | Extending idea of fractal geometry into complex behavioral structures | World out there is not really a world out there | Fractal reality vs fractal ladder | Fractal ladder as a way out of contradictions | Key to climbing the fractal ladder | Story of progress and the physical–vital–mental journey | Climbing the rungs of the fractal ladder to connect inner power to global change | Stepwise journey | Fractal ladder as a fractal for progress | Miracle of progress | Upward and downward causality | Universality of downward causality | Safe passage in the vortex | Personification of progress | Progress as a witness | Creation, power, and change in the world | Qualities of progress: omnipresence, omniscience, omnipotence, omnicaring | Progress as a mother | Relationship with progress | Exceptional beings | Secret of power | Progress and stagnated journeying | Shifting our story of disbelief by completing the Sun-marked physical–vital–mental journey | Our tremendous choice

Introduction

We began this book with the hypothesis that for a person to have a true impact in the world, to "become the change that one wishes to see in the world," would necessitate that the change has a way to ripple out into progressively more complex levels of organization. The change that occurred in a person would need to be able to manifest at the level of a corporation, a market, and a system in such a way that the nature of the change made in the person finds the pathways, or is rather able to influence the very fiber of the progressively more complex layers of organization.

This can only happen if the fiber itself is of a similar substance. To cross, bounds between one type of existence and another would necessarily require some commonality in substance for this to happen. The dynamics which hold true in one kind of structure would need to find a similar substance or medium to so express itself in another kind of structure. Imagine if one were to stir water inside a pot. That stirring motion will cause waves to be created in the water. The waves will, however, cease at the boundary of the pot, primarily because the pot is of a different substance and responds to a different set of dynamics. If, however, there were commonalty of substance between the water, the pot, and the air that surrounds it, then the waves might find expression even in the air. Only so can a dynamic begin in one medium and find expression in another.

When we think of a person, an organization, a market, or a larger system, we generally conceptualize these entities as distinct and as having different drivers and dynamics responsible for their respective functioning. In our explorations of these entities, however, we have begun to conceptualize common building blocks for each of these layers of organization and have begun to build a language to relate and conceptualize this similarity of substance across these levels of organization. Hence, we have identified physical, vital, and mental building blocks across each level of organization and have observed that depending on which of these building blocks or outlooks leads, creation at that level will be of a fundamentally different kind. Not only this, but having found that the building blocks across levels are self-similar, we have begun to make the case that in fact, each level is connected to another by dint of a fractal model, which in the final analysis justifies how one can "become the change that one wishes to see in the world."

This chapter is about linking the various observations we have made through the previous chapters, to establish that indeed what we live in is a physical–vital–mental fractal world. In this world, there is a fractal ladder that connects the different levels together in a unique way. We will examine the notion of the fractal ladder, and begin to explore some of the implications of the existence of such a construct.

Some Fractal Basics

But let us step back for a minute. The term *fractal* has traditionally been applied to geometric shapes and implies a shape that can be split into parts that is a self-similar replica of the whole. The term *fractal* was in fact coined by Benoit Mandelbrot[1] in 1975 and was derived from the Latin *fractus* meaning broken or fractured. Commonly appearing fractals in nature include structures such as mountain ranges, clouds, crystals, broccoli, cauliflower, fern, trees, lightning, river networks, and blood vessels, among many others. Self-similarity in parts implies that a similar pattern occurs across progressively more minute or progressively larger scales of observation. Fractal geometry as conceived by Mandelbrot allowed study of real-life structures which could not be easily handled by Euclidean geometry that essentially focuses on straight lines and curves. In creating this approach, tremendous insight was gained into the handling of *irregular* shapes beyond circles, squares, and triangles. This insight derived from the discovered reality that a seed pattern, such as the broccolette in a broccoli, in fact determined the build-up of the entire structure and the final shape of the broccoli. If one does not see the seed pattern, then the broccoli, as with so many other shapes, can occur to be quite random in nature. If, however, the seed pattern is discovered, then

[1] Benoît B. Mandelbrot, *The Fractal Geometry of Nature* (New York: W.H. Freeman and Co., 1982).

insight, understanding, and shaping power are placed in the hands of the discoverers. In this book, as discussed in Chapter 1, this idea is extended to more complex behavioral structures such as people, organizations, and markets as a whole.

Just as the seed pattern in the broccoli or other fractal occurring in nature determines the final shape, so too, seed patterns in our outlooks, assumptions, behaviors, at the individual level, determines the final and jagged lines of uncomfortable realities such as climate change, toxic pollution, and the range of common social depravities. The world out there is not really a world out there. It is the concrete expression of who we are within, and consequently what we have allowed ourselves to express through the array of choices we continually make through the course of the day. And often the choice, as we have discovered is dictated by a biased or stagnated physical, vital, or mental outlook in a world that demands an objective and progressive physical, vital, or mental outlook. By the nature of the similar physical, vital, or mental medium that cuts across progressively, more complex layers of organization or life, to forms *grooves* of a sort, a magnified expression of a bias is, hence, formed in layers apparently removed from the originating thought impulse.

Fractal reality, the repeating of a self-similar pattern across larger and larger scale, shows us how seed patterns that live in people, manifest as the final *contradictions* so prevalent in our world today. The fractal ladder shows us the way out of these contradictions, to the creation of a progressive and fully sustainable world.

The Fractal Ladder

We have continually drawn the difference between fractal realities and the fractal ladder. Fractal realities will emanate out of myriad seed patterns that may have a random combination of the physical, vital, or mental building blocks as the basis of their creation. The Fractal Ladder is connected by dint of a common pattern that replicates the Sun-marked physical–vital–mental fractal. In other words, there is only one pattern that can create the fractal ladder. This has to be the case if we have observed the same pattern existing in the scale of the evolution of nature, at one end of the ladder, and the same pattern that determines progress in the individual, at the other end of the ladder. A ladder cannot be created unless each rung is similarly created. By *climbing* this fractal ladder, or making active in ourselves the pattern that will allow us to fruitfully connect one level to another, we, in a manner of speaking, can reach the vantage point where what we are creating, regardless of scale, is of the same nature as what we are hypothesizing is the DNA of progress embedded in all Earth circumstance. The key to climbing the fractal ladder lies in using the physical–vital–mental Sun-marked pattern as the step. It is only so that the change we make within, when consistent with that pattern, can have its progressive impact on layers removed from it.

We began our explorations by observation of the Earth–Sun dance, which for all practical purposes is older than history and more containing than geography. When viewed so, it can be thought of as setting the context for all that we experience on the Earth. We observed a pattern, physical–vital–mental that defined the structure of the day and hypothesized that through act of repetition, this pattern of progress was embedded into the DNA of Earth day after day. Briefly, we could say that this is a physical rendering of the situation, based on the observable facts. If one were to consider the mental rendering of this situation, based on ideas, one may in fact say that the physical–vital–mental pattern was already embedded into substance, and is the pathway by which hidden identity is revealed, and that in fact the structure of the day is such that this reality of existence is more fully bought into relief. We will come back to this interpretation shortly.

This is in fact the story of progress that observation of the different rungs of creation seems to reinforce. That is, in order for identity or the uniqueness hidden in each construct of creation to reveal itself, there must be a change from the predominantly physical to the predominantly vital to the predominantly mental outlook. This is no trivial passage, given that many other creations based on a *backward*-pointing, physical leading, or vital leading pattern prevail and perpetuate themselves. It requires abundance of effort to counter the many prevailing oppositions, and in so doing, something of the uniqueness inherent in each construct truly begins to manifest. This cannot but be, since the quieting of myriad and deeply lodged patterns will begin to reveal something of the light and truer substance that might exist behind the noise. This then sets into motion a new fractal that in climbing the rungs on the fractal ladder connects inner power with global change.

We reinforce that of course there is utility in passing through each of the phases of the journey in stepwise manner precisely because the capabilities developed and the experience of each phase better prepares the actor or benefactor of the journey to be a better instrument for any subsequent phase in the journey.

This Sun-marked physical–vital–mental fractal is in fact the containing, contextual, or seed fractal, the fractal that transcends even our canvas of evolution. Quickly summarizing, we have found a self-similar physical–vital–mental pattern repeating itself at progressively larger or progressively smaller scale, depending on which end of the ladder we start from. Let us trace this journey once again. At the largest scale, in the result of the dance of the Earth with the Sun, we have the structure of a day manifesting in three distinct phases—the physical, the vital, and the mental, in that order. At the scale of the Earth, we have the age-long physical–vital–mental evolution fractal, which has journeyed from inanimate matter through vast experimentation and vitality manifest in life, culminating in the mind of the human being. Each stage of the journey has brought more degrees of freedom to nature and allowed more of her innate impulse and possibility to manifest itself. At the scale of the economy, we have traced a similar journey through the agricultural or physical economy, to the industrial or vital economy, to the digital or mental economy, recognizing each of these phases to in fact be subphases of an overarching vital economy. Within the vital economy, the progression through physical, vital, and mental has similarly proffered greater degrees of freedom upon the primary agents of the economy. Somewhat parallel to the scale of the economy, we looked at various instances of *system* level changes, across different systems. Hence, we looked at the digital economy fractal and the Energy Industry Fractal, and found the same journey of progress existent in both these instances. We looked at a couple of fractals related to global politics—in particular, the balance of global power fractal and the exchange rate fractal—and there too, found the three-phased journey of progress repeating itself. We also looked at various systems of thought—physics, biomimicry, and organizational design—and there too, found the similar journey repeating itself. At the level of system, we looked at the fractal for learning and found the same phases repeated in this journey too. At the scale of corporation, we looked at the journey of a progressive organization and similarly found the three-phased journey repeating itself. At the smallest scale, we looked at the person, and there too discovered that progressive action at a more micro-scale and a progressive life at a more macro-scale manifests in the same three-phased journey. This journey is summarized in Figure 7.1.

This constant manifestation of a similar three-phased journey repeating itself at different scales is the definition of a fractal. Again, it is interesting to note that at each scale, the three building blocks

Figure 7.1 The Fractal Ladder

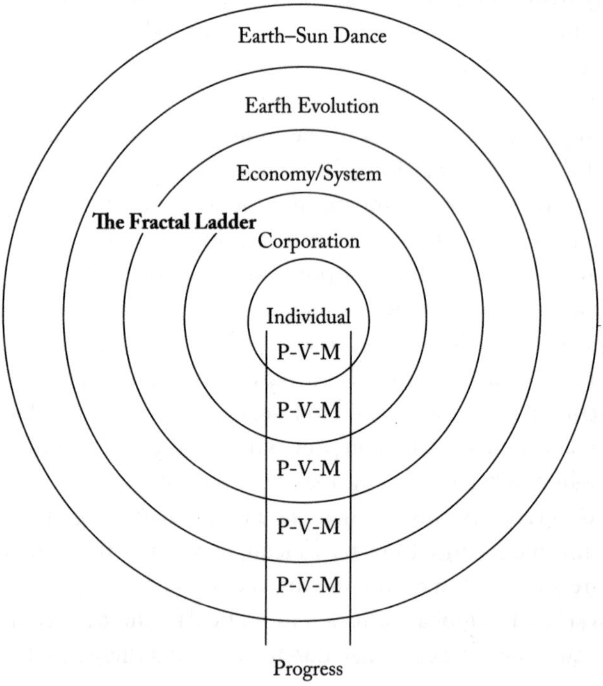

are sufficient to define the nature of the corresponding world. Thus, it is perhaps fair to say that we live in a world that can be entirely defined by the play of physical, vital, and mental building blocks. The progressive world, however, is marked by the physical–vital–mental journey in that sequence. And this pattern of progress, as we have seen, is universal across every scale we have examined, from the level of the person, to the level of the Earth–Sun system. The Fractal Ladder, hence, is a fractal for progress.

Progress

Progress then appears to be an essential quality of our existence. After all, as pointed out earlier, it is not that each of the actors at the level of the economy, or in each independent system, for example, conspired to make a collective shift from the physical to the vital to the mental outlook. In fact, in spite of the major oppositions set up by myriad other fractals emanating from a vast number of habitual and even backward-pointing fractals, the progress was made. Let us think about this some more. In such a milieu marked by vast opposition, for progress to be made, is nothing short of miraculous. It is as though something overrides all the lack of effort, all the vested interests, all the force of habit, and in spite of all contrary tendencies, finds a way for the shift from physical to vital to mental to take place.

When we climb the fractal ladder from the bottom upward, we experience the seed pattern of the progressive fractal as being the shift from a physical to a vital to a mental outlook at the level of a person. At the next level, we see that this shift in leaders running organizations causes those organizations to similarly change their orientation from physical to vital to mental, thereby exercising greater degrees of freedom in their environments. At yet the next level, when collectivity of organizations makes the shift from a physical to a vital to a mental mode of operating, then a larger market or system or economy, correspondingly tends to go through a similar shift. There is however, in our analysis, no causal link between markets and economies, and the next level up, the canvas of evolution. The time periods are too dissimilar, and yet that same shift is observed in the canvas of evolution.

What does this tell us? First, the upward causality is valid only up to a certain point. Second, it is perhaps the downward causality that is universal, for the pattern is fixed in a setting beyond human history and geography and is valid in the entire field of human history and human geography. Third, while the causality is our way of interpreting our observations, perhaps the fundamental take away is not the point of causality at all, but the fact that we live in a vortex comprised physical, vital, and mental building blocks, in which the path of safe passage as it were, the path of progress and fulfillment, is defined by the Sun-marked physical–vital–mental journey, and in following that path we open to the very character and embodiment of progress, in which new creation is possible.

It is almost as though something called progress sits behind the vortex. It is the witness of the physical–vital–mental journey at all the different levels. It sits behind the Earth–Sun dance and manifests in the garb of a day. It sits behind the evolution of nature and perhaps watches more and more complete manifestations of itself surfacing in the Earth play. It sits behind the progress of economy and system waiting for unhealthy limits to be reached so that a new and more holistic phase of progress may begin. It sits behind the development of corporations, waiting for the right actions that liberate rather than limit human possibility. It sits behind the garb of a person, leading and pushing them to embrace the difficult yet empowering Sun-marked physical–vital–mental path so that true identity may manifest. Because it is there, that journey becomes possible. Because it is there, the human can somehow quiet the myriad voices and tendencies that constantly call to it and enter into a space where new tendencies of a very different nature can be forged and released into the world, creating entirely new and progressive fractals. This is creation. This is to own one's power. This is to begin to make a real change in the world.

The fractal ladder shows us that progressive creation is the same at each rung of existence. It shows us that change made in the self is of the utmost importance, for it is only so that corresponding change can be made at levels of organization progressively removed from the person. It shows us the DNA of progress, and even in climbing it, one comes face to face with a largeness that is perhaps synonymous with progress. The fact that it exists is a reason to take notice of it and ask why it exists.

This progress appears to have some unusual qualities. It must be present everywhere, because otherwise it would not be possible for the physical–vital–mental fractal to manifest wherever we see progress happening. It must understand and know what is happening everywhere because otherwise the appropriate shift at the appropriate time could not happen. It must be very powerful because otherwise there is no way amidst the vortex or physical, vital, and mental randomness and of a general downward or backward gravitation that the physical–vital–mental sequence could manifest. It must be connected to all humans because otherwise the right instrument would likely not be able to appropriately make the right progress at the right time. It must be an accomplished designer because otherwise there is no way that a fractal ladder of the type we have come to observe could be etched into the frame of our lives. And it must care for us deeply because otherwise it would have left us to our own devices to sink into the obscurity from which we appear to have arisen rather than seek to lift us up into new worlds of possibility. In other words, at least in the Earth–Sun context, this progress appears to be omnipresent, omniscient, omnipotent, omnicaring, and to possess other astounding qualities.

And if this is so, then what perhaps is the best way to relate to it? If it knows everything, is so powerful, is present everywhere, is connected to everyone, cares for us enough to want to etch a pathway by which we can rise from common trivialities to a mastery of life, then is it fair to say that it can hear us? Is it fair to say that it can see us, and that perhaps even it can respond to us? If so, this opens us out to a very different conception of life and possibility. We live in this *progress*. The *progress* lives in us. We are becomings of this progress. The progress shapes us in its own image. This perhaps is the ultimate fractal: the seed pattern born in progress manifests in the Earth scene as an entity striving to embody progress. And this progress is not just an impartial witness. It lives here with caring and love, like a mother.

Exceptional Beings

We then, are exceptional beings. We wear physical, vital, and mental garbs and possess abilities representative of these three fields of existence. But we are also something more. When we exercise the dynamic of the physical–vital–mental Sun-marked fractal, we partake of an essential quality of creation – we become progressive in nature. Not only that, but if in the continually successful physical–vital–mental journeying we begin to un-create all the surface dynamics of habit and commonality, and gradually enter into the silence behind the thousand voices, where we can more intimately feel our essential nature of progress. There we may come face to face with the larger context that seems to be resident everywhere, and seems to be the context of our lives and can begin to relate with it in a very different way, or even to become it. This is the great secret of our power. In even glimpsing that a new set of possibilities dawn.

Consider for a moment the complexity of comprehending the many tendencies, habits, mores, expectations, judgments, prejudices that each of us in continually enmeshed in. Each of these, we have said, is an uncompleted journeying of the physical–vital–mental Sun-marked fractal. The habit or tendency has found some permanence because it has tended to repeat its act of stagnation. But to successfully cause the completion of the many instances of these incomplete journeys as they relate to ourselves, while perhaps not impossible, can be a mammoth task. What, however, if we were to open up these stagnated journeys to the progress we have glimpsed? What if we were to lay the many tendencies, habits, mores, and so on, before the eye of this progress? Would somehow the essence of what it stands for incarnate something of its essential quality or substance into the constricted entity? If what we have hypothesized is true, that this progress is omniscient, omnipresent, omnipotent, omnicaring, and that it might be possible for us to relate to it as one even relates to a mother, then why shouldn't this type of incarnation be possible? More than anything else, it would require a shifting in our mental outlook to make this story more of a reality. The shifting of the mental outlook is the same thing as making the Sun-marked physical–vital–mental journey on this element of possible disbelief. The act of this journey is the key to climbing the fractal ladder and in so doing opens us out to the possibilities inherent in progress.

On the flip side, choosing not to progress, when this appears to be an essential quality of existence, certainly within the Earth–Sun context, is to consign ourselves to likely extinction. When then we look out at the vast contradictions in our world, we know that what we are facing is a tremendous choice. The contradictions are a result of seed patterns that live in ourselves, and we must make the progress to change these seed patterns. We must complete the many incomplete and stagnated micro-journeys that define who we are being so that the contradictions, whether manifest in social depravities and inequities, climate change, pollution, resource exploitation, among others, can be transformed. This is our test as human beings. We are creators incarnate, and it is our right and responsibility to correctly exercise the tremendous powers resident in our breasts to release the stagnation in the world so that the current set of contradictions can dissolve.

Summary

We started this chapter by revisiting our base fractal hypothesis. We moved on to an examination of the notion of the historical notion of the fractal. We connected together the different rungs of existence and concluded that indeed there exists a fractal ladder that is an instance of a fractal of progress. This fractal ladder has a special meaning in an otherwise random fractal world. The fractal ladder also puts us face-to-face with a contextual progress that we argued must be omnipresent, omnipotent, omniscient, and omnicaring, like a Mother, in the context of the Earth–Sun dance. We further explore our relation to progress and concluded that we are exceptional beings. As beings invested with the kind of power than can be released when one begins to climb the fractal ladder, we have exceptional responsibility. By owning this responsibility, we concluded that we can begin to dissolve the many contradictions that currently prevail in our world. In the next chapter, we will begin to explore in more detail the properties of a fractal world.

8

Fractal Properties

Focus: Examination of properties in a fractal world. These become tools, devices to maneuver through a very different world.

Key Concepts: Application of fractal lens to better exercise our power in the world | Fractal model as an elaborate system view of the world | Progressive state and system evolution | Arranging properties by the triple view | Fractal ladder seed pattern | Physical properties to do with structure | Fractal universality | Universality connecting various fields | From a linear to a system's view | Fractal influence | Influence as giving the fractal ladder its ladder-like quality | Threshold of influence | Magnification caused by fractal influence | Fractal recursion | Recursion as applying fractal to subphase of journey | Recursive property used to piece together likely development of entities | Recursive property used to shed light on structure of entities | Fractal completion | Tendency of fractal to want to complete its journey | Fractal stepwise development | Capabilities of former phases increasing leverage of subsequent phases | Fractal evolution | Evolution alters conditions within which base journey exists | Spiral nature of journey on the fractal ladder | Fractal matrixing | Matrixing as a devise to perpetuate progress by leveraging established insights into progress | Vital properties to do with process | Fractal intersection | Intersection of fractals potentially causes each to progress | Religion fractal | Reviewing world conflicts through the lens of fractal influence | Fractal facilitation |

Facilitation of stagnation by application of physical–vital–mental fractal | Status quo—chaos—questioning | Fractal flow | Flow as a property by which a range of energies enter into a situation | Fractal upscaling | Upscaling implies shifting from a disconnected linear to a one-system view | Mental properties to do with meaning | World-wiseliness | The more physical–vital–mental journeys one masters the more world-wisely one becomes | World-wiseliness and convergence and prevalence of fractals | Mirroring | All is a reflection of an inner state | Nothing lies on the fractal ladder | Affirmation | Successful outcome in the world as a result of the physical–vital–mental journey | Integration | Integration of physical, vital, mental, and underlying purpose | Integration and leadership | Uniqueness | Uniqueness as an outcome of the fractal journey | A fourth class of properties | Alignment with sense of progress | Aspiration for progress | Surrender of difficulties and dilemmas | Rejection of contrary fractals | Love for an omnicaring entity

Introduction

Thus far, we have concluded that we do indeed live in a fractal world. Structurally, there are some key characteristics of this world. The basic building blocks of this world are of either a physical, vital, or mental nature. These fundamental building blocks determine the nature of many rungs of creation, from the personal level, to levels of entire markets or economies and systems. Further, combinations of these building blocks form seed patterns that are responsible for the creation of many different fractals that animate our world. Many of these fractals are backward-pointing or obstinately physical or vital in character. But there is also a fractal for progress, the fractal ladder, which cuts across the rungs of creation to connect micro-movements at the personal level to the very canvas of the Earth–Sun drama in which our lives play out.

This fractal ladder is a symbol of an underlying and essential quality of creation, that of progress. The progress itself appears to be omnipresent, omniscient, omnipotent, and omnicaring, and can be entered into more conscious relation with by beginning to climb the fractal ladder. Climbing the fractal ladder equates to quieting or mastering the many contrary fractals that comprise the active substance of many aspects of our lives. This mastery tends to push us into a space of increased silence within ourselves, the very province of progress, from where our truer identity and more creative fractals that have the power to change our world can emerge. We are, thus, potentially exceptional beings invested with the power of creation, once we choose to climb the fractal ladder, rather than choose to live in the general and surrounding fractal vortex within which all our past creations and habits seem to reside.

The world, hence, when viewed with this fractal lens, takes on a very different hue and dynamic. It sheds a different and more penetrating light on the many contradictions we currently live with and on the power we are each invested with. To more fully understand this world so that we can more fully rise to overcoming the limitations we have ourselves created is an imperative. This chapter seeks to summarize and expand on some of the properties and implications of this fractal world. By so doing, hopefully, just as in the case of the fractal geometer who can now more accurately understand nature's physical symmetries and asymmetries, we too will be able to more fully understand some of our more complex symmetries and asymmetries, and be better able to exercise our power in the world.

In essence, the fractal model we have been discussing is an elaborate system's view of the world. The state of this system is the result of the play of three essential states – physicality, vitality, and mentality in many permutations and combinations, and at many different levels. There is, however, a particular combination, characterized by the Sun-marked physical–vital–mental sequence that is of particular interest to us, because when that occurs, an exceptionally progressive and creative state of the system comes into being. It is this particularly progressive state that we are most concerned with, because it is in this state that meaningful difference is born and that the system itself evolves. It is in this state that inner power can truly connect to global change. In this chapter, we summarize and further elaborate on some of the properties of this most creative state, characterized by the pattern in the fractal ladder.

As has been the approach in this entire book, we will view the properties themselves, from a physical, vital, and mental outlook. The physical outlook will shed light on properties that have to do with the essential structure of this fractal-based world. The vital outlook will shed light on some of the properties that have to do with processes we can employ as actors in this world. The mental outlook will shed light on some properties to do with ascribing meaning to actions in this world.

Physical-level Properties in a Fractal-ladder-based World

Through the course of this book, we have already encountered several properties that have to do with the essential structure or physical field of this fractal-based world. These include properties such as universality, influence, recursion, and completion. Other properties that we will further describe include evolution, matrixing, stepwise development, and feedback.

The seed pattern in the fractal ladder is the Sun-marked physical–vital–mental sequence. In the fractal ladder, it exists in each rung of creation. By knowing the intimacies of this journey or sequence, one can develop significant insight into this similar journey at another level. Thus, for example, in fully living the physical–vital–mental journey as it occurs at the personal level, replete with the nature of the phases and the transitions between the phases, one can have insight into the physical–vital–mental journey as it appears at the level of the corporation or the economy, or even in the evolution of a system of science, such as physics. Many distinct fields of experience and knowledge, which simply have no connection with one another in a linear view of the world, now share an intimacy when viewed as a manifestation of the same underlying fractal. This property is one of *universality*. The implication of this property is that knowledge of progress in one field of human endeavor can be transferred to another field, to gain at least a gut-sense for how progress may happen. Another implication is that if one does one thing really well, thereby by definition going through the Sun-marked physical–vital–mental journey in the mastery of that activity or field, one should be able to not only understand but have sufficient insight into the nature of progress in many different fields.

Fractal *influence* is another property we have discussed throughout the book. This is what gives the fractal ladder its ladder-like quality. Fractal influence is the property by which a shift in the fractal at one level or one rung of the ladder tends to cause a corresponding shift at the next rung of the ladder. Hence, at the individual level, a shift from the vital to mental state of being in a leader may tend to cause a corresponding shift in the functioning of a corporation from the vital to mental state of being. It is to be noted, however, that this will unlikely be a one-to-one mapping. That is, it will require a certain momentum or threshold of influence before an actual shift will be seen at the subsequent level. The fact, however, remains that the shift itself even if emanating from one individual has put a new fractal possibility into place that, as we have discussed earlier, must have its repercussion in the scheme of things precisely because it represents a new possibility in the play of progress. It could also be the case that a shift at the higher level in the ladder can cause a corresponding shift in the lower rungs of it. Hence, if a segment of the economy shifted from a vital to a mental functioning, corporations that may be lagging would need to make this shift in order not to get marginalized. Note, however, that the shift from one phase in the fractal to the next at the level of the economy is per our earlier arguments, made by leading companies where the shift from the physical to the vital or from the vital to the mental outlook has already taken place in the leaders of those companies. Hence, in effect, the influence from earlier leaders is now reinforcing itself from the top-down. This kind of magnification cannot but exist in a world characterized by fractal dynamics.

Another property we have referred to is that of fractal *recursion*. That is, one should be able to apply the fractal journey to any sub-phase within a fractal. For instance, in the previous chapter, we applied a fractal journey to the mental or digital phase of the global economy fractal. Hence, we found that the digital economy itself went through the physical, vital, and mental phases in building its possibilities. Applying recursion upward, we also concluded that the current global economy was in a vital phase and that the agricultural, industrial, and digital phases were all subphases of this overarching vital phase, that is only now hitting the boundary that could possibly lead it into a mental phase, were we to fulfill the conditions of a successful transition. Similarly, we also applied both downward and upward recursion to the evolution fractal. Hence, we explored activity at the atomic and molecular levels through the physical–vital–mental sequence, resulting in the culmination or starting point of matter, the downward recursion, if you will, and subsequently used granular and distinct material building blocks, in an upward recursion to explore the journey through the physical–vital–mental sequence, to arrive at the physical foundation of evolution. In this manner, we saw how the recursive property of the physical–vital–mental fractal can be used to piece together the likely development of entities. In a similar vein, at the level of the individual and the corporation, we have applied the physical–vital–mental sequence to shed light on what physical, vital, and mental could mean within these rungs of creation. In this case, the application of fractal recursion has been used to shed light on the structure of entities, as opposed to the process of development of entities, as in the previous examples.

Another property is that of fractal *completion*. This implies that for progress to happen, the physical–vital–mental sequence must be completed. But it also implies that the fractal wants to complete its journey. That is an essential characteristic of a journey on a rung of the fractal ladder. We have of course examined this notion in some detail throughout the book. At the personal level, for instance, if one experiences anger, a vital state, then introduction of a mental state, bringing in reason into the situation, will diffuse a potentially destructive cycle. At the level of corporation, if the leaders are consumed by greed, a vital state, then unless a higher reason for being, or thinking about the longer term, both examples of mental states, becomes alive, the corporation could experience an Enron-like demise. In the case of a country, such as the USSR, a fixed notion of how things should be run, a physical state, resulted in its demise, perhaps because the country was not able to rise to the next level in the fractal. Hence, for progress to occur, the fractal must be completed. But what we are emphasizing here is that if the person who is experiencing anger or the company that is in the state of greed or the country that is in the physical state, are on the fractal ladder, then completion of their respective journeys is a structural necessity – it is the nature of being on the fractal ladder. If these entities have no impulsion to complete the Sun-marked physical–vital–mental journey, then they, by definition, cannot exist on the fractal ladder, but will exist in the world characterized by the fractal vortex that surrounds it.

There are other properties that shed light on the essential structure of a world characterized by the fractal-based fractal ladder. These include evolution, matrixing, stepwise development, and feedback.

Evolution refers to the fact that engaging in successful physical–vital–mental journeys alters the conditions within which a base journey exists. That is, the nature of the fractal ladder is such that all rungs of it continually go through forms of progress. This implies that the similar physical–vital–mental journeys now repeat themselves under more sophisticated conditions. Hence, for example, an organization that may have successfully risen to the mental or conceptual levels by mastering the use of information technology, say, has altered the physical and vital spaces in doing so. The physical now becomes more *intelligent*, while the vital more effectively dynamic also because of the integration and application of technology. When repeated, this fractal journey, hence, starts from altered and more advanced conditions. This kind of advancement indicates that the fractal journey has been successfully completed. It also implies that an entity on the fractal ladder tends to go through journeys that are spiral in nature so that each time the pattern starts over, it does so at higher initial conditions.

Matrixing refers to the condition of essential connection that exists by virtue of physical–vital–mental journeys successfully completing themselves. Take the example of an accomplished individual in the medical field. Accomplished implies that the individual likely successfully traversed the physical–vital–mental journey in their area of medical specialization. By virtue of successfully completing one such journey, the individual might now be invited to be on a policy board that regulates policy for that whole field – this represents entry into a whole new fractal journey. The individual may also be invited to teach his or her medical knowledge to other aspiring practitioners.

This similarly represents entry into an entire new fractal journey. The individual may also decide to set up a consulting firm, which again represents entry into another fractal journey. Hence, successful completion of the initial journey invited or caused connection to many other fractals each going through their own journeys. This kind of matrixing may be thought of as a device to perpetuate progress by leveraging of established insight into progress, evident by the completion of physical–vital–mental journeying, which of course is the very nature underlying the fractal ladder.

Stepwise development refers to the necessity for the journeying to proceed through the independent stages of the physical, the vital, and the mental in turn and in that order. At each stage, certain capabilities are developed that then allows the next phase to more fully leverage those capabilities to express its possibilities. But also when development at a stage has proceeded to its maximum ability within an overarching context, then the vehicle, instrument, actor, or urge is more ready to have the possibilities of the next phase surface. Stepwise development indicates that it is best when there is a gradual development from phase to phase. Were there to be another phase following the mental, that would find its fullest play if all the capacities of each of the previous phases had already been assimilated by the instrument or actor.

Feedback refers to the property by which any entity on a higher level of the fractal ladder will through dint of the underlying fractal pressure reinforce its raison d'être and way of being at lower levels. Often it is the lower levels that have created the organization on the higher level. In this case, the organization at the higher level reinforces the reality by which it was created, hence engendering more of the same kind of creation.

Vital-level Properties in a Fractal-ladder-based World

Vital-level properties that shed light on processes we can employ as actors on the fractal ladder include intersection, flow, facilitation, and upscaling.

Intersection is a property that holds when two fractals are made to intersect with one another. There is the possibility that both fractals can move to the next rung of their respective journeys through this intersection. Consider the unfortunate destruction of the World Trade Center (WTC). The WTC can perhaps be thought of as the symbol of the global economy fractal. It was destroyed by religious fundamentalists, representative of the fractal that religion is going through. Supposedly vitalistic, that is, egoistic and self-aggrandizing dynamics, characteristic of the present phase of the global economy fractal led to oil-related aggression in the Middle East. This spurred a radical response from fundamentalists that led to the destruction of the WTC. Two vitally centered fractals, both characterized by possibly arrested journeys, were made to collide, and in the shock, perhaps both stand a chance to progress to the next level. On one side, the destruction of the WTC leads to a deeper realization and consequent questioning of some of the methods of modern business, and perhaps forms an important stimulus to the accelerated journey of the global economy fractal. On the other side, peaceful members of a religion the world over are simultaneously led to a questioning of what religion could be made to stand for, thereby also leading to deeper question of what it should stand for—also an important stimulus to the accelerated journey of the religion fractal.

When viewed from this lens, or through examination of this fractal property, a different and hopefully more revealing light might be shed on many conflicts the world over. The conflict should be recognized for what it is—the intersection or collision of two arrested fractals that through the collision are being given a chance to progress to the next levels in their respective journeys. Boundary conditions are always difficult, especially when the resistance to cross over to the next phase is strong. Successful completion of the respective journeys implies integration into the fractal ladder, a state that no doubt represents the very meaning of its existence.

Facilitation is a property that can be applied to a situation that appears to be stuck. Essentially this implies applying a form of the physical–vital–mental fractal to the point or situation of stagnation. The physical–vital–mental pattern can be thought of as a pattern of moving from status quo, the physical, to chaos, the vital, and to questioning or reforming, the mental. Applying the step of *status quo* allows one to more fully grasp the current situation – what are the facts and the visible signs characterizing the situation. Applying the step of *chaos* facilitates movement away from the state of stagnation. The direction in which the move takes place is relatively insignificant; the point is that the movement needs to take place. This sets into motion a new energy of a different nature than that of stagnation. The final step is that of *questioning*, by which a new light is shed on the situation that caused the stagnation, and possible new directions in which the energy that has been introduced through chaos, can now begin to mature.

Flow is somewhat related to facilitation and is a property by which a range of energies, of themselves, enter into a situation. The starting point is that of concentration on the activity at hand. If such a concentrated engagement occurs, then the physical–vital–mental fractal journey manifests of itself. The beginning of the activity, whether it is reading a book, playing tennis, conversing with someone, among many other possibilities, may often be characterized by a state of relative resistance or inertia. This is akin to the physical level. If the activity is pursued with concentration, then a *flow* begins to arise, which makes the activity easier to do. This is perhaps parallel to the vital level. Continued engagement in a concentrated manner will likely result in that same activity becoming effortless, and even perhaps in various insights related to it beginning to arise. This is akin to the mental level. This unrolling of energies is inevitable if indeed we exist in a world where progress, and progress as characterized by the physical–vital–mental sequence, is an essential underlying trait.

Upscaling refers to shifting the context or orientation from a *lower* or previous stage in the sequence to a higher or next stage in the sequence. Shifting from a physical to a mental orientation, for example, necessitates thinking and operating in a wholly different way. From a basic outward or objective orientation, the field of relevance shifts more toward an inward or subjective orientation. Degrees of freedom associated with a situation also changes correspondingly, as does the essential psychology of the actor or instrument exercising the shift. Upscaling is a powerful approach to consider new and different possibilities in any situation.

Mental-level Properties in a Fractal-ladder-based World

Mental-level properties that shed light on the meaning we can ascribe to actions in a world characterized by the fractal ladder include world-wiseliness, mirroring, affirmation, integration, and uniqueness.

World-wiseliness is a property related to the mastery of several different physical–vital–mental fractals at different levels or different arenas of life. The idea here is that the more physical–vital–mental journeys one masters, the more world-wisely one becomes. One experiences a broader range of similar phases garbed in different expressions or languages, and gains more insight into boundary conditions, and the requirements in pushing from one phase into another. A more complete sense of the mosaic underlying progress emerges, and one can more easily perhaps extend one's experience into previously unconsidered areas. The property of world-wiseliness is perhaps very relevant in today's world where many different ways of being are being melded together through force of convergence. World-wiseliness may also shed insight into knowing which converging fractals may prevail, because they are inherently more aligned with the imperative of progress.

Mirroring refers to the fact that regardless of where we look, what we see is a reflection of our inner state. This cannot but be true in a world characterized by a pattern repeating itself on different scales. Seed patterns that live in us, through force of fractal pressure, find expression and manifestation in each rung of creation. Climate change, social depravities, severe resource shortages, are outer expressions or mirror our inner states. In the fractal ladder, nothing lies and all events are signs of changes we must make at the level of seed patterns, in our essential internal outlooks and way of being, if we wish to truly change the world we have created.

Affirmation is a property that reinforces the very notion of progress. This property asserts that any successful outcome in a world characterized by the fractal ladder must have described the Sun-marked physical–vital–mental journey. In other words, anything that is truly successful, in the holistic sense, must be successful because in reality it has described the seed journey that is the key to ascension on the fractal ladder. A simple proof: man is the master of his environment, and not a donkey or rubber plant, precisely because in man the fractal journey has reached a higher level of completion.

Integration is a property with many applications in this fractal world. In its application to leadership, for example, it implies that while leaders may exist at each phase in the fractal journey—the physical, the vital, and the mental—there must be an overriding leader who is a summary of the fractal journey. That is, he must possess mastery over all levels, while being led by the very sense underlying the meaning of the fractal ladder. It is only such a leader who can successfully integrate and coordinate all that is going on in an organization and yet ensure a constant freshness in direction and approach. A leader, hence, who draws inspiration solely from the vital or financial level, for example, will not be appropriate in times of major change. On the other hand, a leader who just has an intuitive sense of the underlying progress, without having mastery over the material or physical, the financial or vital, and the conceptual or mental realms, may be relatively ineffectual in getting things done.

Uniqueness emerges as fractal journeys are completed and may, to some extent, be defined by the particular shades, circumstances, or capacities experienced and developed along the way. Uniqueness uses the journey to emerge from the trials and tribulations of it. Crossing between or through phases often necessitates encounters with contrary fractals that force something essential that is experiencing the journey to begin to express something of itself. Finally, there must be a shaking off of the physical, vital, and mental garbs used on the way for something to emerge from within that then may use the experienced physical, vital, and mental capacities to more fully express itself.

Other Properties

While we have outlined several properties of a physical, vital, and mental nature, the fact is that in a world characterized by the fractal ladder, there is another class of properties that are equally if not more important. The physical, vital, and mental blocks and properties that correspond to these are of course fundamental to an understanding of the practical dynamics of such a world. At the same time, there is a teleological sense and meaning in such a world, as is made apparent by the possible omniscience, omnipotence, omnipresent, and omnicaring characteristics of progress. In a world where there is the presence of something of this nature, there cannot but be another class of properties that have to do with the notion of relationship with such an entity. Such properties may be those of alignment with the sense of progress or even perhaps something more active like aspiration for that reality of progress. They may include a laying out of current difficulties and dilemmas or even perhaps a sense of surrender, to such an all-knowing, all-present entity. They may include a resolve to detect fractals or sub-beings of a contrary nature and to reject their influence and reality in us, because only so does it seem that we can truly find a way onto the fractal ladder. Properties may even include conversing with or a love for such an omnicaring entity.

Summary

The properties discussed in this chapter help us more effectively understand, relate to, and live in a world characterized by the fractal ladder. These properties are summarized in Figure 8.1.

Application of these properties should help us solve some of the difficulties and dilemmas we are currently faced with.

Figure 8.1 Fractal Properties

Physical	Vital	Mental	Other
Universality	Intersection	World-wiseliness	Alignment
Influence	Flow	Mirroring	Aspiration
Recursion	Facilitation	Affirmation	Surrender
Completion	Upscaling	Integration	Rejection
Evolution		Uniqueness	Love
Matrixing			
Stepwise development			
Feedback			

The Nature of Progress

9

Focus: Examination of the nature of progress and how that interacts with and ultimately shapes the fractal ladder.

Key Concepts: The initial state | Creation has proceeded under the aegis of progress | Reviewing manifested creation in understanding properties of progress | Insight into transitions and trajectories when properties understood | Sequence to progress yielding to a fourth state | Insight into seed state providing guidance in selecting emerging pathways | Who we become determined by nature of progress | All-presence of progress | All-knowingness of progress | All-power of progress | All-caringness of progress | Properties coexist and act in simultaneity in management of fractal ladder | Top-down versus bottom-up analysis of properties | Manifested states or physical, vital, and mental building blocks tell us something about progress | *Perfection* and *service* at the physical level | Parallels between the top-down and bottom-up observations | All-presence and the physical state | Limitations of properties of progress in nature | Power of energy versus light of energy | Adventure as proceeding under the aegis of power | All-power and the vital state | *Adventure, energy, assertiveness, growth* as characteristics of all-power | Questioning and the heart of knowledge | All-knowingness and the mental state | Impersonal and personal qualities of progress | Omnicaring and heart | The fourth state—intuition | Intuition as a border state connecting the top-down with the bottom-up | Rule of heart | Fragmented creations of manifested nature | Physical, vital, and mental states as fields of possibility | Changing action of properties of progress in different fields of possibility | Fixed grooves of the physical | Physical–vital conglomerate | Uniqueness and identity manifest at the mental level | Intuition and more direct action from nature of progress | Observed nature | Service as observed nature of property of omnipresence | Adventure as observed nature of property of omnipotence | Knowledge as observed nature of property of omniscience | Harmony as observed nature of property of omnicaring | Application of the physical–vital–mental architecture to progress | Physical aspect of progress as physical, vital, and mental, intuitional states | Vital aspect of progress as service, adventure, knowledge, harmony | Mental aspect of progress as omnipresence, omnipotence, omniscience, omnicaring | Secret names behind the operation of the fractal ladder | Reduction of rigidities in building blocks through action of intuition | Darker or shadow states of physical, vital, and mental | Structure, process, and meaning of fractal ladder evolving rapidly | Basis of operation shifting from narrow one-dimensionality to holistic multidimensionality | AUM and the fractal ladder

Introduction

In the previous chapter, we posited the notion that progress is a living entity that is all-present, all-knowing, all-caring, and all-powerful, at least within the context of the Earth–Sun dance. It is only so that the same physical–vital–mental pattern can repeat itself at different rungs of creation, in spite of overwhelming opposition. In this chapter, we will try and shed some additional light on the nature of this progress. In doing so, we may gain a glimpse into the way in which each rung of the fractal ladder, and the way in which the fractal ladder itself may progress. Such insight will help us understand how the current transition between the vital and mental phases of the global economy fractal and perhaps many other fractals that we have already surfaced might proceed.

At the start of the Earth–Sun dance, the Earth was characterized by inanimate matter. Yet an entire creation has proceeded from this state. This state, however, as we have begun to see, could not have been the initial state. Given that we are suggesting the presence of an all-present, all-knowing, all-powerful, all-caring progress, it is fair to assume that this progress has preceded all creation, and in fact, creation is a result of this progress. It is under the aegis of progress that creation has proceeded. This is evident from the fact that progress seems to bear one and the same signature to it, the physical–vital–mental sequence, regardless of the level of activity or organization we consider.

Progress then is the initial state, and in trying to isolate some of its relevant properties, we can perhaps look at manifested creation itself, since all creation has proceeded from this initial state. But why is such an examination important? Precisely because what we are aiming to do is understand transitions and trajectories in the light of creative acts of individual power. Further, if we are saying that there is a sequence to progress, then is that sequence fully captured by the physical–vital–mental phenomena? Or is there another state, a fourth state, perhaps that the oft-seen and oft-repeated sequence must yield to? Because of where we currently stand in the scheme of things, and because of what we seem to have assimilated into our functioning and way of being, will progress itself reveal another element to it, because we now stand more ready to embrace it and make it our own?

Not only an attempt at examining the nature of progress can reveal this, but also the nature of the tree in the nature of the seed. If we can better understand the seed state from which all seems to have proceeded, then perhaps we can also gain insight into how the tree in process of growing will continue on its journey of progress. This is important where we stand at the moment because in the flux of contradictions, a clearer guidance may help us better choose or recognize the emerging pathways toward the future. Since we do not live in the consciousness of progress in the same way that progress does, recognition of pathways that are resonant with progress itself will perhaps be a useful way by which we can more successfully navigate toward the best future.

Finally, if as individuals we are successful in completing, offering, or silencing the many tendencies, manifestations of the incompleted physical–vital–mental journey that live within us or that we live in close proximity to because they are the constant shadows of our play with life, then we must of necessity enter into a state of quietness where we come closer to progress because all else is progressively being unmade in us. Then who we become in this state of creativity, must be determined by the nature of progress itself. Under such circumstances, the nature of progress more fully incarnates in our nature. This is the act of creativity. This is how our inner power manifests in the world. Because now something new and powerful from the fount of progress itself, finds expression in the world through the resultant fractals that play themselves out with the new incarnated quality in us as the seed state.

The Four Qualities of Progress

We have already concluded that because the same pattern of progress manifests everywhere, regardless of scale, and regardless of field, that progress must be all-present. This then must be an essential quality of progress. We have also concluded that rogress must be all-knowing, because somehow, the right instrument is used, or the right circumstance is leveraged, to push toward the next stage in the physical–vital–mental sequence. We have also concluded that the act of progress, in spite of the formidable opposition that is present in all fields of endeavor from the personal to the societal levels, must require an incredible amount of power. Progress, hence, has to be all-powerful. Nothing can withstand it once it chooses that the next stage in the physical–vital–mental sequence must occur. Finally, we concluded that for such a scheme of progress and possibility to even exist in the Earth–Sun dance, a scheme by which each person and each level of creation can come to terms with and even discover something of their individuality and true bases of power, and further be helped along the way, indicates that progress must be all-caring. This then is also an essential quality of progress.

These qualities are, of course, derived from a top-down view. We arrive at these qualities by applying logic to the apparent design of circumstance as they occur in the fractal ladder. But what if we view the situation from the bottom-up or from the point of view of what has already manifested in the Earth–Sun creation? Will the same qualities or further insight into their essential natures reveal themselves? For a quick answer to what has manifested, we can of course refer to the fractal ladder itself. The building blocks for each rung are the physical, vital, and mental states. Let us probe into the nature of these states once again since these states must also tell us something about the nature of progress.

The physical state is characterized by all that the eye can see. It is the essential matrix of creation, the substance into which all else manifests. It is also the index of all that has successfully manifested and that has become an essential part of life. And it also reveals the incredible detail and level of perfection that has gone into the manifestation itself. Take a sweeping look at the detail, intricacy, and beauty of nature and this quality of perfection seems to arise. Take a look at the incredible patience with which matter awaits the intervention of other dynamics, whether of vitality or mentality, and a sense of service seems to arise. This substance that is all-present then seems to be imbued with a character of detailed perfection and a quality of service. In fact, the principle of service and perfection seems to stand behind the play of the physical state. And if they stand behind the physical state, it is likely that they form a link between what is manifested and the seed state from which all has manifested.

One cannot but see a parallel between the top-down observation of progress being all-present, and the bottom-up observation of the physical state as being all-present. One cannot but observe that there appears to be this sense of inherent service present in both of them. These are perhaps parallel states, with the all-presence manifesting as the physical state. But in the process of manifesting, something also seems to have been left out. While omnipresence transcends barriers of time, there is mortality in physical nature. While the general forms are perpetuated, individual constructs cannot sustain themselves and decay and die in relatively short order. There seems to be a general quality of stagnation that accompanies the birth of omnipresence into finite forms. Since progress is the ultimate designer, we must conclude that the creation of such a shadow state is of strategic importance. Hence, while the omnipresence manifests as the physical state,

Figure 9.1 Physical State Relationships

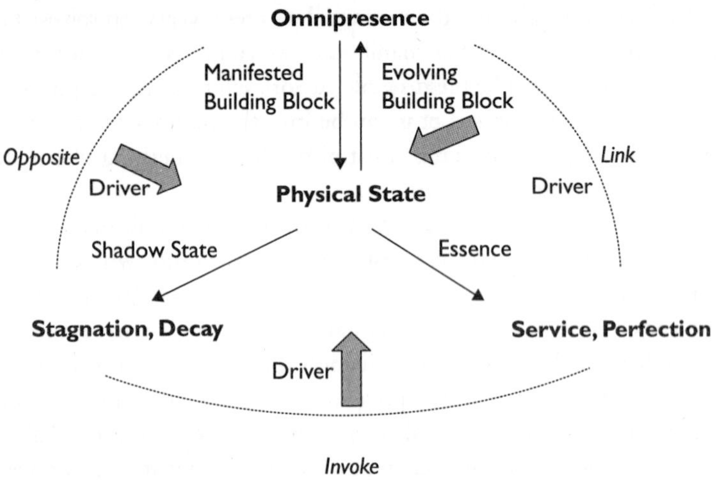

it seems to almost do so from an opposite position of stagnation. Growth of possibility occurs through invoking service and perfection, the essence that stands behind the physical state. Such invocation would likely not take place unless there was a felt shortcoming. The combination of these drivers then becomes the means by which the physical state progressively embodies more of omnipresence. These relationships shed further insight into the quality of omnipresence and are summarized in Figure 9.1.

The vital state is characterized by an essential state of energy, experiment, and adventure. It is an index of the rush of possibilities colliding with each other and reforming themselves into new possibility. It is not light of energy but power of energy that determines outcome. The essential character, hence, seems to be that of power. In the matrix of manifested life, this seems to play itself out through the trait of adventure. Each type of energy adventures toward an expression of itself, adventures toward clash and battle, and toward unknown outcome. But all this adventure and experiment can only take place under the aegis of power. Else, what would dare to seek fulfillment or self-destruction in such manner? The vital state, therefore, seems to be the manifested state of the quality of omnipotence.

Adventure, energy, assertiveness, and growth seem to be some characteristics of its quality.

We must note, however, that whereas in its aspect of top-down omnipotence, this essential characteristic seems to have an inevitable force and power that is ultimately irresistible, in its manifestation in the strivings of nature's constructs the power is child-like and weak, perhaps precisely because the base through which this quality is manifesting is fragmented and strapped by limited tendencies of all kinds. As suggested, this must be a strategic decision on the part of that ultimate designer, progress. Hence, while the omnipotence manifests as the vital state, it seems to almost do so from an opposite position of weakness. Growth of possibility occurs through invoking adventure and power, the essence, that stands behind the vital state. Such invocation would likely not take place unless there was a felt shortcoming. The combination of these drivers then becomes the means by which the vital state progressively embodies more of omnipotence. These relationships shed further insight into the quality of omnipotence and are summarized in Figure 9.2.

The mental state is characterized by the play of the idea as the principle means of organization. While at its far rim mentality is an

Figure 9.2 Vital State Relationships

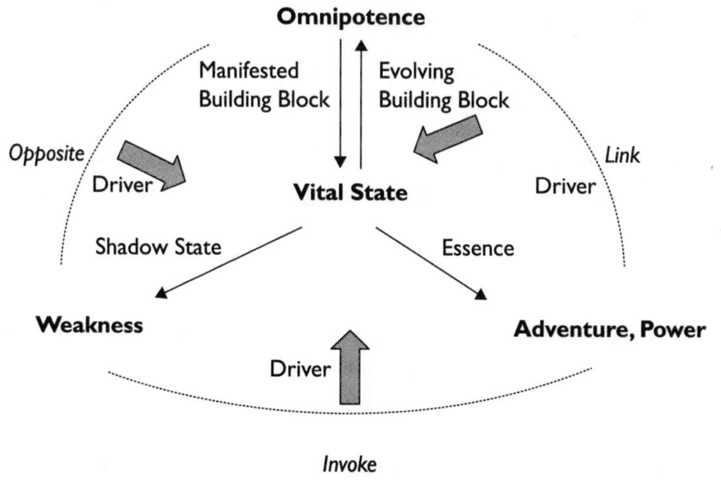

index of future possibility, in its central orb it appears to be more of an index of organizing around reason and rationalization. Increasing knowledge, consideration from many more points of view even in the organization of smaller and smaller matters—a dawning wisdom hence, seems to be essential characteristics of its quality.

But in its play, it seems that while it yields insight and makes better choices possible, yet it cannot reveal the heart of knowledge. No doubt, mentality is the manifested quality of progress' omniscience, yet while there is vast and intricate play and pushing of possibility in its top-down aspect, from the bottom-up, mentality is marked much more by error and ignorance. This again, must be a decision of strategic importance. Essentially, while the omniscience manifests as the mental state, it seems to almost do so from an opposite position of ignorance. Growth of possibility occurs through invoking knowledge and wisdom, the essence, that stands behind the mental state. Such invocation would not likely take place unless some shortcoming was felt. The combination of these drivers then becomes the means by which the mental state progressively embodies more of omniscience. These relationships shed further insight into the quality of omniscience and are summarized in Figure 9.3.

Figure 9.3 Mental State Relationships

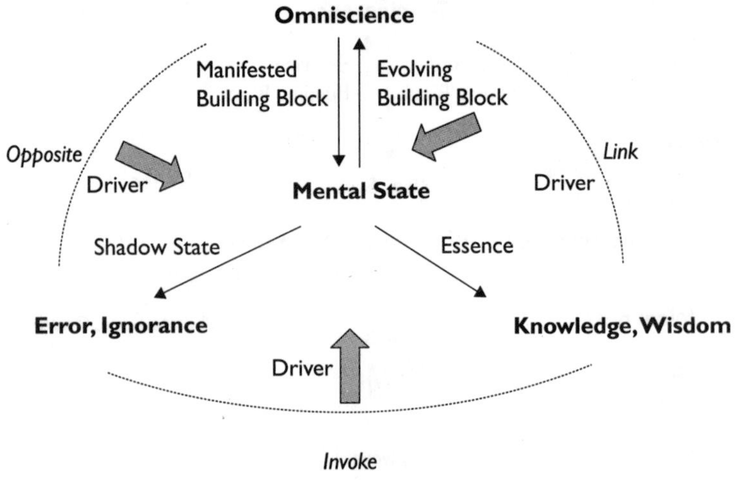

Let us pause for a moment and observe that the essential qualities of progress have indeed manifested themselves in the evolution of life. The physical state is related to or is more accurately perhaps a reflection of omnipresence, the vital state a reflection of omnipotence, and the mental state a reflection of omniscience. Hence, any effort to understand the nature of progress must be useful since it will likely give us insight into perhaps even how circumstances and events may unroll in the future.

If the physical state is related to omnipresence, the vital state to omnipotence, and the mental state to omniscience, then what about the state of omnicaring? What does that relate to in practical terms? Surely it must also have a place in the scheme of things. Omnicaring is that sense of deep caring, of deep love that progress seems to have for its creation. If it did not care in this manner, it would have left the creation to sink in the obscurity of its own machinations. Instead, it has continually intervened, and even constructed this means by which we can not only rise above the pettiness of our own natures but even transform it, by beginning to ascend the fractal ladder.

In a sense this property of progress seems even to be more core than the other ones. There is a measure of impersonality in the properties of all-power, all-knowledge, and all-presence. But all-caring seems to be much more personal. It perhaps manifests as heart, as that ultimate movement that gives a very different sense to everything. Progress happens because of an essential love. Progress has an essential love for its creatures, by which it forms them into reflections and images of itself. Omnicaring makes everything its child. And these children grow through the travails of life into wiser, more loving beings, who can more easily embrace all of life in a grasp of power.

This property is all about establishing a growing harmony. It is almost as though something significant, characterized by the heart, is growing behind the essential physical–vital–mental journey. And yet in its growth, fundamental limits of the mind itself are breaking and leading the being into states of intuition, whereby manifested possibility can more easily touch the heart of progress and be more securely molded by it. This is the likely fourth state, intuition. While heart seems to be behind the journeying, the next phase in an incomplete and evolving physical–vital–mental sequence seems to be that of intuition. This is a broader state that seems that it will more securely connect the top-down properties of omnipresence, omnicaring, omniscience, and omnipotence with the bottom-up physical, vital, and mental states and make the different rungs of the fractal ladder more ready for the rule of heart.

Increasing Action of the Qualities of Progress

This brings us an important insight that we need to further develop. When viewed from the top-down, the essential qualities of progress seem to act in simultaneity. Omnipresence, omnipotence, omniscience, and omnicaring seem to coexist. In manifested nature, however, they replete with the many fragmented creations cut off from each other by limitations of the essentially physical, vital, or still-evolving mental outlooks, or some combinations of each, only some aspects of the qualities of progress and certainly incomplete combinations of them can find expression. Hence, thinking of the physical, vital, and mental states as fields of possibility, it seems that each field progressively allows more of the four identified qualities of progress to act simultaneously and fully. This is depicted in Figure 9.4.

At the physical end of the spectrum, possibility manifests in fixed grooves. The essential expression is of the past, of what has already been brought into the manifestation. In such a matrix, the more dynamic, light-filled, and loving aspects of omnipotence, omniscience, and omnicaring, respectively, act behind the surface in whatever way they can, precisely because the means for their overt action and way of being has not still been adequately brought. The physical field is still too rigid, inert, and obscure to allow any meaningful expression of these possibilities. Hence, while it appears that the omnipresence aspect of progress presides over the physical field, the omnipotence, omniscience, and omnicaring aspects are quite hidden.

In the vital stage, energies and dynamism have infused the physical, and the very physical–vital conglomerate now allows many more possibilities to manifest. While it is perhaps the omnipotence aspect

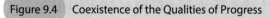

Figure 9.4 Coexistence of the Qualities of Progress

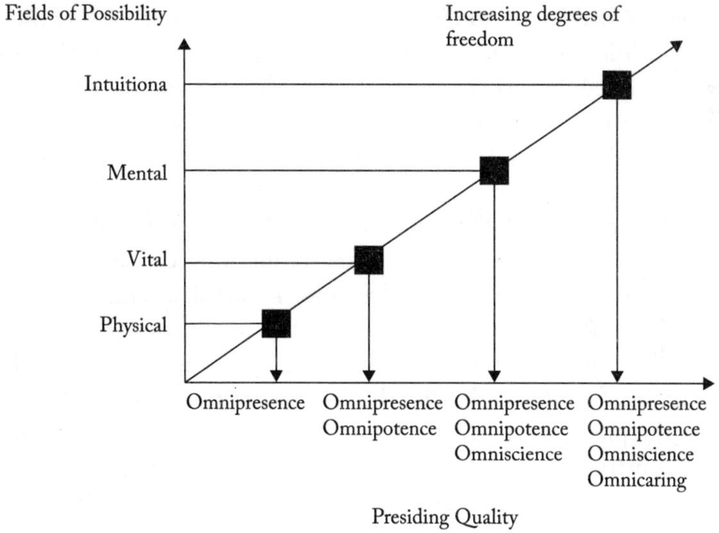

of progress that presides over this conglomerate, the substance of the field is still not malleable enough perhaps to allow the possibilities resident in omniscience and omnicaring to meaningfully manifest. Even, of course, omnipotence, given the nature of the vital field, can only appear as a reflection of itself.

At the mental level, the essential field has been even further altered to allow a more advanced play, relatively speaking, characteristic of a more intense reflection of omnipresence, omnipotence, and omniscience. These essential qualities of progress can shape possibility, and uniqueness and identity can more meaningfully manifest.

But still, these fields have more of a bottom-up quality. They are still too tied up to physicality and the backward look. With the advent of the fourth state, intuition, there is now a more direct action from the essential nature of progress and its four qualities will likely find far more meaningful expression. Further, there will likely be a higher degree of simultaneity in their action, more akin to the essential quality of their unfettered top-down action.

Application of the P-V-M Fractal to Progress

When we had begun to identify the essential traits of each of these four qualities of progress in their interactions in the Earth play, we had suggested that service and perfection were the observed nature of the quality of omnipresence. Adventure and power were the observed nature of the quality of omnipresence. Knowledge and wisdom was the observed nature of the quality of omniscience. And harmony was the observed nature of the quality of omnicaring. While omnipresence, omnipotence, omniscience, and omnicaring can appear to be very abstract terms, service, adventure, knowledge, and harmony[1] seem to be much more practical terms and certainly easier to grasp. While the former set of terms can be thought of as end goals in the evolution of the fractal ladder, the latter set of terms can be thought of as the presiding motive forces under which the fractal ladder has been constructed and by which it more immediately progresses.

It is interesting to note that through the analysis we have just conducted, we have essentially applied the physical–vital–mental fractal to the very nature of progress. In its physical aspect, that which we see all around us manifest as each rung of the fractal ladder, it appears as the physical, vital, mental, and intuitional states. In its vital aspect, the link state which is leading through experimentation and expression, it appears as service, adventure, knowledge, and harmony. In its mental aspect, that which is its hidden meaning and identity, it appears as the states of omnipresence, omnipotence, omniscience, and omnicaring. In other words, service, adventure, knowledge, and harmony are secret names behind the operation of the fractal ladder. We shall examine their role more closely in the next chapters when we consider alternative bases to our current vital foundation of business and leadership. The most secret names behind the fractal ladder are of course omnipresence, omnipotence, omniscience, and omnicaring. This is what the fractal ladder must have the potential to transform into some time in the distant future.

[1] In his book *The Mother* (Pondicherry: Sri Aurobindo Ashram, 1950), Sri Aurobindo describes four active powers Maheshwari (Knowledge), Mahakali (Power), Mahalakshmi (Harmony), and Mahasaraswati (Service and Perfection) that govern manifested existence. The four terms arrived at here have similarities with these four powers.

Figure 9.5 Architecture of the Fractal Ladder

M-State (identity)	Meaning	Omnipresence	Omnipotence	Omniscience	Omnicaring
V-State (link state)	Drivers	Service and Perfection	Adventure and Power	Knowledge and Wisdom	Harmony
P-State (manifested nature)	Building blocks	Physical	Vital	Mental	Intuitional

This architecture of the fractal ladder resulting from the application of the P-V-M fractal is summarized in Figure 9.5.

Through the action of intuition, it is possible that rigidities in the fundamental building blocks can be reduced. This is inevitable since the action of intuition, by definition, means that the fundamental building blocks are themselves completing their fractal journeys, since intuition is the fourth state, beyond the mental. As a result, the physical, vital, and mental building blocks, more easily admitting of the unfettered qualities of progress, of which they are reflected or shadow states in our analyses, can begin to admit a different mode of operation. Hence, the rigidity, obscurity, inertia, dullness, and opposition to progress that mark the shadow side of the physical, might more easily begin to give way to their opposites. The egoism, desires, demands, vanity, anger, fear, aggressiveness, jealousy, among other shadow states of the vital, might similarly also begin to give way to their opposites. The fixed notions, beliefs, constructions, narrow ideas, and noise that mark the shadow side of the mental, might also begin to give way to their opposites. As a result, the physical, vital, and mental fields will begin to go through a progressive transformation. These fields will become more capable of incarnating qualities of progress and allowing a higher degree of simultaneous action of each of the four qualities to take place.

If the very building blocks of each rung of the fractal ladder goes through such a transformation, then imagine what may happen to the creation on each rung and the fractal ladder itself. Opposition to the fractal journeys will diminish and they will be completed far more rapidly. Fractal influence, completion, universality, recursion, matrixing, evolution, stepwise development, and feedback will become more pervasive and the very structure of the fractal ladder will evolve with rapidity. More fruitful experimentation and adventuring will take place as the fractal qualities of intersection, flow, facilitation, and upscaling find more and more avenues to be expressed. The very meaning of individuality will change as world-wiseliness, mirroring, affirmation, integration, and uniqueness become more prevalent. As a result, the fourth state, intuition, will find forms and circumstances much more malleable to its influence, thereby even further opening out the essential structure of the fractal ladder to the secret names that stand behind it. The exercise of alignment, aspiration, surrender, rejection, and love will increase and constructs will open and manifest in their very natures the essential motive forces of service, adventure, knowledge, and harmony. The bases of individuals, or corporations, of society, of all manner of systems, of the very notion of leadership, will change from within, proceeding now on a multidimensional platform of holism as opposed to the long-experienced one-dimensional platform of exploitation. Progress itself will more openly manifest in all the workings of the fractal ladder.

In the Mandukya Upanishad,[2] there is reference to the four states of AUM. "A" is the Waking State where there is consciousness of the form of things. This is akin to the consciousness of the physical, vital, and mental building blocks, the physical or P-state in the emerging scheme of the fractal ladder. "U" is the Dream State where there is consciousness of the play of principles behind forms. This play of principles can be thought of as the motive forces of service and perfection, adventure and power, knowledge and wisdom, and harmony, the V-State in the emerging scheme of the fractal ladder. "M" is the

[2] Please refer to Sri Aurobindo's *The Upanishads* (Pondicherry: Sri Aurobindo Ashram, 1981) which has a translation of portions of the Mandukya Upanishad relating to AUM.

Sleep State, the consciousness of the principles themselves. These principles can be thought of as omnipresence, omnipotence, omniscience, and omnicaring, the M-state in the emerging scheme of the fractal ladder. The combination of A, U, M, forming AUM, is the transcendent state, the witness, that which is everywhere, and which manifests past, present, and future. The stringing together of P, V, M results in the emergence of progress, that witnesses state, that is similarly present everywhere, and is the seed state of the fractal ladder. If this analogy holds, then the seed fractal of the fractal ladder, progress, is none other than that revered and ever-present mystic syllable that promises to be the ultimate secret behind all manifestation, AUM. Let us consider this more deeply. AUM in its visible manifestation is the physical, the vital, and the mental. For the physical is the form of things, the vital is the play of possibilities seeking for expression, and the mental is the idea or principles themselves. Hence, not only the fractal ladder in its three aspects represents AUM, but each of the rungs which string the physical, the vital, and the mental together also represents AUM. In other words, the fractal ladder as a whole, each of the rungs on the fractal ladder, and therefore every type of progressive organization from a person to entire system is also a manifestation of AUM. This then stands as the most secret nature of progress. This analogy is depicted in Figure 9.6.

Summary

We began this chapter with a restatement of the top-down qualities of progress. We then looked at the fractal ladder, as the instance of manifested progress, to surface from the bottom-up other insights into the nature of the qualities of progress. We arrived at the notion of deeper principles or motive forces, service and perfection, adventure and power, knowledge and wisdom, and harmony, behind the established building blocks of the Fractal Ladder. We then considered the coexistence of the essential qualities of progress as they preside over the fields of possibility set up by the physical, vital, mental, and intuitional building blocks. We applied the P-V-M fractal to progress itself, to surface a deeper architecture of the fractal ladder.

Figure 9.6 AUM and the Fractal Ladder

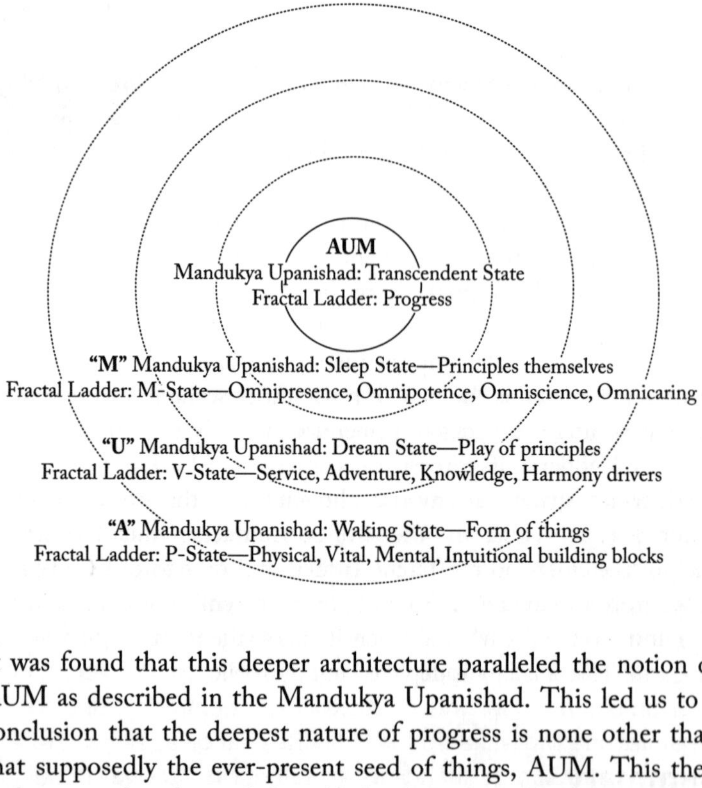

It was found that this deeper architecture paralleled the notion of AUM as described in the Mandukya Upanishad. This led us to a conclusion that the deepest nature of progress is none other than that supposedly the ever-present seed of things, AUM. This then perhaps stand as the seed-fractal behind the fractal ladder.

The next chapters will look at an alternative bases for business and leadership, leveraging off some of the findings in this chapter, particularly the motive forces of service, adventure, knowledge, and harmony.

Remaking the Business World 10

Focus: A look at what business and the corporation may become as the fractal ladder continues to progress.

Key Concepts: Comprehension of current problems through examination of related business fractals | Consumerism fractal, business fractal, global economy fractal, global society fractal | Choice of consumption as dictated from the physical, vital, and mental ways of being | Walmart and testament to being at the vital level of consumer fractal | Changing the root dynamic to bring about progression of related business fractals | Extent of impact of the root dynamics and the wake-up call | Climate change as essence of the wake-up call | Climate change as a result of the vital way of being | Business fractal at the vital level | Global economy fractal on vital side of boundary between vital and mental | Nature of boundary | Global society fractal and business standards of judgment | Progress of society as synonymous with progress of business | Global society fractal at the vital level | Pervasive vital-centeredness indicating severe loss of balance | Climate change as a rebellion of matter | Individual consciousness as the root of the world fractal | The remaking of business through shift in individual consciousness | The essence of CSR | CSR can give the appearance that a real shift in consciousness has occurred | False solutions and other disequilibrium as severe as climate change | Climate hange as a wake-up call to the vital way of being | Nature of transition from the vital to the mental way of being | Different ways to accelerate shift from the vital to mental way of being | Mobilization of secret names of progress | New creation of business must have four motive forces as foundation | People being allowed to follow their essential way of being as key to new creation | Organizations with enduring power have mobilized something of four motive forces simultaneously | Instability caused by following shadow state of one motive force only | The great tragedy of current corporate life | Modern business versus grass-roots community-driven development | Nature of leadership as the deciding factor

Introduction

Thus far, we have suggested that our world is marked by a fractal reality. Within the vortex of fractal dynamics, there is a Fractal Ladder that is the signature of progress. We have examined various rungs of creation on this ladder from the point of view of the fundamental building blocks that determine the active dynamics of that rung, and the necessity of the completion of the Sun-marked physical–vital–mental fractal, were progress to happen at the level of that rung. Following the physical–vital–mental fractal is the key to enter the fractal ladder, which by its nature allows and promotes dynamics of accelerated and sustainable progress. We have also examined fractal properties that exist on the fractal ladder and have taken a deeper look at progress itself, that remarkable dynamic, to gain insight into the secret names behind the construction and operation of the fractal ladder. These examinations and the alternative model of reality that they suggest are showing us pathways to a more sustainable world that is within our grasp.

We know that the current intensity of problems we are experiencing at the global level, from climate change, to a general financial breakdown, to increasing resource shortages, to increasing prices of commodities, to destruction of biomes and species, among many other severe problems, is the result of living a primarily vitally centered life at many different levels. The effects of a big business can no longer be ignored, and the choices we continue to support as a society must go through a radical change. In order to fully comprehend the nature of our problem, it is necessary to examine several distinct but related fractals. These include the consumerism fractal, the business fractal, the global economy fractal, and the global society fractal. We live in the vital sphere in each of these, and through dynamics of influence and feedback, there is the reinforcing of an unsustainable way of being that must be altered at the root.

In this chapter, we will look into each of the mentioned business-related fractals, and the resultant nature of the wake-up call. We will then seek to understand the serious global problems at its roots. We will conclude this chapter by considering possible approaches to then address the problems at its very roots by bringing about the needed shift from the vital to the mental way of being.

The Consumerism Fractal and the Nature of the Wake-up Call

As consumers, we have a choice of consuming dictated by the physical, vital, or mental way of being. In the physical way of being, there are certain set habits that determine our choices of consumption. Things we are used to doing, foods we are used to eating, and clothes we are used to wearing determine our on-going choices of consumption. We will not much deviate from that way. In the vital way of being, there is far less stability in our choices, and stoked by desires, whims, and opportunities to experience immediate satisfaction, we become conspicuous consumers. In this way of being, the disposable type of product is promoted. There is little value for what it takes to create product and what the implications are of churning out more product on the environment and the segments of societies that create the often many inputs for the products or the products themselves. There is little or no thought or consideration given to the fact that there is an equilibrium that must be maintained with the Earth of which we are a part. Reason rarely dawns at the height of the unrefined vital level. As long as base emotions—vanity, easing of jealousy, desire, among

Figure 10.1 The Consumerism Fractal

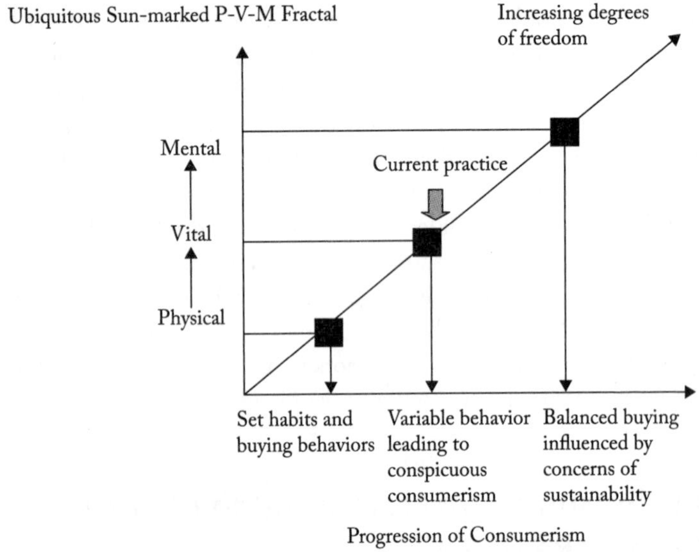

others—are fulfilled, that is all that counts. In the mental way of being, there is a dawning and even a more rigorous intervention of thought. In this case, consumerism will tend to become more sustainable in its essence, as larger impacts of buying decisions are progressively factored in the buying decision itself. This progression through the consumerism fractal is depicted in Figure 10.1.

Generally speaking, it is the immediate satisfaction of a desire, or a particular tendency that we ourselves may have created, or that may have incarnated in us as a result of affinity with that particular influence, that drives our buying decisions. Even though at the leading edge there is the emergence of green consumers, that fact that the Walmarts of the world, with all their questionable impacts on social, cultural, and environmental dimensions are still growing so rapidly is a testament to the fact that we are, primarily speaking, at the vital level in the consumerism fractal. This positioning is also depicted in Figure 10.1.

It is not thought, but desire that drives much of our decision when it comes to buying. And yet, this is because those desires live in us and obviously dominate our active consciousness. Unless this root dynamic is changed, the consumerism fractal will always remain at the vital level, and by nature of its reality and fractal influence, will cause other fractals, at progressively more complex levels of organization, such as the business fractal, the global economy fractal, and the global society fractal to tend to remain locked at the vital level as well. So long as a questionable way of being is confined within boundaries, it may be allowed to continue to exist in its suboptimal way of being. When its influence effects the very foundation on which all boundaries depend and if there is a meaning to that foundation, and we have seen that there is meaning in our lives as is evident by the existence of progress, then there has to be a wake-up call that fundamentally attempts to realign the way of being, and in this case the many business-related fractals, with the Sun-marked physical–vital–mental fractal that is the very symbol of that progress. This relationship is depicted in Figure 10.2.

Figure 10.2 The Necessity of a Wake-up Call

Arrestation of Global System Fractal at Vital Level Requires Global Wake-up Call

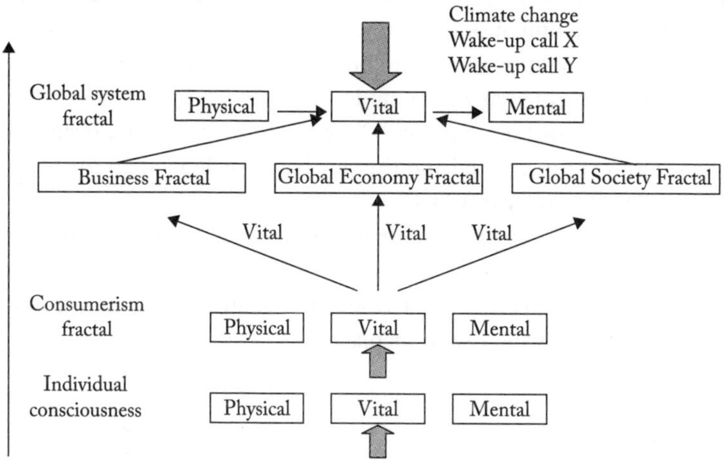

Climate Change is the very essence of that wake-up call. It is causing the base dynamics and the long built-up equilibrium of our physical world to shift substantially. The increase of carbon dioxide and other greenhouse gases, due to manmade causes, increases the heat trapped in the atmosphere. As a result, temperatures shift upward causing more intense weather and storm systems around the world. Coastal towns and cities in the path of these storms get devastated.[1] But, as the polar ice melts, the water level of seas and oceans increases and then coastal regions, cities, and natural dams and wetlands get flooded and destroyed. As the oceans get warmer, fundamental water currents that have maintained the rhythm of seasons and weather of all continents gets compromised and radical and results in destructive shifts to much larger ecosystems. The increased atmospheric temperatures also result in alteration of ecosystems and long-established equilibrium of plants and animal species and contribute to their extinction. Diversity of life is compromised. The increased carbon dioxide levels also increases the acidity of oceans, destroying the formation of base species such as plankton at the very bottom of the marine food chain, thereby also throwing all marine life into substantial disequilibrium and progressive extinction as well. As the fundamental equilibrium of oceans and lands and the many ecosystems that exist in these systems alters, base services that nature offers us, whether of carbon sequestration, purification of air and water, enrichment of soil, flood control, diversification of species with their many known and unknown benefits such as pollination, provision of medicinal compounds, creation of all types of food, among many other services that allow us to live as a human species, gets severely compromised and the very basis we depend on for all our lives gets pulled away from us.

As Figure 10.2 suggests, climate change has to be addressed by addressing the root cause responsible for it. If this does not happen, then other wake-up calls—X, Y (indicated in upper right hand corner of Figure 10.2)—will arise in its place.

[1] There are many books on Climate Change. For a deeper treatment of climate change, you may refer to: Tim Flannery, *The Weather Makers: How Man is Changing the Climate and What It Means for Life on Earth* (New York: Grove Press, 2001).

Other Related Fractals and Their Status

In Chapter 3, we have already discussed the physical, vital, and mental outlooks of a business corporation. Our earlier analysis of business was focused more on looking at why the Sun-marked physical–vital–mental fractal was the optimum path for business. But even as we look at where business is today, we must conclude that it too is at the vital level. The very fact that human life and humane working conditions require a business case to be justified shows the short-sighted, self-seeking, and narrow focus that is characteristic of the vital level of operation. We would not expect otherwise, since the reason or prize of markets, the consumer, is himself at the vital level as just discussed.

The global economy fractal is also, as we have discussed in Chapter 4, on the vital side of the boundary between the vital and the mental. This boundary, by nature, must bring up the essence of being vital in all its force so that by understanding this and overcoming it, the very engine of the transition from the vital to the mental can come into being. Hence, it is to be expected that all the depravities of this way of being must surface. Wars for oil, diamonds, and other metals, pillaging and ravishing entire countries and continents and sending millions into a subhuman state of life; shortages of fundamental resources such as water and clean air; shortages of staple foods as they become raw material for substitutes for oil; exploitation and destruction of biomes and long-formed and essential creations of Earth, such as forest, wetlands, and watersheds; and trading of human beings as commodities to sold into labor and satisfaction of pleasure, among other depravities promises to unleash further havoc on our already increasingly fragile way of life.

The global society fractal is in such a stage that all of its institutions are currently judged by their ability to prop up and feed the engines of business. We seem to have forgotten knowledge for its own sake, but judge its value in its ability to create more money. We seem to have forgotten the promise of freedom contained in beautiful art and music, and have in a miserly deal, revalued these in terms of the money they can generate. Love is sold in the marketplace, and when a child is educated, it is often with the goal of churning out another asset that can at the end of the day benefit the bottom line of business. Today, we talk of the triple bottom line, and while this represents a progressive step away from the depravities of business, it is still the bottom line and the institution of business that drives our meaning and worth. At the end of the day, we have even forgotten that we can be something other than cogs or even fountains in the game of business. We have forgotten that there are other drivers of progress that if pursued along their own paths of development may result in a balance of creation necessary for truer sustainability. The sense of business has pervaded our very lives so strongly that the meaning of societies and their very progress has become synonymous with the progress of business. This state of being indicates that the global society fractal is also in the vital phase. But again, why should we expect anything different if in our basic stance as individuals we view life from a vital perspective.

The Root of the Problem

If all the rungs of our life are centered at the vital level and if the meanings of our lives have become synonymous with business, then we are in essence out of balance. The degree of this loss of balance is severe, as evident by the response from Earth itself in the form of climate change. For, in its essence, climate change is nothing other than a rebellion of matter. We are aware of rebellions through history, of a social nature, as means to bring development back into balance. But a rebellion of matter on the scale we are seeing today is perhaps unprecedented in recorded history. But why shouldn't there be a rebellion of this nature, if indeed Earth system is a living being, with a trajectory of development that is in essence being compromised by the short-sighted way of her constructs? There is perhaps no other way for the trajectory of progress to continue as it should, unless individual consciousness, the root of the world fractal we see playing itself out now, were itself to progress to the next phase in its own Sun-marked physical–vital–mental journey. That is the need of the hour. This change lies at the crux of the remaking of business to bring about true and meaningful sustainability.

There is no other way to promote true sustainability. Today, we see the rise of the Corporate Social Responsibility (CSR) movement.[2] In its essence, CSR is about integrating more holistic environmental, social, and governance considerations and factors into the strategy and operations of business. At its best, it is about pushing the business fractal from a vital to a more mental mode of operation. But at the end of the day, there is a real business case for adopting CSR, which means that business actors have a business incentive to follow through with what CSR brings to the table. The shift from vital to mental, from operating without more holistic environmental, social and governance considerations to operating with these considerations will allow a business to generate more profit. This is because more customers and stakeholders from the public to the investment community expect this behavior from business and, therefore, reward it, which is because it has also proven to minimize a variety of production and operating costs, thereby increasing margins. Moreover, it is because consideration of environmental, social, and governance factors also provides stimulus to the redefinition and creation of new products, thereby enhancing revenue generation. The point is that there is a business reason to make these changes, and therefore the mode of operation will tend to be centered in the unrefined profit motive which is essentially vital in nature. Because of the business case, business actors can remain fundamentally at the vital level, while doing all the things that CSR will make them do, to give the appearance that there has been a real shift to the mental level. But, no real shift has occurred, and the base fractal at the individual level remains at the vital level continuing to have its prolonging, and as we have seen, negative effect on world dynamics. At best, more mental force has been drawn to the service of the central vital principle.

The dangers of climate change may be immediately assuaged and we may live comforted that we have successfully addressed a potential calamity. But this is an illusion. The calamity has only been pushed back into the future. The fundamental way of being remains vital,

[2] For an overview of CSR, please refer to: John Elkington, *Cannibals with Forks: Triple Bottom Line of 21st Century Business* (Oxford, UK: Capstone Publishing Ltd, 1999).

and therefore this dynamic is what will continue to ripple outward to the limit of the Earth, just as in the case of climate change, which has rippled out to the limits of the Earth.

We know, for instance, that the increase in electronics introduces a distortion to the natural electromagnetic field that surrounds each living being. We are essentially electromagnetic entities and this continued vital hunger for electronics of all kinds, in every facet of our lives, will continue to compromise the basic dynamics of our individual chemical equilibriums. For all chemistry that occurs in us is a result of a subtle electromagnetic equilibrium that stimulates cellular level chemical reactions.[3] With the increase of electronics, and even with their increasingly being implanted into our very bodies, whether through devices such as attachable cell phones and receptors or probes that enter into the bloodstream, the possibility that we are setting ourselves up for a severe disequilibrium as catastrophic as climate change cannot be ignored.

But there are so many other micro-threats of this nature that compromise our very equilibrium as individual entities. There is also the infiltration of harmful chemicals that alters our body chemistry, whether through intake of industrialized and processed foods and pharmaceuticals, application of cosmetics that immediately enter into our bloodstreams, use of cleaners, washers, paints, and other materials that exist in our dwellings, regular contact with surfaces such as processed textiles, plastics, automobiles, and other forms of transport that are themselves centers for the release of myriad harmful chemicals, and ingestion of non-renewable energy sources such as oil and gas that again pervade every aspect of the society and life we have today created for ourselves. There are a thousand ways that we are oblivious of whereby compromising chemicals can enter into our body. And there are a thousand ways in which they also enter into the very fiber of nature, right from wastes released during manufacturing, leakages during transportation, off-gassing during storage, not to mention as wastes released from us through course of daily activity. All industries that we have created—consumer

[3] For a more detailed treatment of this subject, please refer to Robert Becker and Gary Selden, *The Body Electric: Electromagnetism and the Foundation of Life* (New York: Harper Paperbacks, 1998).

products, energy, food and agriculture, transportation, information technology and electronics—have through our vital lust become means to kill our very vitality.[4]

Climate change is in fact a wake-up call to this vital way of being, and so long as we are able to penetrate into the true cause of it and grapple with the root fractal of which it is the result (see Figure 10.2), climate change will have done a great service to humankind by causing the needed shift in our way of being from a vital to a more mental way of being. The root pattern at the individual level is what must be changed. If, however, we reduce greenhouse gas emissions, create clever trading schemes, even create markets for promoting services of nature, and force regulation and legislation that causes business to alter action without affecting the root cause, we will have done ourselves little favor, and will be pushing back the inevitable catastrophe, which may incarnate in another form, whether of a fundamental poisoning of life through chemical overdose, a destabilization of living matter through alteration of base electromagnetics, or some other way that we are not foreseeing.

Facilitating the Shift from the Vital to the Mental

The shift from the vital to the mental level at the individual level is an imperative. The transition must be made, either willingly through sincere individual, corporate, and societal effort, or unwillingly through potential catastrophes of the nature of climate change. The movement from a vital to a mental way of being is at the crux of the matter, and the question is what can business do or how must it be remade in order to promote that shift? Several potential approaches have suggested themselves through the course of the book.

One is to have people consciously examine the tendencies that exist within them, and through reason and thought invigorate the

[4] For a detailed illustration of how the oil and gas and the automobile industries have compromised our lives, please refer to: Terry Tamminen, *Lives Per Gallon: The True Cost of our Oil Addiction* (Washington, DC: Shearwater, 2008).

arrested journey that has caused the tendency to anchor around its state of particular dysfunction. This is no doubt a difficult approach that few may be inclined to follow. Another approach that has suggested itself is to consciously enter into relationship with progress and lay everything before it. If this can be done, it is probably the best approach and we will have more to say about this in the next chapter. Given the fact that the business world is primarily at the vital level, however, and that this type of thought may be too much of a leap for it, this too may be a difficult path to follow. A third approach is to mobilize the secret names of progress. We had posited a fourth phase, that of intuition, which lies beyond the mental phase. That phase is alive with a dynamic array of motive forces, the secret names, that we found are also responsible for the very creation of the fractal ladder that cuts across creation. These motive forces are service, adventure, knowledge, and harmony.

These motive forces are at the heart of progress, and given that we are all constructs of progress, it must be that these motive forces lie at the heart of what drives us too. The physical, vital, and mental states are settled though unrefined formations of service, adventure, and knowledge respectively. Harmony stands behind it and emerges more as we move into the fourth or intuitional state. Hence, service, adventure, knowledge, and harmony are embedded in each living entity. In the vast play of nature, differentiation seems to manifest as unique combinations of these four motive forces. Countries, communities, mature companies, and people, each seem to have different combinations of these four forces that determine their uniqueness. Each living being, hence, likely has one of these four forces as a dominant driver of their being, with the other motive forces settled around or supporting the prime driver in different ways. This is depicted in Figure 10.3.

For illustrative purposes, Figure 10.3 depicts Entity-1 as ruled by a dominant adventure/power component and Entity-2 as being ruled by a dominant service/perfection component. Entities could be people, companies, collectivities, or countries, among other mature organizations.

In the new creation of business, it is these fundamental drivers, hence, that must be mobilized as the bases of the foundation. In today's world, we are all mobilized as pieces in the global business

Figure 10.3 The Play of Uniqueness

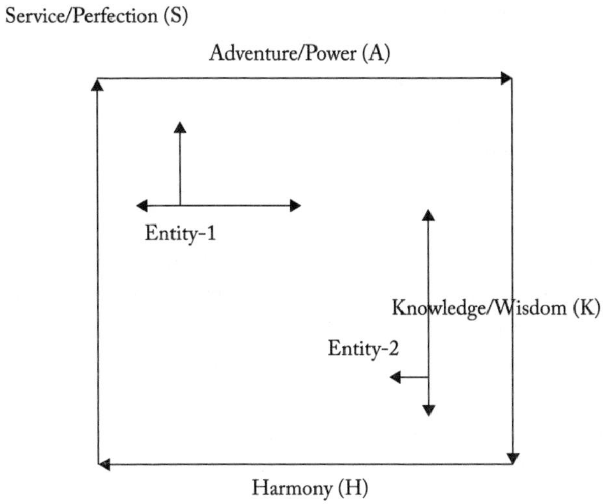

puzzle. All the possibility of what we stand for is reduced to one questionable motive force: exploitation in the name of business. In the remaking of business, this reality has to be changed. The four motive forces that must stand at the bases of any vibrant creation have to be consciously brought forward. Even though their fuller action may belong to the fourth or intuitional state, a conscious over-reaching of the mental way of being to mobilize these four powers cannot but result in even a more fruitful journey into and through the mental phase. This has to be the case if these four powers stand as the basis of uniqueness, and as we have posited, the very essence of the mental way of being is to question and therefore to anyway more rapidly arrive at this very sense of uniqueness, which is embodied by various combinations of the four motive forces at the heart of progress as illustrated in Figure 10.3.

Business to-date has proceeded along the vital dimension which is the shadow state of adventure. In this shadow state, the prime motive force has often been that of exploitation at any cost. This is for obvious and already observed reasons a miserly and unsustainable basis for organizational foundation. This very foundation has to be changed to include the four dimensions of service, adventure, knowledge, and harmony. It is only so that the true and sustainable springs or progress will be mobilized. It is only so that people will find that their raison d'être coincides with the activity of business, and it is only so that the very nature of progress can incarnate in the activity of business, thereby changing its fibers forever. The incarnation takes place through the root component – people. It is people allowed to follow their essential and innate way of being that creates the reality of progress at the individual level, and then by fractal pressure at each subsequent level.

Climate change and other threats of a similar nature can only be securely changed when the pattern at the root of the global fractal is allowed to move to the next phase in its own journey through mobilization of the deep forces that stand at the heart of progress. Even a brief study of sustainable society, countries, or other complex organizations through history will reveal that those with enduring power have managed to mobilize something of the four motive forces simultaneously. Severe instability is caused when only one motive force, which thereby, by definition, lacks influence from the other motive forces and is unable to move out of its unrefined state, remains the basis of organization.[5] Witness the current degeneration of countries as different as USA on the one hand and Pakistan on the other, that seem have been locked into an adamant and single way of being, thereby destroying their very springs of progress. As mentioned, in the business world today, all are subsumed to exist for the unrefined vital urge of exploitation. This may take other, more pleasant names, but at the end of the day, if a business does not fulfill its financial goals, all manner of idealism is often jettisoned. This standardization at the people level to force thoughts and acts to be of a certain kind only is the great tragedy of current corporate life.

The question as to whether the institution of business can remake itself to allow a balanced play of the four motive forces simultaneously, lies at the heart of its sustainability. On the one hand, it can be envisioned that current business organizations may rise to the challenge and truly allow the four ways of being to incarnate at the

[5] For an illustration of the instability of a narrow one-dimensional societal focus, please refer to: Jared Diamond, *Collapse: How Societies Choose to Fail or Succeed* (New York: Penguin, 2005).

very foundation of their operations. On the other hand, it can be envisioned that the poison runs just too deep, and that this type of model will need to be newly incubated into being. In the second scenario perhaps, it is at the grass-roots community level that the new models will come into being. After all, some of the perversities of modern business are attributed to its separation from ground realities and from accountability to society in general. A grass-roots community level organization will perhaps be more likely to reinforce these checks to thereby minimize the vital exaggerations that more naturally accompany a context of minimal accountability. A grass-roots community level organization also has the added advantage of more naturally nurturing the four motive forces in close albeit perhaps independent proximity to each other. The proximity may allow for more intimate interaction from the start, thereby evolving more robust organizations over time.

Though a particular form of the organization may tend to allow the more balanced play of motive forces, it cannot be the deciding factor. The deciding factor is the kind of leadership that exists at the individual level. The individual leader is going to determine the degree to which the heart of progress can be mobilized. The individual leader is going to determine the degree to which uniqueness and the countering of established ways of being can come into being.

Summary

In this chapter, we studied several fractals related to business to understand the nature of the problem we face on a global scale. The degree of the problem is apparent in the nature of the wake-up call—climate change. We argued that climate change is only a symptom and unless it is addressed at its very roots, by shifting the seed fractal at the base of the related business fractals, we are doing ourselves little long-term favor. We discussed the nature of the root and suggested approaches to remaking the business world so allowing a fruitful transition from the vital to the mental way of being. We suggested that mobilization of motive forces and effective leadership were the keys to facilitating the needed shift. In the next chapter, we will examine the criticality and nature of the required leadership.

11 Creating Enterprises of Tomorrow

Focus: A look at some critical factors in creating the enterprises of tomorrow.

Key Concepts: Cogs in a machine | Physically-centered puppets | Unkowing instrument | Element mastery | Holistic leadership | Substance from the heart of progress | Unique personalities of deeper substance | Highest possibility of leadership | Dynamic being | Centers of creative power | Dharma | Physical–service–perfection–omnipresence conglomerate | Vital–adventure–courage–omnipower conglomerate | Mental–knowledge–wisdom–omniscience conglomerate | Intuitinoal–harmony–mutuality–omnicaring conglomerate | Radically redefined building blocks | Apotheosis in space and time | Incarnations of the fractal ladder | Sunlit path | Fractal ladder as key to the system | Unendable progress | Attuning to raison d'être | Turning our world view on its head | Altering equilibrium between objectivity and subjectivity | Sea change in psychology | Becoming heroes | Co-responsibility | Becoming a compelling center | Hidden orchestration of progress

Introduction

We live in a world predominantly animated by the physical and the vital, to some extent the mental, and less so by the intuitional way of being. Examination of several rungs of creation reveals that it is these very states that form the building blocks of these levels of creation. So long as the preponderant state at a level remains the physical or vital or even the lower mental way of being, as opposed to the side of the mental approaching the intuitional, conditions at that level of creation will tend to be more yesteryear as opposed to progressively focused. This means that our thoughts, behaviors, and actions will reinforce a surface rendering of ourselves, and we will continue as cogs in a machinery set in motion through yesteryear's laws. We will continue an existence as puppets of dominant physically-centered, backward-pointing forces.

The prime task of leadership in building the enterprise of tomorrow, hence, regardless of field, is to bring about this shift from a physical–vital to a mental–intuitional mode of operation. That is, an organization's Sun-marked physical–vital–mental fractal, regardless of type of organization and respective playing field, must be completed.

In this concluding theoretical foundation chapter, let us look at the type of leadership needed, the future scenario that must emerge, and the imperative recontextualization that must take place to get us there.

Type of Leadership

If progress is a reality and the examinations in this book conclude that this must be so, then there have to be circumstances in the affairs of life that perforce move in a direction consistent with the Sun-marked physical–vital–mental fractal in spite of any number of forces to the contrary. This is how progress happens. For this to occur though the particular circumstance must be the field of an instrument by which the necessary shifts occur along the needed trajectory. If it is an unknowing instrument, that is, one who is not aware of the intention and hand of progress in the movement of circumstance, yet he or she must likely have mastery over some critical elements—be it physical, vital, or mental—the application of which allows the circumstance to move in the needed direction.

The physical mastery may take the form of precise knowledge of the rules and the resources that have established past stability, and therefore of insight into the right application of these variables to ensure that stability continues or incrementally changes in the needed manner. The vital mastery may take the form of power to be able to shift players who make rules, through insight into what their emotional or resource levers of change are. Mental mastery may take the form of insight into root causes of stability and shifts in the situation and the adjustment of these to bring about sizable changes in circumstance. In the case of the unknowing instrument, it is still the intent of progress that likely acts in a subtle manner to cause the unknowing instrument to choose in a particular way so that overall progress in the circumstance occurs.

The mastery over the physical, the vital, or the mental elements of the situation is no doubt manifestation of leadership. This kind of *element* leadership is, however, different from the integral, holistic leadership that is the need of the hour in that it is in a manner of speaking disconnected from progress and therefore incomplete. Were it to be consciously connected to the very fount of progress, it would admit to a whole other way of operation because it would by definition be open to the mysteries and possibilities inherent in progress and through this influence would likely be stretched beyond anything it could possibly effectuate in the absence of that influence. The contrast in type of leadership is summarized in Figure 11.1.

Connection and mobilization of progress will allow the substance from the heart of progress to project more of itself forward, and truer, more spontaneous, more creative and more sustainably enduring renderings of service and perfection, of adventure, of knowledge, and of harmony will manifest. In other words, truer, and more unique personalities of deeper substance, radically different from the established personalities and commonly accepted stereotypes of leaders of the past will be experienced. This is not to say that these types of personalities have not manifested in the past. They surely have. Conscious contact with progress, however, will likely cause more of these types of leaders to manifest.

It is this type of leadership that is the need of the hour. This is so because it is nothing less than an *omniscience* or *omnipotence* or *omnicaring* or *omnipresence* of the type possessed by progress that is perhaps needed to successfully handle the many different complexities humanity is currently embroiled in. It is also the need of the hour

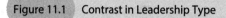

Figure 11.1 Contrast in Leadership Type

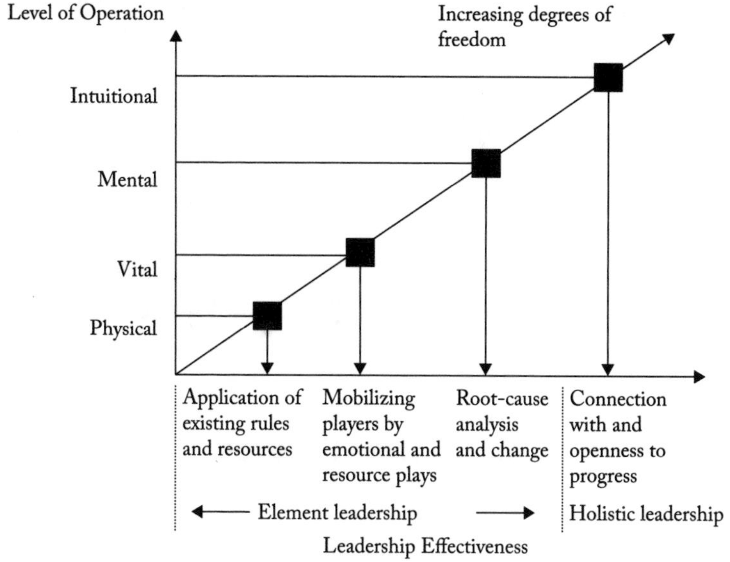

that true personalities with power to counter established tendencies and habits arise. If a personality is composed of the same dynamics and habits already present in established physical, vital, and mental building blocks, then by definition this is likely only going to reinforce yesteryears rule. It is only by new and unestablished dynamics manifesting and restructuring the existing building blocks that past habits have a chance of being countered. Such personalities can only incarnate by being in more conscious relation with progress. This is the only sure way for a habitual difference that becomes permanent to be created. Anchoring of newer possibility to anything that is the result of the past, even a mental idea, is potentially too replete with contradictions, subtle or overt, to be the basis of a new creation.

This highest possibility of leadership can only take place when the instrument or leader has disengaged from the physical, vital, and mental trappings so that it is not their dynamics that move it, but the deeper intent resonant with progress that in fact guides the physical, vital, and mental instrumentation toward the needed outcome.

The highest possibility of leadership can only take place when a new personality summarizing new possibility emerges in the play of life. When this occurs, the leader has truly become a dynamic being because the inner has been integrated with the outer thereby also creating the conditions for maximum affectivity.

To connect inner power to global change means that it is not physical power, not vital power, and not even mental power that must be the fount of our existence, though each of these will and even must be used in our expression of leadership, but the deeper essence of our realities, that essence that finds its meaning and motive in progress itself, inner power, that must become the fount of our being. It is progress that must incarnate in us. Only so will we become centers of creative power.

Recognizing Alternative Futures

The existence of progress is a sure indication of the overall direction of development for humanity. The architecture of progress, as indicated by its three aspects—physical, vital, and mental—further indicates the trajectory of this development, since in one way of looking at the architecture the physical is about established reality, the vital is about reality in process of being created, the mental is about possible reality. In its present *physical* incarnation, the fractal ladder is animated by relatively unrefined physical, vital, and mental building blocks. As the intuitional element surfaces, and as humans follow their inspiration, deeper drivers, or dharmas—service and perfection, adventure and courage, knowledge and wisdom, and harmony and mutuality will more surely come to the surface. The very structure and possibility of the fundamental building blocks will alter and the physical will morph more into a physical–service–perfection conglomerate, the vital into a vital–adventure–courage conglomerate, the mental into a mental–knowledge–wisdom conglomerate, and the intuitional will be more firmly established as an intuitional–harmony–mutuality conglomerate.

This will alter the base fractal of which the fractal ladder is a creation, and hence each of its rungs will themselves become projections of the radically refined building blocks. Much of experienced creation, from the individual to corporations to countries to society to the environment to planet Earth, will begin to function in a more enlightened and obviously sustainably progressive way far more aligned with the deeper drivers of progress. This can be thought of as the vital incarnation of the fractal ladder. But that is only a step along the way.

Even further in the future, one can foresee the deeper *mental* aspect of progress – of which omnipresence, omnipotence, omniscience, and omnicaring are qualities – further altering the manifested character of the fundamental building blocks so that the physical further morphs into a physical–service–perfection–omnipresence conglomerate, the vital morphs into a vital–adventure–courage–omnipotence conglomerate, the mental further morphs into a mental–knowledge–wisdom–omniscience conglomerate, and the intuitional further morphs into an intuitional–harmony–mutuality–omnicaring conglomerate. This can be thought of as the mental incarnation of the fractal ladder. The fractal ladder further alters and all possibility and apotheosis is then perhaps more obviously present at each and every moment of space and time. This is no doubt an astounding future.

The timing of these futures, of the manifestations of the discussed incarnations of the fractal ladder is, however, the issue in question. Depending on choices we make now and in the foreseeable future, the promising incarnations of the fractal ladder will occur sooner or later. The interim passage is variable and expresses alternative paths, which because of the possibility of taking decades or even perhaps centuries will for all practical purposes need to be thought of in terms of alternative futures. The existence of progress and its signature across creation, in the form of the fractal ladder, indicates that the promising incarnations are inevitable. Whether we arrive there through a path of major upheaval and destruction or through one of relative ease and joy, a sunlit path, depends on the degree to which we are able to complete the myriad Sun-marked physical–vital–mental fractal journeys that each of us is continually on. The root, of course, of all the myriad journeys we all have the privilege of being on, which fractal mirroring, fractal influence, fractal evolution, fractal completion, and fractal matrixing, among the other fractal properties points to, is the state of consciousness—physical, vital, mental, or intuitional—that we tend to operate from. The alternative futures that we will experience over the next few decades and even perhaps centuries is an outcome of the general state of consciousness that as a race we choose to be in.

Basis of the Intuitional Scenario

At its crux, the fractal ladder indicates a reality of deep connection and integration. All is connected to all and all is integrated around a reality of progress. Progress itself is the secret of the one system, and the fractal ladder represents the character of that progress. The fractal ladder is the key to the system. Stepping on to it unveils a world of sustainable and unendable progress. It indicates a conscious, meaningful reality in which there are no accidents but all is the result of particular base patterns representative of the Sun-marked physical–vital–mental pattern in the consciousness of its primary actors. These base patterns themselves get their reality from the possibility inherent in progress and through force of creativity manifest as different actors represented by different types of organization on each rung of the ladder. It is possible too and at present far more likely that the physical, vital, and mental building blocks arrange themselves in other ways unaligned with the Sun-marked pattern, in which case the organizations of which they are the constituents falls outside of the fractal ladder, in the region of the system characterized by a general fractal vortex. These organizations can also step onto the fractal ladder if they are able to complete the fractal journey that characterizes their current reality. Completion of the fractal journey implies that uniqueness and true personality are beginning to manifest. For it is only so that the generally accepted realities of yesteryear, that run counter to progress, can be overcome and the price for entry onto the fractal ladder, as it were, paid as a result of that. Truer personality is aligned with the deeper drivers of progress and begins through its action to even more rapidly change the very nature of the building blocks and the fractal ladder.

Realization of the reality of this system means that the actor, whether individual, corporation, collectivity, or country, is operating at the intuitional level. For already comprehensiveness of vision and inspiration is animating the general outlook of the actor, and possibility, meaning, action is driven by a reality very different from that driven by the other building blocks of possibility. This outlook will likely result in a shorter, more joyful, and easier path toward the future and inevitable incarnations of the fractal ladder. On this path, each type of actor more quickly embraces the uniqueness they are capable of. Hence, people more quickly attune to their raison d'être, and casting aside the false promises of making the quick buck by becoming a part of the global business engine, follow the possibilities of service, adventure, knowledge, or harmony, as their dharma or character dictates. A new array of fractals arises, and all manners of changes at each more complex level of organization—corporation, community, collectivity, country, society—come into being.

The Imperative Recontextualization

As a global society, we operate more in the physical–vital realm than the mental–intuitional realm. The limits of the physical–vital orientation have today become abundantly clear, and it is an imperative that at all levels comprising the global society we must make the shift toward a mental–intuitional orientation. To not do so is to consign ourselves to decades of needless upheaval and inevitable debilitation from the level of the individual to our very planetary system. Our very view of ourselves, our corporations, and all manners of other organizations, our concept of money and markets, our view of other resources, our view and understanding of countries and international relations, and our view of the planet and our very Earth–Sun system itself have to be recontextualized in the light of the progress-centered fractal system that has emerged as the possible reality of our world system. In other words, our very world view has to be turned on its head. There is no choice in this matter since of necessity the very *world view fractal* has itself to shift from the physical–vital orientation, where it has centered itself for perhaps centuries, to a mental–intuitional orientation in order to complete its own Sun-marked physical–vital–mental–intuitional journey and begin to arrive at fruition. In this progressing journey, the equilibrium between objectivity and subjectivity will be reversed as internal and more subjective dynamics begin to account for more than the external and more objective dynamics. This is nothing less than a sea change. Its time, however, has come.

Recontextualization, hence is the need of the hour. There are instances of organization and pervasive dynamics where it is more immediately critical that such recontextualization takes place. This is because these instances of organization and dynamics hold a central place in the affairs of our lives. These include the individual and her development at one end, country at the other, and commerce as the general air in between that fills our waking and perhaps even our sleeping moments.

Our reality does not end with what the eye can see. This is where it begins. There is the whole informing edifice of which what the eye can see is only the final outcome. To focus only on the physical, on that which can be seen, is to focus on the surface of the edifice only, and by definition misses the causal dynamics that marks the real meaning and intent behind the physical. To focus on the physical only is to focus on established reality and to miss the reality of all the possibility that is seeking to manifest from within the heart of the edifice. And being that the heart of the edifice, the heart of progress, is the real center around which the entire edifice and all physical manifestations revolve, to focus only on the physical, as though it were an independent reality with no connection to anything deeper, is to miss the context of life.

To imagine therefore that each of us are entities existing in a physical world to fulfill a part as determined by our common and most likely programed physical–vital orientations is to consign ourselves to littleness and lack of possibility. We each then become a cog in a wheel, and depending on the randomness or luck or even effort of construction of our physical resources or vital capabilities, we will play either a more or less central role in driving or moving a wheel that is headed ultimately toward its own destruction. If there is power in this, it is not power to bring about global change, but power only to accelerate debilitation of a poorly perceived and believed world system.

Meaningful change can come about only when the reality of one's relation with the heart of the system is rightly perceived, and by identity, the dynamics of the heart of the system begin to determine the dynamics in oneself. For this to happen though one's psychology has to go through a sea change, and the existence of a progress-centered, fractal ladder marked, universal fractal system, of which each of us are potentially significant or insignificant fractal actors depending on if we choose to step or not to step onto the fractal ladder, respectively, must become a reality. In other words, a basic recontextualizing, so that rather than experiencing ourselves as independent and isolated entities existing in the world to fulfill or aggrandize a narrow physical–vital view of ourselves by catering to dominant physical–vital dynamics abroad in each institution of life, we must begin to experience ourselves as part of the just described larger fractal system.

Such a recontextualizing implies that we become heroes because every manner of limitation as evidenced by the pervasive and incomplete physical–vital outlook will then need to be faced, overcome, and successfully replaced by the mental–intuitional outlook that by definition begins to open us to the heart of progress. The recontextualizing in fact begins to become more real, with each stagnating or opposing fractal that we successfully overcome. In this view, we are not just cogs in a wheel but creative centers of a continually and sustainably progressing world system for which we are each ultimately co-responsible. There can be no more power than this.

In the face of boundary situations and currently as already described, we appear to be at a very significant boundary condition vis-à-vis the shift from the vital to the beginnings of the mental phase in the global economy and global society fractals, it is all the more necessary for this to be led by leadership at the individual level. The price we will pay for individuals not making the shift in their own personal fractals from a vital to a mental way of being will increase in exorbitance with every passing day.

Further, this surfacing of individual leadership must be at the core of the development of the next level of organization – be it the evolution of the business corporation or any other manner of nonprofit organization. Change by arbitrary or even logically thought out strategy or policy will never be as sustainable as change that is the result of a shift in consciousness and the consequent and organic surfacing and development of a unique personality, thereby also organically reshaping or remaking the rules of life in their own areas of influence. A person, for instance, who is able to enter into the place of creative stillness in the eye of the fractal storm, to thereby begin to approach or even to enter into the heart of progress and from there remake themselves, based on, say, some unique combination of courage, knowledge, and sense of service, will of necessity become a compelling center for the creation of a new organizational reality.

This is what must lie at the heart of the recontextualized business or other type of organization. The usual equilibrium whereby an organization functions as a cog in the business-as-usual world must be toppled to yield to an equilibrium where organization is an expression of a deeper truth that finds its roots in the very heart of progress itself. Such an organization, if it is a business organization, will not solely exist to increase profit or market share or revenues, but to express such a deeper possibility and even to be an instrument among instruments tied together by the hidden orchestration of progress, for the further development of the world system. For is not progress that astounding reality that has brought about shift after shift in every manner and type of fractal journey across every level of organization from the individual to the planet itself, in the face even of audacious odds?

Conclusion

Creating the enterprise of tomorrow demands a shift in leadership, the ability to recognize the path one is on, and an imperative recontextualizion to shift this path. The shift must be one that is intuitional and in alignment with the progress-centered, fractal-ladder-marked universal fractal system, of which each of us and each of the organizations and enterprises we are a part of can at the end of the day be incredibly significant fractal actors, if we so choose to be.

PART II

Exercises

Exercises

1 The Pattern

Chapter Statement

The following questions are designed to assist you in enhancing your understanding of the chapter material. In this chapter, we introduced:

- New language to introduce a fractal-based world system
- The notion of a universal pattern across the world system
- The notion of physical, vital, and mental
- The specific fractal pattern of progress

Application Questions

1. Reflect on the quotation attributed to Gandhi "Become the change you wish to see in the world." What does this mean to you?

____

____

____

____

____

____

____

2. What self-repeating patterns do you observe around you?

3a. How has the author defined the terms physical, vital, and mental. What do these words now mean to you?

Physical:

Vital:

Mental:

3b. Do you see instances of these in aspects of your life, or in the world around you?

____

____

____

____

____

____

____

4. For each of the three lists, tick mark the descriptors that apply to you. Count the total number of tick marked descriptors and write the total number at the bottom of each list. The column with the highest score indicates your current tendency to operate with this fractal pattern.

Physical	Vital	Mental
__Stable	__Energetic	__Idealistic
__Structured	__Adaptable	__Questioning
__Status-quo-based	__Competitive	__Reasoning
__Sense-based	__Networks	__Thought-based
__Solid	__Spontaneous	__Innovative
__Well-defined	__Emotion-based	__Purposeful
__Likes boundaries	__Dynamic	__Analytical
__Proven	__Experimentation	__Introspection
__Conservative	__Action-oriented	__Reflection
__Stabilizer	__Risk-taker	__Progressive understanding
__Organized	__Likes variety	__Futurist

5a. Consider different situations or outcomes around you. Make a list of outcomes where only the physical was active. Make a list where both the physical and vital were active and where the vital leads. Make a third list where all three states are active but the mental leads.

Physical leads	Vital leads	Mental leads
______________	______________	______________
______________	______________	______________
______________	______________	______________
______________	______________	______________

5b. Now compare the nature of the outcomes on each list. How do they differ? Was there something more complete about one kind of outcome versus another?

____

____

____

____

____

____

____

Impact Questions

6. What would be the benefits of being able to see fractal patterns on a daily basis? In your personal life? Work life? Spiritual life?

____

____

____

____

____

____

____

7. What are the potential lost opportunities of not seeing these fractal patterns: physical, vital, and mental?

Advanced Question

8. Reflect on the base pattern versus other patterns. How do these patterns differ?

Rhetorical Question

9. Are you ready to explore and unlock your inner powers?

Exercises

2 The Person Pattern

Chapter Statement

In this chapter, we introduced:

- The make-up of a person in physical, vital, and mental terms
- Tendencies/habits as comprised of physical, vital, and mental elements
- The notion of alteration of habits
- The emergence of identity

Application Questions

1a. Describe yourself in words: ______________________________

____

____

____

____

____

____

____

1b. Now place these words in the respective physical, vital, or mental column:

Physical	Vital	Mental
______________	______________	______________
______________	______________	______________
______________	______________	______________
______________	______________	______________
______________	______________	______________

2a. Looking at the examples on pages 20–21, make a list of the tendencies/habits (PVM fractal patterns) within yourself that you are aware of: as a child, as an adolescent, and as an adult.

Child	Adolescent	Adult
______________	______________	______________
______________	______________	______________
______________	______________	______________
______________	______________	______________
______________	______________	______________

2b. Now order these by strength so that it is the loudest or most apparent tendency at the top. Also label these habits by physical, vital, and mental depending on which element leads or is the central nexus around which the habit is organized.

Child	Adolescent	Adult
______________	______________	______________
______________	______________	______________
______________	______________	______________
______________	______________	______________
______________	______________	______________

2c. Are any of these patterns consistent?

2d. Which of these patterns are healthy and move you forward? Which of these patterns are unhealthy and may possibly be getting in your way of progress?

Impact Questions

3. What Sun fractal pattern changes (180 degree change or quantum change) would you like to see in your life?

4. How by looking and working within yourself might you truly alter life in the world? Envision how you would like to see yourself in the future. What are the new tendencies that surfaced? Are they physically, vitally, or mentally led? Are you progressing along the continuum from where you are today?

5. Thinking of the concept, "tomorrow's realities are today's ideas," create a mental picture of what you want your future to look like. Visualize this future state daily for the next 21 days.

Advanced Questions

6. "When such tendencies admit of the paradigm of progress, a totally different dynamic is set up in a person. It is the nature of organization that is of importance." What is the pattern order (pages 21–25) you would like to see in your life?

7. Why do you exhibit a unique combination of tendencies? How do these unique combinations help you or hinder you?

8. What does the phrase *Earth becomes an Earth–Sun* mean to you (pages 26–28)?

Rhetorical Question

9. What insights into yourself did you gain through an understanding of fractal patterns into your uniqueness?

Exercises

The Business Pattern 3

Chapter Statement

In this chapter, we introduced:

- The make-up of a business in physical, vital, and mental terms
- The concept of mental, leading in the successful running of an organization
- The link between the thoughts and feelings of a leader and the state of an organization

Application Questions

1a. Brainstorm a list of words that describe your current organization. Analyze the words. Are they physical, vital, or mental?

____

____

____

____

____

____

____

1b. In thinking of the rule of thumb for the physical—"that which the eye can see"—what other words come to mind to describe your organization from the physical perspective?

1c. In thinking of the rule of thumb for the vital—"the play of energies"—what other words come to mind to describe your organization from the vital perspective?

1d. In thinking of the rule of thumb for the mental—"reality as shaped by thought"—what other words come to mind to describe your organization from the mental perspective?

2. Remember that a fractal is a pattern that repeats itself on different scales. Taking one of your answers to describe the physical, vital, and mental from the question above, reapply the physical, vital, and mental to that building block or descriptor to help further elaborate the fractal-pattern concept.

   Physical: "that which the eye can see"

   Vital: "the play of energies"

   Mental: "reality as shaped by thought"

3. For each function given in the left-hand column, choose the correct option from the right-hand column and write its corresponding number in the space provided. You can also make primary, secondary, and tertiary choices for each function.

Marketing	____________	Physical – 1
Finance	____________	Vital – 2
Sales	____________	Mental – 3
Engineering	____________	
R&D	____________	
Quality	____________	
HR	____________	
Other	____________	

Impact Questions

4. What would you like your organization to be down the line in four years? What is the business model, the culture, the leadership approach, and your position? Use descriptive words leveraging of the physical, vital, and mental orientations to describe these.

   Business model

   ____

   ____

   ____

   ____

   ____

   ____

   ____

Culture

Leadership approach

Your position

5. Think about your current position as a leader, a change agent, or an educator. What do you need to do to lead from the mental, energize from the vital, and stabilize with the physical?

Lead from the mental

Energize with the vital

Stabilize with the physical

Advanced Questions

6. From a logical consideration, why is it important to integrate the physical, vital, and mental orientations in the running of an organization? Think of this from the perspective of limitations and possibilities.

7. Why does a shift at a corporate level from the physical to vital or the vital to mental require a corresponding shift at the personal level? Elaborate on this with the help of an example in your organization. What did you do to manage the change?

8. Why is it desirable for a business to incarnate some properties of the sun—timeless, solid, vast, and self-lit?

Rhetorical Question

9. What are you doing to move yourself and your company forward?

Exercises

The Economy Pattern 4

Chapter Statement

In this chapter, we introduced:

- Physical, vital, and mental manifestations in the economy
- Progress in the economy as determined by the physical–vital–mental fractal
- Degrees of freedom and the necessity of moving from the physical to the vital to the mental
- The multiplier effect and the difficulty of larger change

Application Questions

1. In your own words, describe the existence of the physical–vital–mental fractal at the level of the global economy.

____

____

____

____

____

____

2a. Brainstorm a list of words that describe your current industry sector. Analyze the words: are they physical, vital, or mental? Put them in the appropriate column.

Physical	Vital	Mental
______________	______________	______________
______________	______________	______________
______________	______________	______________
______________	______________	______________

2b. In thinking of the rule of thumb for the physical—"that which the eye can see"—what other words to describe your industry sector come to mind?

____

____

____

____

____

____

____

2c. In thinking of the rule of thumb for the vital—"the play of energies"—what other words to describe your industry sector come to mind?

____

____

____

____

____

____

____

2d. In thinking of the rule of thumb for the mental—"reality as shaped by thought"—what other words to describe your industry sector come to mind?

3. Remember that a fractal is a pattern that repeats itself on different scales. Taking one of your answers to describe the physical, vital, and mental from the question above, reapply the physical, vital, and mental to that building block or descriptor to help further elaborate the fractal-pattern concept.

Physical: "that which the eye can see"

Vital: "the play of energies"

Mental: "reality as shaped by thought"

____

____

____

____

____

____

____

4. In the space next to each industry in the left-hand column, write the corresponding number (from the right-hand column) of the physical, vital, and mental orientation that most applies to the way that industry functions. You can make primary, secondary, tertiary choices for each indsutry below if you like.

Oil & Gas	____________________	Physical – 1
Healthcare	____________________	Vital – 2
Airlines	____________________	Mental – 3
IT	____________________	
Retail	____________________	
Food & Beverages	____________________	
Pharmaceuticals	____________________	

5a. The following are different percentage blends of physical, vital, and mental that run a hypothetical economy. How would Economy-1 differ from Economy-2 and Economy-3?

Economy-1: Physical – 80%, Vital – 15%, Mental – 5%
Economy-2: Physical – 10%, Vital – 60%, Mental – 30%
Economy-3: Physical – 20%, Vital – 35%, Mental – 45%

____

____

5b. Of the three economies in 5a, which one would likely be the best run? Why?

Impact Questions

6. How does the notion of *Degrees of Freedom* provide you with the insight into your own action? Action of the organization you work in? Action of the industry sector you are in? Action of the global economy?

   Own action

Industry sector

Global economy

Advanced Question

7. What does the phrase "the organization we create and the society we have created are indices of our own personality" mean to you (pages 54–56)?

Rhetorical Question

8. Trace how the physical–vital–mental sequence embedded in the DNA of life manifests in the economy.

Exercises

The System Pattern 5

Chapter Statement

In this chapter, we introduced:

- Physical, vital, and mental manifestations in system instances
- Progress in system instances as determined by the physical–vital–mental fractal
- Degrees of freedom and the necessity of moving from the physical to the vital to the mental
- General applicability of fractal for progress model

Application Questions

1a. What are the fractal patterns in your industry?

____

____

____

____

____

____

____

1b. How are these fractal patterns similar to/different from other industry fractal patterns that you are aware of?

2a. What political systems appear to be physical or vital or mental? Why? Consider socialism, communism, and democracy, among others.

2b. Where do you see the system-wide global politics fractal today in relationship to the physical, the vital, and the mental? Have we progressed, digressed, or stayed constant?

2c. If a political system were made up with the following constitution (physical – 70%, vital – 20%, and mental – 10%), how would it likely deal with industry failure? For example, if the banking industry failed, what would government likely do?

____

____

____

____

____

____

____

2d. If a political system were made up with the following constitution (physical – 20%, vital – 40%, mental – 20%), how would it likely deal with industry failure? For example, if the banking industry failed, what would government likely do?

____

____

____

____

____

____

____

3. What are the appropriate blends of the physical, the vital, and the mental in each of these institutions:

a. Science Physical: ______ Vital: ______ Mental: ______

Why?

____

____

____

____

b. Education Physical: ______ Vital: ______ Mental: ______

Why?

c. Industry Physical: ______ Vital: ______ Mental: ______

Why?

d. Government Physical: _____ Vital: _____ Mental: _____

Why?

e. Art & Music Physical: _____ Vital: _____ Mental: _____

Why?

f. Other Physical: ______ Vital: ______ Mental: ______

Why?

Impact Questions

4a. As you consider your interaction with or use of the Internet, does it tend to be physical, vital, or mental?

4b. How about for your children, or the younger generation's use of the Internet?

4c. How about for your partner or spouse?

4d. How would your relationship with these different groups differ based on this? How might it be harmonized?

Advanced Questions

5. Thinking about yourself as a life-long learner in the context of fractals, is it possible to live in one or two of the physical, vital, and mental states?

6. Would any of the system changes described in the chapter have occurred absent of leadership?

Rhetorical Question

7. How does understanding the fractal pattern for progress help to understand the world?

Exercises

The Evolution Pattern

6

Chapter Statement

In this chapter, we introduced:

- Physical, vital, and mental phases and subphases in evolution
- The application of the fractal for progress in a trans-human setting
- Soft voices as often indicative of the future

Application Questions

1. How does the evolutionary process through the physical/vital/mental as described in this chapter compare to your beliefs on evolution?

   Your belief:

   ____
   ____
   ____
   ____
   ____
   ____
   ____

What supports it?

What dispels it?

2. This chapter shows how the physical–vital–mental sequence is embedded in nature. How does such a realization change your view of life? Your view of self?

View of life:

View of self:

Impact Questions

3. Give examples of leveraging recursion (that is, applying the fractal to the fractal) when employing fractal analyses. How has this manifested in your own life? In life around you? How does leveraging recursion help to see things differently? What have you done differently as a result of this?

   Your own life:

   In life around you:

Seeing things differently:

Doing things differently:

4. The author states "the human species has yet to become the true metal being. Perhaps in 1000 years" (pages 81–84). What do you believe is the work that needs to be done by man to transition to the truly mental orientation? How can it be done in 100 years? 25 years? 10 years?

100 years?

25 years?

10 years?

5a. Reflect on a soft voice within yourself. Has this been able to guide your decisions and actions? Why or why not?

5b. What are some instances of soft voices in your home and work environment?

5c. In your industry?

5d. Contrast these with the louder, prevalent voices.

5e. Which voice is more appealing to you? Why?

5f. Do you see the softer voices as indications of the future?

5g. Over the next 3 days, write down what your soft voice tells you:

5h. Analyze your messages in terms of physical, vital, and mental.

Advanced Questions

6. "At the end of the day this fractal model is about connecting your inner power with global change." How would you ultimately like to be heard?

7. How might the existence of a fractal ladder affect our interpretation of life?

Rhetorical Question

8. With religion in mind, how nature or some divine entity might have used fractals when creating heaven and Earth?

Exercises

7 The Fractal Ladder

Chapter Statement

In this chapter, we introduced:

- The notion of the fractal ladder as a conduit to connect inner power with global change
- The notion of progress as the system within which we exist
- Characteristics of progress

Application Questions

1a. There is only one pattern that can create a fractal ladder. What is it?

(a) Physical–vital–mental, mental leading
(b) Vital–physical, physical leading
(c) Physical–mental–vital, vital leading
(d) Mental–physical–mental, mental leading

1b. Why?

____

____

____

2. In climbing your fractal ladder, what are the physical–vital–mental Sun-marked patterns that need to be traversed (Figure 7.1)? What is a change you would like to make?

Impact Questions

3a. Often what we do is "dictated by a biased or stagnated physical or vital or mental outlook in a world that demands a progressive physical or vital or mental outlook." What in this statement is true for you?

3b. What opportunity does this present to you?

4a. How many "new fractals" have you brought into existence? Describe them?

4b. What impact have they had on the environment?

4c. If you have not brought any new fractals into existence, why not?

Advanced Questions

5a. We live in *progress*; *progress* lives in us. What does this statement mean to you on a personal level?

5b. What is your relationship with *progress*? Describe this.

5c. How has this relationship helped you?

6a. What are the physical, vital, and mental garbs that you wear?

6b. Once you have stripped away these garbs, you may come face-to-face with the secret of your power. To what extent have you experienced this power?

6c. How have challenges changed when you experienced this power?

7a. What stories/*noise(…)* do you live in?

7b. Describe these stories in physical, vital, and mental terms.

7c. How would you change them through your understanding of fractals?

____

____

____

____

____

____

____

Rhetorical Question

8. Do we live in an essentially random or an essentially ordered world?

Exercises

8 Fractal Properties

Chapter Statement

In this chapter, we were introduced:

- The structural (physical) properties of a fractal-ladder-based system
- The processes (vital) we can employ as actors in a fractal-ladder-based system
- The meaning (mental) we can ascribe to actions in a fractal-ladder-based system
- Properties that have to do with developing a direct relationship with the fractal ladder system

Application Questions

1. Match up the given definitions with the right fractal ladder physical–level properties

Universality	Where any entity on a higher level of the fractal ladder will reinforce its way of being at a lower level through fractal pressure
Influence	Refers to the necessity of the journeying to proceed through the independent stages of the physical, the vital, and the mental in turn and in that order

Recursion	For progress to happen, the physical–vital–mental journey must be completed
Completion	Being able to apply the fractal for progress to any subphase of a progressive journey
Evolution	Knowledge of progress in one field can be transferred to another field
Matrixing	Shift in fractal at one level of the ladder tends to create a corresponding shift at the next level of the ladder
Stepwise development	Refers to conditions of essential connection that exists by virtue of physical–vital–mental journeys successfully completing themselves
Feedback	Engaging in successful physical–vital–mental journeys alters the conditions within which a journey exists

2. Match up the given definitions with the right fractal ladder vital-level properties

Intersection	A property by which a range of energies are made to enter into a situation
Facilitation	A property that holds when two fractals are made to intersect with each other to thereby cause progress along their respective journeys
Flow	Refers to shifting the context or orientation from a *lower* or previous stage in the sequence to a higher or next stage in the same sequence
Upscaling	Applying the physical–vital–mental fractal to a stagnated situation

3. Match up the right definitions with the right fractal ladder mental-level properties

World-wiseliness	Refers to the fact that regardless of where one looks, what one sees is a reflection of one's inner state
Mirroring	Refers to the fact that any successful outcome in a fractal-ladder-based world must be so because it has completed the physical–vital–mental journey

Affirmation	For best outcomes, this must be true—that is, the physical, vital, mental must be integrated around the sense of the journey of progress
Integration	It uses the journey to emerge from its trials and tribulations
Uniqueness	Refers to the fact that the more physical–vital–mental journeys one masters, the more world-wisely one becomes

Impact Questions

4. Answer any three of the following, from a through g, that all refer to fractal ladder properties at the physical-level:

   a. *Universality* refers to the transference of knowledge of progress in one field to another unrelated field. Consider an area in which you have made significant progress. Chart out the physical, vital, and mental stages of this. How can the stages, the learning, the transitions between the stages be applied to a completely different area? Where else have you seen this property of *universality* at play?

   ____

   ____

   ____

   ____

   ____

   ____

   ____

   ____

   b. *Fractal influence* refers to a shift in the fractal at one level of the fractal ladder tending to create a corresponding shift at the next level of the fractal ladder. Where have you seen fractal influence at play?

c. *Fractal recursion* is being able to apply the fractal for progress to any subphase of a progressive journey. Give examples of how fractal recursion is used in both understanding the structure of entities and the process of development of entities.

d. *Fractal completion* refers to the fact that for progress to happen, the physical–vital–mental journey must be completed. Thinking about this property, how would a person on the fractal ladder deal with anger? How would a person not on the fractal ladder deal with anger?

e. *Fractal evolution* is when engaging in successful physical–vital–mental journeys alters the conditions within which a journey exists. Recall instances of fractal evolution in your personal, family, or work life.

f. *Matrixing* can be thought of as a device to perpetuate progress by leveraging off established insight into progress. Where have you seen this?

g. *Stepwise development* refers to the necessity of the journeying of progress to proceed through the independent stages of the physical, the vital, and the mental in turn and in that order.

Think of a change in your personal life. Did you intuitively use stepwise development? How did that effect the outcomes? How would the outcomes have been affected had you not used it?

5. Answer any two of the following, from a through d, that all refer to fractal ladder properties at the vital-level:
   a. *Fractal intersection* is a property that holds when two fractals are made to intersect with each other to thereby cause progress along their respective journeys. Consider a difficult situation you are in. Can you reframe this as being the intersection of two stagnated fractals? Seeing the situation this way, how might it change?

   b. *Facilitation* refers to applying the physical–vital–mental fractal to a stagnated situation. Consider a stagnated situation you are in. How can applying the physical–vital–mental fractal to that situation change it?

c. *Flow* refers to the phenomenon by which a range of energies are made to enter into a situation. Consider a time where you have applied concentration to alter a situation. What is the process that happened? Can you interpret this process in terms of the physical–vital–mental journey?

d. *Upscaling* refers to shifting the context or orientation of a situation from a *lower* or previous stage in the sequence to a higher or next stage in the same sequence. Consider a situation that seems difficult to work through. Using upscaling, how can additional degrees of freedom be bought into that situation?

6. Answer any two of the following, from a through e, that all refer to fractal ladder properties at the mental level:

   a. *World-wiseliness* refers to the fact that the more physical–vital–mental journeys one masters, the more world-wisely one becomes. Consider someone who you look up to as being wise. What are major challenges they faced? What accomplishments have they made? Would you say this person has completed a lot of physical–vital–mental journeys? Elaborate.

   b. *Mirroring* refers to the fact that regardless of where one looks, what one sees is a reflection of one's inner state. Reflect on the property of mirroring. Have you personally experienced it? How do you see this playing out in your world?

   c. *Affirmation* refers to the fact that any successful outcome in a fractal-ladder-based world must be so because it has completed the physical–vital–mental journey. Think of your personal successes and failures/shortcomings. To what extent are these related to having completed/not completed physical–vital–mental journeys?

d. *Integration* must be true for best outcomes to occur—that is, the physical, vital, and mental must be integrated around the sense of the journey of progress. What can you do to increase your reality of integration? How might this alter the circumstances you are in?

e. *Uniqueness* uses the journey to emerge from the trials and tribulations of it. Are you unique? Reflect on this. How can you become more unique?

7. Where can you use the fractal properties of *alignment, aspiration, surrender, rejection, and love* to develop or improve your life?

Advanced Questions

8. How does an understanding of fractal properties help us better understand some of the symmetries and asymmetries in our world?

9. Can one experience a progressive state multiple times in one's life or does it tend to be one epic event?

Rhetorical Question

10. Why are fractal properties important in bringing about system-level change?

Exercises

The Nature of Progress

9

Chapter Statement

In this chapter, we were introduced:

- Deeper look at the system behind the system
- The top-down qualities of progress
- The bottom-up qualities of progress
- The relationship between the top-down and bottom-up qualities of progress
- The notion of deeper drivers and secret names that belong to the system behind the system
- A look at what are the deeper drivers that may be responsible for development

Application Questions

1. We posited the notion that progress is a living entity that is all-present, all-knowing, all-caring, and all-powerful, at least within the context of the Earth–Sun dance. Why is it important to understand the nature of progress?

____

____

____

2. Name and discuss each of the top–down qualities of progress. What do they mean to you? Have you had any personal experience of any of these?

   Quality 1: ______

   Quality 2: ______

   Quality 3: ______

Quality 4: ____________________

3. Why is it important to consider the bottom-up qualities of progress? How do the bottom-up and top-down qualities relate?

Impact Questions

4a. "The physical state is characterized by all that the eye can see. It is the essential matrix of creation, the substance into which everything else manifests. It is also the index of all that has successfully manifested and that has become an essential part of life. It also reveals the incredible detail and level of perfection that has gone into the manifestation itself." What is the most beautiful object you know or have seen? What is its essence?

4b. How has it evolved?

4c. What is its shadow state?

5a. "The vital state is characterized by an essential state of energy, experiment, and adventure. It is an index of the rush of possibilities colliding with each other and reforming themselves into new possibility. It is not light of energy, but power of energy that determines outcome." Think of a change you personally made that you are extremely proud of. What was the essence of the change?

5b. What were the building blocks?

5c. What was the shadow state?

6a. "The mental state is characterized by the play of the idea as the principle means of organization. While at its far rim, mentality is an index of future possibility, in its central orb, it appears to be more of an index of organizing around reason and rationalization." In your organization, what innovation could fundamentally change the way you do business for the betterment of mankind? What would be the essence of that change?

6b. What would be the building blocks?

6c. What would be the shadow state?

Advanced Questions

7a. Which of the following pairs drives you the most. Indicate with a relative percentage breakdown:

Service–Perfection: ______________________

Knowledge–Wisdom: ______________________

Adventure–Courage: ______________________

Harmony–Mutuality: ______________________

7b. Look at the percentages you have entered. What does this tell you about yourself? Is this consistent with your sense of whether you are driven by a physical, vital, or mental orientation? Please comment.

____

____

____

____

____

____

____

8a. As you consider the layers behind the operation of the physical, the vital, and the mental, what thoughts do you have? What feelings does this incite?

____

____

____

____

____

____

____

8b. How does this help to reframe situations you may currently be in?

9. What does AUM mean to you?

Rhetorical Question

10. Knowing what you have in this book, are you on the right path?

Exercises

10 Remaking the Business World

Chapter Statement

In this chapter, we were introduced:

- Key fractals that comprise the business world: consumerism fractal, business fractal, economy fractal, society fractal
- Climate change as a wake-up call
- Necessity of addressing climate change and other global problems through shifting the root pattern
- Notion of uniqueness and redesign of the business world by mobilizing four powers

Application Questions

1a. What kind of consumer are you (physical, vital, or mental) for consumer goods and major purchases? Elaborate.

Consumer goods:

____

____

____

____

____

Major purchases:

1b. If you are the physical or vital level, what will it take for you to shift to the mental level?

2a. What is the consumerism wake-up call? Why does it have to be this?

2b. What is it going to take for today's business model to shift from making money to serving the greater good?

3. "Industries that we have created through our vital lust, become the means to kill our very vitality." Comment on this.

4a. Is your organization engaged in CSR? What is the program?

4b. Has there been a shift to the mental level as a result of this program? Please discuss.

4c. What are you personally doing to drive CSR?

Application Questions

5a. The author states, "for in its essence climate change is nothing other than a rebellion of matter." What are the rebellions you are wrestling with today?

5b. Are they physical, vital, or mental? Are the levels out of balance?

6a. Referring to Figure 10.3, sketch out your own uniqueness diagram using the four motive forces of knowledge/wisdom, service/perfection, harmony, and power/adventure?

6b. Sketch out the uniqueness diagram of someone close to you.

6c. How do these diagrams compare? Does the comparison shed insight into the relationship?

____

____

____

7a. Sketch out your organization's uniqueness diagram.

7b. How does your uniqueness diagram compare with that of your organization's? Are you a fit for your organization?

____

____

____

____

____

____

____

8a. Sketch out your country's uniqueness diagram.

8b. Sketch out the uniqueness diagram for a neighboring country.

8c. How do these compare? Does it help to explain the nature of the relationship between the two countries?

Advanced Question

9. "The standardization at the people level to force thoughts and acts to be of a certain kind only is the great tragedy of current corporate life." Comment on this statement. Are people in your organization allowed to live their uniqueness? What are the results of that?

Rhetorical Question

Q. Is it possible to remake the business world? How would you go about doing this?

Exercises

Creating Enterprises of Tomorrow 11

Chapter Statement

In this chapter, we were introduced:

- The notion of elemental and holistic leadership
- The necessity that leadership assists in completing stagnated fractals by shifting the physical–vital to the mental–intuitional

Application Questions

1a. What is leadership's responsibility in shifting their people, culture, and organizations from the physical–vital to the mental–intuitional?

____

____

____

____

____

____

____

1b. As you look at successful instances of leadership in your organization and around you, to what extent has that leadership bought about a shift from the physical–vital to the mental–intuitional mode of operation?

1c. How have you seen this done?

1d. What can you do as a leader?

2. Why is the notion of progress so important in leadership? What happens if a leader does not support the notion of progress?

3a. Analyze your level of mastery at the physical, vital, mental, and intuitional levels. What is the relative dominance of each type of mastery in your leadership make-up?

3b. Are there particular kinds of situations in which this relative dominance changes?

3c. As you consider your mastery at the intuitional level, what kind of unique personality seems to be forming for you?

Impact Questions

4a. Leadership is about manifesting the truth of who we are. "Holding up a mirror to yourself," what kind of leader are you?

4b. What do you stand for, what do you want your legacy to be?

4c. What are you willing to do to make the shifts required to leave this legacy?

5a. What would it be like to live in a world of service and perfection, adventure and courage, knowledge and wisdom, and harmony and mutuality? Describe.

5b. What would it take to replicate this in your own life?

Advanced Questions

6. What are three things you are willing to do to adopt a more dynamic nature (dharma) within you?

7. Describe an instance where deep and sincere questioning has created a powerful change in your life. If this has happened, then what is it? If this has not happened, describe why not?

8a. Think about a very difficult problem in your organization or market. Why has this remained a difficult problem?

8b. What kind of leadership (physical, vital, mental, and intuitional) would be required to solve the problem?

9a. How does your organization currently define itself?

9b. As a leader, how would you redefine the organization and its dynamics so that situation in interpreted from a mental–intuitional as opposed to a physical–vital perspective? Think about fractal ladder qualities and relationship with progress in this redefinition.

Rhetorical Question

10. In today's world, why is a holistic leader much more effective than an elemental leader?

Bonus Exercises: Creating Your Personal Manifesto

1a. Write your personal manifesto. What fractal patterns does it encompass?

____

____

____

____

____

____

____

____

____

____

1b. How do you operate differently?

____

____

____

____

____

1c. How are you unique?

1d. How does an organization around you operate differently?

1e. What is your relationship with progress?

1f. How do you redefine and recontextualize stagnated fractals in different spheres of your life?

1g. How do you make the change happen?

1h. Describe instances of this. Does it create a better world?

1i. How does life around you look in 10, 20, and 40 years?

PART III

Reflections and Analyses

A Personal Experience of Fractals

When I was a child, I used to have a recurring experience during episodes of high fever. Perhaps it was that during such times, the veil between the material and other realms becomes thin because of which the experience became possible. But whatever the reason be, it left its impact in my consciousness.

The experience was the following: I would see myself looking at a drop of falling water. In the drop, I would again see myself looking at a drop of falling water. In that drop, the same thing would happen, and this seemed to repeat itself many times over. Therefore, there was a fractal reality to the experience. Further, the passage of time would change. Everything seemed to slowdown. The end result of this space–time modification was that I would come *out of myself*, and it seemed that consciousness was being repeated on smaller and smaller scale. Interestingly, this coming out of myself would cause me to sweat, and my fever would break with the release of many, many drops of *water*.

So when I was introduced to the concept of a fractal—a pattern that repeats itself on different scales—about a decade ago, there was an immediate resonance with it. While fractals were being abundantly used to understand the geometry of irregular objects on the physical plane, I was predisposed to seeing it as describing repeating dynamics and phenomena in complex behavioral systems. Perhaps in addition to the *drop* experience, this impulse has definitely derived from studying a magnificent piece of work by Sri Aurobindo, Savitri, in which the very structure of existence is laid out in a comprehensive poetry. To me, Savitri also represents the most comprehensive end of a gradation in the use of fractals. Definitely the seed, root, or overarching consciousness of which all other phenomena are diminished reflections as in drops within a drop, within a drop.

At the other end of this gradation is the very work of Mandelbrot, who coined the term fractal and who formulated the Mandelbrot Set, which has been termed by Arthur C. Clarke, as *the thumb-print of God* because of the possibility of a vast array of objects, plants, and animals, as being potential offshoots and images of the underlying Mandelbrot Set.[1] The Mandelbrot Set looks like a turtle of sorts, and the logical next question is as to what could possibly give this pervasive, spherical-like structure the stability that allows all the shapes we see around us to persist?

This takes us to a deeper level in the gradation and to the work of Nassim Haramein whose use of fractals describes the very structure of space.[2] Haramein leverages the most stable geometrical structures known, and abundantly used and popularized by Buckminster Fuller in his own comprehensive work, the tetrahedron and the octahedron.[3] Haramein proposes a unified theory connecting atomic-level structure with stellar and larger-level structure where the tetrahedron, octahedron, and a 64-tetrahedron grid emerge, as it were, from the density of vacuum, to form dynamic structures that possess equilibrium at the micro- and macro-level.

The octahedron, comprised of eight tetrahedrons pointing inward, is balanced by the star-tetrahedron comprised of eight tetrahedrons pointing outward, and symbolize the basic polarity inherent in any unit of space. The 64-tetrahedron grid provides the dynamic structure with which the energy streaming out of a singularity or mini black hole in the vacuum *clothes* itself. Rotational movement, caused

[1] Nigel Lesmoir-Gordon and Arthur Clarke, *The Colours of Infinity* (Bath: Clear Press, 2004).

[2] Nassim Haramein, E.A. Rauscher, and M. Hyson, "Scale unification: A universal scaling law for organized matter," Proceedings of the Unified Theories Conference, Budapest, Hungary, 2008.

[3] Buckminster Fuller, *Synergetics: Explorations in the Geometry of Thinking* (London: Macmillan Publishing, 1982).

by the bending of space–time in the vicinity, gives a boundary to the rotating grid that then appears as the spherical-like structures of Mandelbrot's Set. Space–time torque, the result of the rotating object, streams back into the black hole and a sustainable source of energy results.

But then, the next logical question is as to where does all the possibility and tremendous scheme of things inherent in the vacuum come from? This leads us right into Savitri, and I quote a few lines from this 24,000-line poem:[4]

> At first was laid a strange anomalous base,
> A void, a cipher of some secret Whole,
> Where zero held infinity in its sum
> And All and Nothing were a single term,
> An eternal negative, a matrix Nought:
> Into its forms the Child is ever born
> Who lives for ever in the vasts of God.
> A slow reversal's movement then took place:
> A gas belched out from some Invisible Fire,
> Of its dense rings were formed these million stars;
> Upon earth's new-born soil God's tread was heard.

My use of fractals, attempting to follow the source of its inspiration, is therefore more comprehensive, also exceeding its common use of describing physical-level structure and phenomena only. I have used a dynamic fractal, comprised of fundamental elements, that will cause events to precipitate in a certain way depending on the combination of elements active in the fractal. Further, as descriped in Part I, there is a disposition in the fractal itself to tend toward a certain combination of elements, that in fact is defined by a universal pattern of progress observable regardless of scale.

In the gradation of the universal pattern of progress, we start from the Mandelbrot Set—the visible structure before us. This represents the physical state in a ubiquitous journey. We then enter into the dynamics upholding the visible structure as elaborated by Buckminster Fuller and Nassim Haramein's—the vital state. We then enter into

[4] Sri Aurobindo, *Savitri* (Pondicherry: Sri Aurobindo Ashram Press, 1950).

the cause behind, that which seeks to clothe itself in the dynamic structure of space—the mental state.

To me such a structuring of phenomena is a practical matter. Links between the micro and the macro in complex behavioral systems become clear. The logic of consciousness repeating itself on different scales becomes apparent. So too therefore does the set of actions required to reverse seemingly irreversible macro situations.

Reflections at the Individual Level

We are entering into a radically different space. There are no shortcuts. There are no quick fixes. A new mood arises. We turn from the outer to the inner. The times demand this.

To pronounce that we are done with recession is to not see the true demands of the time. The true leader would say: "Listen. Quieten down and hear the footsteps of the future. They lead us into a space of wealth where all shines with native light. Not the light of false sources, of money made by deceit, manipulation, greed, and fear, but made by the light of inner strength unveiling its face in the depths of our heart. Hear its voice and the call of its song. It beckons us to abandon our attachments to the small and the petty, and to arise as conquerors of our own nature. It beckons us to become who we really are and in that manner open the floodgates of inner wealth."

Imagination? Then, quieten down more and with objective eye see the hand of strength that in an instant has cleared the path toward the future. It says, "The apparent keepers of wealth are being toppled. And this is only the beginning. The fury of my breath grows in tornado and storm and the heat of my insistence is felt in the rising temperature around the globe. The blind demands of the selfish has created a facade. And now I am about to rip it down."

Resource constraints and a reality of overshoot, signifying that the demand for Earth's resources has exceeded the supply, have bounded the possibility of unending growth as it has been understood for centuries. Yes, wealth will still increase, but rather than that barbaric notion of wealth by which we have driven activities over the last couple of centuries, we are now entering a phase of increasing inner wealth.

It is inner wealth that must become the driver of future development. It is that possibility peeking out, or felt silently behind the inner facades and acts of constant and pervasive prostitution, that must be latched onto if we are to truly increase the pie so that we can create a truly sustainable world. Courage, justice, liberty, equality, strength, love, compassion, wisdom, sincerity, humility, and service, among a hundred other possibilities must step out from behind the veils and take their place on the world stage to reshape our coming years.

Under the crass veil of blind moneymaking active in every manner of institution, starting from the person and ending with the canvas of society itself, we have lost or are fast losing connection with our inner songs, to become a senseless cog in a wheel hurtling toward its own destruction. The connection has to be re-established, and bought into a decisive focus. It is only so that the seeming inevitability of destruction will be reversed, and we emerge as co-creators of a world forever recreating itself in images of greater and greater possibility and sustainability.

The drivers behind the creation of product and service have to be recast so that products and business process becomes green. The definition of wealth has itself to be altered to more comprehensively put into focus the full range of human endeavor. The pathways by which economic activity have tread have to be relaid. The seeds of creation have to be multiplied and diversified so that many ways lead to many beautiful and surprising outcomes.

Our inner songs have to rise to replace the standardized drone that has created the score of our recent paths. It is time to create a new symphony comprised of liberating notes formed in the silence of our own hearts.

The Desert Flower: Journey to an Ideal

Rare is it when a person's life becomes an ideal. Rarer still when a person's life is true to their name. Yet the life of Waris Dirie meaning Desert Flower, depicts how this became true in her case.

Born into a nomadic Somalian family, she was subject to the traditions that bound such people, and at the age of five suffered the procedure of female genital mutilation. At age 13, she was being forced into marriage with a 61-year-old, and it was then that she fled from her home and hazarded the journey across the desert to Mogadishu.[1]

What does it take to flower in the desert, to overcome all nature of challenge, and flower out into an ideal that becomes an icon of hope and light?

After all, this situation is true for most organizations, regardless of scale. Whether the organization is a person, family, community, corporation, or country, it is much easier for the organization to maintain the status quo—to continue without change, simply subscribing to the forces that had been in existence even before its own. This phase of maintaining the status quo is like the physical state in the three-phased ubiquitous journey and can easily continue indefinitely.

A first step away from this has to be taken so that a different set of dynamics can begin to come into being. In Waris Dirie's life, this was her act of running away from the familiarity of her home and all her known relationships. An act such as this often requires one to be open to a different voice, something much deeper than that which visible life offers us.

But when that first decisive step is taken, and an organization opens to a different order of being, to the possibility present in the ubiquitous journey, then something different begins to manifest. In Waris Dirie's life, this something different was finding herself being moved to London, UK. The journey could have ended there, but continual opening to that deeper impulsion so that thought and action are driven by something beyond the comfort and easy familiarity of one's own, allows entry into the vital or second stage of the three-phased journey.

Here there is a growth in different directions, and an increasing interaction with a larger range of forces and circumstances. In Dirie's life this is perhaps captured by her quickly becoming a supermodel. In fact these external forces and circumstances reshape the

[1] Waris Dirie, *Desert Flower: The Extraordinary Journey of a Desert Nomad* (London: William Morrow Paperbacks, 2011).

organization in ways it could never imagine, and if there continues to be that opening to the deeper voice of the ubiquitous journey, then the mental stage of the journey can be reached.

Then all the stages of the ubiquitous journey are seen for what they really were, a preparation by an *intelligence* far vaster than one's own, to create a springing board for something that transcends the limits of the little person. This is where the idea resident in the seed comes into manifestation, the intent and purpose of the journey becomes clear, and the *ideal* begins to develop a life of its own. This is where the little girl born into a life, tremendously pitted against her, can turn it around and change the established tradition into something far more meaningful.

It is the reaching of such ideals that makes life worth it and that reshapes possibility along the unimaginable contours, surfaces, and beauty of even unknowable flowers.

The Importance of Managing Stress

Managing personal stress is more important that one can imagine. There are of course the common reasons that existence of stress compromises the functioning of the body and results in its accelerated breakdown. But here, I focus on a couple of uncommon and equally important reasons.

First, who one is being, through fractal pressure, invites the reality of one's circumstance and creates the reality of one's world. This theme has been amply explored in *Connecting Inner Power with Global Change*. If one lives in states of physical, emotional, and mental stress, then those states act as attractors of corresponding physical, emotional/vital, and mental stresses in layers of organization more complex and removed from the organization characterized by the level of the individual, to ripple out to the layer of organization characterized by the global playing field itself. In my perception, hence, global symptoms such as climate change and the global financial crises have their roots in states of stress experienced at the level of the person.

Further, living in states of stress keeps one locked into the surface of one's being. One is driven by myopic surface-oriented physical, emotional/vital, and/or mental states of being. At the same time, one is locked out of deeper possibilities resident within oneself. Lack of managing personal stress, whether it be states of the physical nature such as inertia or fatigue, or states of the emotional/vital nature such as fear, anger, jealousy, doubt, or depression, or states of the mental nature such as anxiety, mental noise, or short-sightedness, perpetuates the trivial and wasteful reality of these states of being.

On the other hand, managing these states of being so that they do not exercise themselves or form the kernel of one's action in the world means one is now potentially open to deeper possibilities that are no doubt resident in the depths of one's being. It is only when the common surface dynamics we are habitually used to can seize to be operative, through a process of managing stress, that one can enter into meaningful silence and become more aware of who one is at one's core and who one stands for in the play of the world.

Personality Types

In the corporate world, there has been increasing focus on personality types and as CPP Inc, the publishers of the Myers-Briggs Type Indicator (MBTI) state, as many as 2 million MBTI tests alone are taken per year.[2] Such typing is meant to be a measure of preference in using certain faculties of consciousness, as opposed to a measure of ability. Yet, it is often, as is the case in any general physical–vital anchoring, positioned as determining the very type of an individual, and if so, is a dynamic that can become stagnating as opposed to freeing.

In a study of the system we live in (see Part I), progress is inevitable and as suggested tends to happen from the physical orientation, to the vital orientation, to the mental–intuitional orientation is significant. Further, this pattern of progress is found to exist regardless of industry, regardless of region, regardless of field, regardless of race, regardless of person, regardless of circumstance, and in the end the

[2] CPP Inc., https://www.cpp.com/company/index.aspx, 2013 (downloaded July 11, 2013).

fact that this pattern manifests in spite of tremendous opposition to change, without preference to location, with incredible intelligence seizing on any opportunity for progress, and with an overarching principle of love and caring, signifies fundamental properties of the system we live in—omnipotence (overcoming all opposition to change), omnipresence (happening all over), omniscience (happening with an incredible practical intelligence leveraging levers, people, and circumstances magically), and omnicaring (happening with an overarching care).

In fractal fashion, where a seed pattern repeats itself on different scales, these fundamental properties of our containing system manifest in more practical terms or types, as power or strength (omnipotence), service and perfection (omnipresence), wisdom and knowledge (omniscience), and harmony and mutuality (omnicaring). These types then also reproduce themselves in fractal fashion and are the very soul force of different personality types.

Yet, so long as we as individuals are caught at the egoistic end of this ubiquitous pattern, the physical–vital end, these types are going to remain hidden to us. It is only when we overcome the dysfunctional and egoistic patterns that define our behaviors that we can progress along this journey, and in opening more to the mental–intuitional end, become aware of that deep soul force that in reality drives us.

Any personality-type test or indicator that does not map or suggest these two fundamental dynamics of: (1) moving along the P-V-M-I journey and (2) reorienting our meaning and inner drive to the four soul forces are incomplete and can never provide a progressive framework to align and move us in the direction that all life is inevitably moving in. And such an alignment is arguably of increasing importance in today's world where decades old operating assumptions are simply falling apart. In fact, in giving too much credence to the test that does not capture these two fundamental movements, the types so derived will, as mentioned, tend to forever lock us into one insignificant frame or another.

The axis of introversion–extroversion is perhaps the most illuminating feature of the common MBTI test. It parallels the journey from the physical (outward, sense-based orientation), through the vital (energy-based orientation), to the mental–intuitional (thought and even deeper, inner-based orientation). The importance of an integration of these modes of operating manifests in the age-old and archetypal journey a prince makes in becoming a king or a princess in becoming a queen.

While we might say that a prince starts from an attitude of often-foolish self-assertion (the egoistic, vital anchoring), through the resulting adversity and fall becomes the king, more tempered by freeing thought and even inner sight. The foolish extrovert becomes the wiser extrovert–introvert (a mental–intuitional anchoring). On the other hand, we might say that the princess generally starts from an attitude of shyness (the egoistic, physical anchoring, or perhaps a form of subdued introversion) and through the resulting adversity and fall becomes the wiser queen, more open to the powers of elevated introversion and necessary extroversion.

Both the king and the queen typify a fundamental balance between introversion and extroversion and are the result of a personal journey in which many contrary fractals emanating from one's own self had to be faced and overcome. The fruit of the journey is the accumulation of a treasure beyond measure—full awareness and assimilation into active being of the soul force that drove one from behind.

The other abilities referenced in MBTI, Sensing and Intuition (different from the intuition suggested in the P-V-M-I model), and feeling and thinking, when seen from this perspective, are lateral or horizontal capacities only indicating preference in information processing (sense or intuit) and decision-making (feel or think) in the fundamental journey to balance introversion–extroversion. They are not in fact exhaustive capacities, but something that was obviously in the field of Jung's experience at that time.

This sense of the journey, of change as a result of the journey, and of the journey leading to a goal or true type that was implicit and hidden, must be the true value in any personality test. It is, hence, and based on the deeper insight of the fractal for progress that the web-based tool, PowersWithin,[3] that seeks to help a person identify the soul force or deep driver that they are within them, is designed. It is also based on the deeper insight of the fractal for progress and

[3] Aurosoorya, Powers Within, http://www.aurosoorya.com/powerwithin.html (2013a; downloaded July 11, 2013).

the practical and personal limitations that the deeper soul force may manifest as, that the web-based tool, EmotionalIntelligenceBuilder,[4] has been designed. EmotionalIntelligenceBuilder provides an index of common fractals and contrary fractals that may drive one's journey and that have to be overcome. PowersWithin provides insight into the deeper soul force that indicates truer and deeper personality. The juxtaposition of the four soul forces and the P-V-M-I framework provides insight into how the soul force is likely seeking to develop practically.

Recreating the World Around Us at Every Instant

When one takes a good, hard look at oneself, one will find there many active voices housed within the self. There may be a voice that wants fast promotion in the workplace, a voice that wants to balance work and family life, a voice that is continually frustrated by one's own boss, a voice that is driven by idealism, a voice that is somewhat scared and shy, a boisterous and self-righteous voice, and a voice that is enamored of technology, among many other voices.

These voices are not unlike different *players* within one's small self, and in this manner of looking, it is as though one *were* a team comprised of many different players or members.

Sometimes these team members are at odds with one other, sometimes one member imposes their will to the dismay of all other members, sometimes the team seems to be getting absolutely nowhere—lost in a task that can hardly be defined, and sometimes there is forward movement—at the cost of delayed retribution because one of the voices feels that its agenda has been severely compromised, for now.

The dynamics of self when considered from this point of view is not unlike the dynamics of team, as illustrated by the forming–storming–norming–performing model. In fact, these dynamics repeat themselves on different scales and are therefore *fractal* in nature.

[4] Aurosoorya, EmotionalIntelligenceBuilder, http://www.aurosoorya.com/emotional.html (2013b; downloaded July 11, 2013).

Note though that it is *not* that there is this happy, coincidental similarity between the way a team functions and the possible dynamics in one's small self. Quite the contrary, the dynamics in the small self is the dynamics of the many voices, and this is causative, fractal in nature and ripples out so that teams are in fact an accentuating mirror held up to throw into relief the conflicting dynamics in oneself.

After all, if one find's frustration in interacting with another team member, it is not that the team member is fundamentally frustrating (they after all are themselves a conglomeration of many possibilities), but it is that a *voice* in oneself gets triggered into frustration because that voice has stagnated around a dysfunction that is particular to one's self.

If immediately, when this voice of frustration arises, there is a stronger movement in oneself that coalesces around a voice of compassion or a voice of love, then the whole external dynamic will shift and the apparent frustration that was beginning to crystallize will get dissolved.

In other words, if the myriad team members in one's self coalesced around the emergent leader of compassion and love, then the forming–storming–norming–performing dynamic would accelerate through its stages and the team (or self) would display attributes of *performing* (the reader may recognize that this movement through forming–storming–norming–performing is none other than the movement through the all-present physical–vital–mental fractal for progress, where physical = forming, vital = storming, mental = norming + performing).

When looked at from this point of view, each one of us is a repository of incredible resourcefulness, possibility, and power. A whole environment can be understood if one learns that the environment is a reflection, an image, a projected world, with its origin in the dynamics in one's self. A whole environment can be shifted if one learns to shift what one is feeling and thinking when in that environment. A whole environment can also be recreated if one recreates the dynamics one experiences in one's self.

It seems that the human was after all made in the image of God. We are powerful beyond measure. And knowingly or not, we create and recreate the world around us, at every instant.

"A Man Does What He Can, Until His Destiny Is Revealed"

This quote from *The Last Samurai*, an inspiring 2003 movie, becomes meaningful when taken from the perspective of a fractal system's architect.[5] In the movie itself, it refers to a situation when the Samurai Lord, reflecting on a series of conversations with a captain of the US army focused on Custer and his attacks on the Native Americans, is about to attack a far larger imperial Japanese army. Death of the outnumbered Samurai seems certain and that is when the captain says, "A man does what he can, until his destiny is revealed."

The movie was inspiring for a number of reasons. It portrays the bravery and nobility of a wise warrior clan fulfilling its dharma without calculation. It captures the dynamic of sacrifice to awaken a country to its soul. And it ends with a synthesis in which finally the old and new are both respected and become the guiding light for a more meaningful integration.

But these inspiring outcomes are the result of significant shifts that occur in the character of key people. The life of a person, after all, is the conglomeration of many different fractals,that is, repeating patterns on different scales. These fractals determine how the person will perceive, behave, and act. These fractals will consequently also draw circumstances consistent with their root pattern. Hence, the texture and significance of one's life will be determined by the conglomeration of underlying root patterns.

If man does not do what he can, then he will forever be subject to a class of fractals that will keep him locked into a certain way of being. In such a case, the past lives on, often unendingly, and it is only when powerful external patterns intersect with the existing ones, in an act of Grace, that the resulting shock and pain may cause these habitual and stagnated patterns to dislodge and progress on their respective dynamic journeys.

If man does what he can, on the other hand, meaning, if all the myriad journeys that he is composed of are completed, then something

[5] Wikiquote, *The Last Samurai*, http://en.wikiquote.org/wiki/The_Last_Samurai (2013; downloaded July 11, 2013).

else can be revealed. When all the journeys are completed, then stagnation whether at the physical or vital level is overcome, and the past is transcended. History is undone, and in the moment of *now* so created, something other than habitual physical, vital, and mental patterns can step forward. This is destiny, this is creativity. This is to live.

In the contemporary movie portrayal of Thor, of Norse mythology, the power he possesses is subject to stagnations at the vital level. Hence, Thor is impulsive and short-sighted. For him, to own his power, for it to become the platform of his destiny, he must fall—and this is so because he is unwilling, and even quite unaware of what he must do to overcome his stagnations. In other words, the patterns that animate him must intersect with other powerful patterns so that the stagnation can be undone. When he is stripped of his power, and has fallen, and is willing to die for a greater cause, it is then—when the stagnated patterns have completed their respective journeys—that his destiny is revealed, and he is able to return to his home as a wiser heir apparent.

Whether with the sword or the hammer or any instrument—internal or external—a man must do what he can to overcome his physical, vital, and mental stagnations. It is only so that Destiny, the living ambassadress from Earth's glorious future, will consent to incarnate in him.

Reflections at the Organizational Level

The Dark Knight and the Fractal for Progress

In the recent *Dark Knight* trilogy, society in Gotham City is portrayed as decadent, and the extinction of Gotham City positioned as the solution by the League of Shadows, to maintain a balance between forces of light and darkness. At its very base such a solution is counter to the fractal for progress in which all organizations have an in-built urge to transcend their littleness. It is only when that is at all costs not possible, that extinction naturally becomes a possible outcome.

And certainly, the costs were stacked high by the machinations of the League of Shadows, and in the *Dark Knight*, the second movie in the trilogy, *The Joker*. In *Batman Begins*, the League of Shadows is intent on destroying Gotham City and this outcome is reversed through the heroics of Batman. Like the mythical Atlas, he shoulders Gotham City's burden—in this case of decadence and continually reverses the intended outcome. In the *Dark Knight* another force, of extreme anarchy, is released through the character of The Joker. So strong is this force of chaos that even the overt hero, the District Attorney, is transformed into evil and emerges as the doomed Two Face.

In terms of the ubiquitous journey, The Joker is the overt and dark vital force causing a society to move away from its established status quo of decadence. The Joker's ferry experiment like his unintended creation of Two Face reinforces the volatile yet dark bias inherent in the society of Gotham City. The Dark Knight has no creative power, but exists only to arrest Gotham City's movement into anarchy. Anarchy is avoided by The Dark Knight shouldering the burden of sin and allowing Two Face to emerge as the hero that he thinks the city needs.

Such a dynamic is clearly an early stage in the fractal for progress, whether of society or the hero, and is marked by maintaining the status quo and erecting a false hero that will satisfy a small sense of greatness that perhaps people are adequately moved by. Atlas remains Atlas, and as Ayn Rand suggests in Atlas Shrugged, "Atlas would simply shrug with the added burden of an increasingly decadent society".[1]

In the finale of the *Dark Knight* series—*Dark Knight Rises*, the fractal for progess surges ahead, and the timeless and never-moving Atlas, who thus far seemed to use all his power to arrest the plunge into anarchy, is able to emerge as something different. This ability was accompanied by a subtle yet corresponding transformation in society itself. In response to the seeding of possibility through the figure of the future Robin, and the more important growing collective urge for change, the downward pointing anarchy that had held the Dark Knight as a dark knight, changes and he becomes more of a knight in shining armor.

He becomes an ideal, something greater than any human, and in that movement embodies more of the intent and intuition at the progressive end of the ubiquitous fractal for progress.

This dynamic is then perhaps the secret of any organizational development. The hero or champion shifts the set of possibilities available to an organization by furthering the fractal for progress in herself or himself. The organization embraces this possibility and also surges forward in its own journey.

The Brave New World of Organizational Development

In *Connecting Inner Power with Global Change*, I present a fractal framework, built through observation of progress, which unifies different layers of complex organization, from the person, to the

[1] Ayn Rand, *Atlas Shrugged* (New York: Signet, 1996).

team, to the business unit, to the corporation, to the market, and to the containing system. These different layers emerge as expressions of an underlying unified system, which in fact is perceived as being intelligent, loving, all-present, all-powerful, and more.

Further, I identify common dynamics that exist across each of these layers of organization, which I term broadly as physical, vital, and mental dynamics, that in fact completely determine the behavior of each of these layers of organization. I posit that this behavior is the result of how the physical, vital, and mental strands combine together, and that there is in fact one particular pattern, termed the P-V-M fractal that is progressive and allows the system to arrive at the most sustainable and fruitful outcome possible.

As suggested, there is a tight and causal relationship between the base patterns existing at the level of the person, and the patterns at each of the subsequent layers of organization, from the team all the way through to the market and system itself. Hence, the key to solving seemingly complex problems, whether they exist at the system, market, or corporate levels, is in fact the physical, vital, and mental dynamics that exist in root form at the individual level.

For after all, if everything is essentially One, and as practitioners if what we experience out there actually lives in such fractal, or root form in our own beings, then the question is as to how much control can each of us have over our environments, and how should the field of Organizational Development be reconstructed because of this? In *Connecting Inner Power with Global Change*, it is clear that every single individual is bestowed with *great power and therefore great responsibility* in changing this World. In such a view, there is no such thing as a victim, and the only thing that has to be done is for the individual to awaken to the often deeply ingrained fractal programming that drives them, and *complete* the many stagnated fractals resident in their own being so that each of these progresses along the eventually inevitable P-V-M arc.

This may seem theoretical, but in fact as one experiments with the completion of stagnated fractals in one's own space and sees the impact in the world around, it will be found to be quite practical. A documented case in point, structured in a different language and background, but I believe, based on the same underlying principles is that of Dr Hew Len clinical psychologist who worked at the Hawaii State hospital in the high security ward for the criminally insane from 1983 to 1987, where he cured an entire ward of violent mentally ill patients using the simple ancient Hawaiian healing method of Ho'oponopono.[2]

In a nine-part YouTube interview conducted by Rita Montgomery and Dr Rick Moss,[3] Dr Hew Len talks about *data* that is running everyone. In fact he posits that perception itself is the end product of this data that lives in everyone's subconscious. He says that we are not free but are always driven by this data. There are millions of bits of this data that constantly drive us. Ho'Oponopono is the practice of letting go of this data.

To me this is remarkably like the myriad stagnated fractal patterns that drive us. *Cleaning this data* or *erasing the data* is like completing the stagnated fractals that not only animate one's own perception and behavior, but by fractal contagion much of what is around us. One can only become free when they have let go of the data. Healing another entails first becoming aware of the data in oneself, when one thinks off or experiences another. Then through a process of surrender to the *one reality*, and knowing that each and all are emergences form that one reality, of offering the data in oneself to *that* and asking *that* to forgive or complete it. As a result, what may change is the data in oneself, which by fractal effect may change the data in another.

To me it is such a practice that constitutes the brave new world of organizational development. In a talk I gave recently in Silicon Valley on leveraging fractal technology to scale change initiatives,[4] I emphasized how organizational development (OD) is going to be the most important profession in the world. I said this precisely because of the focus that OD practitioners have on dynamics at the

[2] Joe Vital, *Zero Limits: The Secret Hawaiian System for Wealth, Health, Peace, and More* (Hoboken: Wiley, 2008).

[3] YouTube Interview with Dr Hew Len, http://www.youtube.com/watch?v=OL972JihAmg (2013; downloaded July 11, 2013).

[4] Aurosoorya, "Leveraging Fractal Technology to Scale Change Initiatives," http://www.slideshare.net/SBODN/leveraging-fractal-technology-to-scale-change-initiatives (2013c; downloaded July 11, 2013).

individual and team levels, and their resultant fractal effects on much larger corporate, market and system outcomes.

But for this to happen, the focus of OD practitioners has to shift from *out-there* to *in-here*. OD practitioners have to become acutely aware that their own being is a precise field that mirrors many, many dynamics in the corporations they may be working in. It is by shifting the nature of dynamics in oneself that dynamics can be shifted in the world around oneself. Mahatma Gandhi summarized this well in his statement: "Become the change that you wish to see in the world."

An Equation for Organizational Creativity

It has been said that the universe is recreated at every instant.[5] But even if we cannot wrap our minds around that insight, it is evident that we are continuously creating.

Every instance of our lives is a creative act. We cannot but help that. It is our inherent nature. If from nothing else, this should be evident from the fact that we are at least the result of the interaction of two generously creative entities—the Earth and the Sun.

But the question is "What is it that we are creating?" More often than not our acts of creativity reinforce the past that exists. Being so, we do not notice what is being created because the output already exists. This dynamic is captured by the equation: P(centeredness) + V(centeredness) > M(centeredness) where P signifies the physical orientation, V the vital orientation, and M the mental orientation.

What this is telling us is that the sum of our P-centeredness, that is centeredness in what the eye can see and hence the past, and V-centeredness, that is centeredness in self-referencing energy or egoistic movements, is greater that our M-centeredness, that is centeredness in genuine curiosity and progressive questioning. In other words, we are subject to stagnated patterns that are generally anchored around the physical or vital orientations.

[5] Sri Aurobindo, *Isha Upanishad* (Twin Lakes: Lotus Press, 1986).

It is only in completing the stagnated patterns that something other than what had already structured the past can appear.[6] When stagnated patterns are completed, then our creativity, which is happening ALL the time becomes more visible since what is produced is something OTHER than what had existed before. The equation that describes this condition is: P(centeredness) + V(centeredness) < M(centeredness).

Being that every element is creative, and in fact seeks to reinforce its raison d'être wherever it can, it can be said that creativity is fractal in nature, that is, it tends to repeat itself on different scales. This insight suggests that the set of equations are true for organizations at different scales. Hence, the psychology of a person, practically determined by the play of P-centeredness, V-centeredness, and M-centeredness, will also determine the creativity that may or may not exist at a department, unit, corporate, market, system, or global level.

[6] Pravir Malik, *Connecting Inner Power with Global Change: The Fractal Ladder* (New Delhi: Sage, 2009).

Reflections on Organizational Design

We live in unprecedented times. The confluence of crises ranging from climate change, signifying a fundamental macro-level restructuring of the very physical foundation we have come to rely on, at one end, to the global financial meltdown signifying the breakdown of the very vital foundation replete with various flows our economy and present-day society have come to rely on, leads us squarely into the necessity of a basic mental level reorientation at the other end.

Our conception of ourselves must of necessity alter such that the subjective powers, the powers within, begins to count for more than the objective. It has become a necessity that we restructure all manners of organization so that these PowersWithin may find a more concrete platform to exercise their influence in practical life. It is only in the re-equationing of the fundamental balance between subjectivity and objectivity that whatever is seeking to express itself through the chaos of the time will find its most secure surfacing.

PowersWithin can be thought of as those exceptional drivers that come to the surface where the oft common journey characterized by the physical–vital stages comes to an end. Hence, these are perhaps those dynamics that were inherent in the seed. Utilizing or tapping into these drivers can provide exceptional stability to organizations because of this.

The time for leveraging PowersWithin has arrived. There are several concrete indications of this:

- The knowledge of the physical world has increased to such an extent that it is trying to break its own bounds. The search for

the bases of matter is leading to more and more subtle particles that are themselves increasingly subjective in quality.
- The veil between the outer and inner physical, vital, and mental capacities and powers are breaking, and the outer physical, vital, and mental possibilities are awaiting to get more power from within rather than from the external material level as in the past.
- Manifestation of excessive vital powers and its practices in the material world exerts such a high pressure that it has resulted in the formidable problems such as climate change and the global financial meltdown and is leading to the collapse of the very foundation we have based much of our activity on.
- Conventional industry is dying before it is even declared as sick.
- There is an increase in the collapse of all hierarchical and patriarchal structures around the world.
- Any contemporary crises are very deep rather than superficial.
- The consequence of practicing falsehoods is becoming concretely visible.
- Nothing can be hidden any more.
- The strength of women, naturally more subjective beings, is on the rise.
- There is more and more awareness of and focus on the unknown.
- There is a growing urge toward freedom and equality.

Every thought, word, and act, which already is a means for the vaster powers of *all-love*, all-knowledge, all-presence, and all-power, to manifest themselves, must more completely surrender to that which is seeking to manifest. For on closer examination, one can perhaps see that it is indeed these powers from within—harmony and mutuality, knowledge and wisdom, service and perfection, power and energy—that stand behind all that we see manifest around us.

Consider a simple example of a chair. For centuries perhaps, people sat on the ground or on boulders. Then one fine day somebody had a flash of insight and the concept of sitting on a movable, comfortable chair became real. The concept itself was the result of the *power of knowledge*. Having had the sure vision of the thing to be done, the force and energy to do it became real. This is the result of the *power of energy*, a derivative of all-power. Now, of course, was the issue of making the concept real. Elaborate plans were then drawn out, specifying materials to be used, implements to be used, alternative end designs, and even the process of production. This was the result of the *power of harmony and mutuality*, a derivative of all-love. Finally, the blueprints needed to be executed. The skill and workmanship and overseeing of the project had to be embarked upon. This was the result of the *power of service and perfection*, a derivative of all-presence.

Or consider the example of the human body. One can again see the action of the archetypes in the very creation of the human body. Thus, the archetype of wisdom and knowledge creates the thinking ability resident in the brain and mind. The archetype of harmony and mutuality creates the lungs and heart, by whose action the individual can remain connected to the rhythm of the vaster breath all around and keep connected the different parts of the body whose individual rhythms are in tune with the heart within. The archetypes of power and energy create the entire digestive system by whose action food is assimilated and provides power and energy for all that the body needs to do. The archetypes of service and perfection combine micro-elements into atoms, and these into molecules, these into plasma for cell, these into organs, and these into the body itself, which then becomes the sac within which all the other archetypes and their representatives can act.

The Archetypes of the Powers Within

When the researcher, thus, is seeking after a new insight, it must be done with a one-pointed commitment and concentration so that the very wells of knowledge resident in hidden Sun's feel compelled to reveal their great secrets. When the manager is seeking to motivate his team he must do so with such conviction and energy that the very powers of the wind and fire feel compelled to manifest in the team. When the organizer is seeking to design and arrange parts of an organization, he must do so with such a sense of rhythm and harmony that the beauty of nature becomes apparent in the designed forms. When the engineer is constructing his device, he must do so with such a sense of accurate detail and attention that perfection itself arises through his touch.

These four powers must be allowed to express themselves in their purity. Currently, and in accordance with the unrefined vital tendency of the age, all the sub-powers of the four powers have submitted themselves to the dynamics of commercialization, itself an unrefined power of mutuality and harmony. Thus, art is created and valued for its ability to generate monetary wealth. Sports too have become big business. Knowledge is valued only for its ability in generating monetary gains. And so on. When we say that everything must express itself in its purity, we mean that knowledge must be pursued for the sake of knowledge, art to express beauty, sport to perfect the body, enhance organization skills, and develop many other noble qualities, and so on. But it also means that the myriad capacities contained within these four powers will more easily exercise themselves in our functioning.

Thus, the development of the archetype of knowledge within oneself will perhaps imply not only the seeking of knowledge in areas related to one's immediate work, but even seeking of knowledge in other areas, of a need to research and create new knowledge, of a temperament that is calm and turned to introspection and even meditation, of a tendency to want to dominate all emergence of passion and vital tendencies by reason, by the urge of wanting to spread knowledge among all, and by the seeking after truths too profound to perhaps even be contemplated.

The development of the archetype of mutuality and harmony within oneself will perhaps imply the understanding of rhythms of all kinds, the understanding and even mastery of the great laws of interchange by which organizations are built, of the need of amassing in order to throw out in even larger measure in order to create an even greater return, of even the ability of compelling others to unite through harmony, and of turning insights into practicalities—of making even abstract thoughts and ideas manifest practically.

The development of the archetype of power, leadership, and energy within oneself will perhaps imply the development of an unflinching courage, of the ability and need to be a leader in noble causes, the need to protect the down-trodden, the ability to muster and possess great energy for any new endeavors, the ability to see the new and needed, and the ability to convince others of the worthiness of new adventures.

The development of the archetype of service and perfection within oneself will perhaps imply an extraordinary attention to detail, a need to labor at any discipline in order to achieve perfection, a giving of oneself to that which one loves without concern of the self, a sense that nothing is too small to be the object of attention, and a sense of what has already been accomplished and what remains yet to be accomplished.

Powers within and the Creation of a Stable Mega-organization

Once each power is developed and expressed in purity, then only will multiple motive forces become the engine of development. When this happens, then truly robust organizations, flowering organizations, can begin to come into being.

Consider the example of Silicon Valley. While it may be primarily a commercial organization, yet we begin to glimpse something of what may become possible when the powers just talked about can begin to interact with one another in free fashion. That is, without the motive of doing everything for the sake of generating only money. In the case of Silicon Valley, we see that the climate and beauty of the Bay Area began to attract many talented people into the vicinity. Over time, the talent pool became progressively diversified. Educational institutes, such as Stanford University and University of Berkeley cropped up and became centers of cutting-edge research. The Armed Forces were attracted to the area for the same reason, and came with their huge requirements for research for research's sake, and their huge funds in support of the area. Graduates from the universities started companies that began to in turn support the universities with handsome funds. Talent moved around from company to company like people from department to department. Thus, we see that even when individual companies failed, Silicon Valley functioned as a larger organization and was able to retain the talent in the area, was able further, to buffer the shocks to some extent, hence preparing the ground for future waves of innovation.

Pragmatically speaking, this dynamic of functioning as a larger mega-organization meant that some level of commercial immunity began to develop so that people losing their jobs were not necessarily considered as that stressful an event. There was a freeing, thus, from the purely commercial element. If the various powers of beauty, aesthetics, knowledge, power in the form of money, plus the myriad streams of talent—from engineers, scientists, managers, lawyers, and so on—did not exist in such close proximity, and further, if the various professionals could not thus support each other through their continued informal meetings, through the urge to create the next wave of innovation, through the urge to pursue progress for the sake of progress, then they would have left for other areas and the phenomenon of Silicon Valley would never have been.

Modern day organizations cannot provide these various buffers and opportunities for interaction that Silicon Valley provides and, hence, when hit with adversity, more often than not, simply crumble. This is perhaps due to the fact that it is always only one-dimension that drives them, and when the health of that is threatened or falls, the organization resorts to tactics that will ensure that the dimension looks good at any cost in the bargain, sacrificing the development of the other dimensions and therefore its longer term health.

The PowersWithin-led organization will be something like a community. Having attained freedom from an exaggerated commercial impetus, people will *live* their *jobs* because it is what fulfills them. Such a freedom is what will allow the four primary powers to manifest to greater and greater degree within them and their environment. Seeing, thus, their ability to become centers of knowledge and wisdom, or mutuality and harmony, or power and leadership and energy, or perfection and service, or some unique combination of these primary forces, so increase, a sense of satisfaction with life will more easily accompany all that they continue to do. Under the freer flow of these powers, their uniqueness will be refined and flourish, and correspondingly, so too will the uniqueness of their respective organizations.

An organization may be political and, hence, be primarily driven by the power of leadership and courage, or it may be social and hence be primarily driven by the power of service and perfection, or it may be commercial and hence be primarily driven by the power of mutuality and harmony, or it may be research oriented and academic and hence be primarily driven by the powers of knowledge and wisdom, but always each of the other powers will also be behind it, fulfilling and completing its primary urge. Even the number of PowersWithin *savants* will continue to increase, become guiding lights so that the community will spontaneously begin to move in holistic directions consistent with the urge of people, of the suborganizations within the community, of the community itself, and of the larger system of which the community or mega-organization is a part.

Even perhaps, something that may be behind the four archetypal powers, something that may be behind the building of all uniqueness—individual and organizational—if something like that exists, that is, may be compelled to come forward, seeing how developed its means of expression and action have become.

Reflections on Industry Development

Deeper Symbolism of the BP Oil Spill

As I consider the confluence of some recent global business events (Eurozone crises, continued Japanese deflation, rippling stock market depression, and BP oil spill), the conclusion that we are witnessing the death of an old-way of being cannot but be reinforced.

Fractal system architecture analyses at various levels reveal that we are at a significant transition between the physical–vital and a more mental way of being. The physical–vital is all about appropriating energy flows to reinforce a myopic perception of self and build it to be even larger, bigger, and become even more aggressive so that it can more effectively do more of the ineffective same. This is the operative mentality that has so far driven our corporations, markets, and economies.

The short-sighted growth of these constructs has interestingly been driven by a carbon-based energy source which, chemically speaking, is nothing but crushed and pressurized remains of eon-old physical and vital beings (less evolved and even supposedly gigantic plants and animals). So, from a symbolical perspective, we have the remains of eon-old physical–vital beings fuelling an essential consciousness that is physical–vital in its manner. That we are approaching or by some estimates are in a reality of peak-oil is in this analysis significant since it suggests that peak-oil too is a sign that an essentially old-way of being is reaching its end.

Transition always tends to bring an old way of being vehemently to the surface, if for no other reason than to try to fight an emerging new way of being to prolong its reign. In this perspective, the BP oil spill may symbolically be viewed as bringing that old physical–vital energy source and consciousness that flowed unseen in subterranean passages or pipes, vehemently to the surface. This old way now openly spreads its poison and a valiant battle, which does not include throwing golf balls and tires at it,[1] which by the way is what BP did to try to control the out-spewing of oil, must take place between the old and the new until the new spreads its wings and makes us soar to new heights.

In this light, the Eurozone crises, continued Japanese deflation, stock market depression and crises must be seen as a deep need to want to disengage from a maddening physical–vital way of being. The irony is that our analysts, commentators, regulators, and other economic and public stakeholders continue to see these events in the old physical–vital way of being and continue to want to resuscitate this dying and outdated way so that it may live again.

It cannot be resuscitated though. Way has to be given for a new, more mental way of being in which possibility can more abundantly come to the surface. De-monopolization of power in all its forms is the inevitable future before us. Realization of this will help all involved to more effectively transition through and manage what is seeking to taking birth.

Walmart's Entry into India: A Time for Tests and New Measures

Walmart has tied up with Bharti to create wholesale stores in India. Beyond marking a new phase in the Indian retail environment, application of the fractal for progress indicates why this also marks a crucial phase in the Indian and global developmental cycles.

[1] Harvey Morris, "BP abandons 'top kill' efforts on oil spill," http://www.ft.com/intl/cms/s/0/832b7b5e-6a4a-11df-b268-00144feab49a.html#axzz2YIQFcCUR (2010; downloaded July 11, 2013).

Walmart's success to date has been driven by consumer desire for an increasing array of diverse products offered at low prices. Walmart leverages its tightly managed global supply chain to offer just such a mix. But what are the hidden costs of this equation? Insight into this is gained by dwelling further on the nature of the driver behind Walmart's success.

1. This driver is consumer desire, an aggressive vital-level dynamic. Such a dynamic seeks for satisfaction of its want immediately without considering the factors that have allowed the product to be supplied in such a manner. The cost, hence, tends toward a marginalization of all longer term, more sustainable solutions.
2. As this dynamic is reinforced, there is a ripple effect and a similar short-term vital-level dynamic becomes alive at the local, national, and global levels. Affected journeys at these levels include the consumer journey, the business journey, the supply-chain journey, the culture journey, and the society journey, to mention some key ones. In other words, the progressive realities possible to each of these entities are stalled at the vital level, resulting in a slew of additional costs. Cycles of conspicuous consumerism, of business-as-usual, of questionable supply chains, of stalled culture, and of misplaced society, respectively, are reinforced. To illustrate some of these:

    a) Vital-level consumer desire reinforces and strengthens vital-level global supply chains. Such vital-level supply chains often operate at suboptimal levels increasing the social and environmental costs to humanity in their wake. These costs remain unfactored in the final price of the product and are borne by the locality that has come into contact with the ever-expanding supply chain. Ironically, as the companies managing such supply chains show increasing profits, they are rewarded by investors, and the very dynamic that it would make most sense to move away from is given additional impetus to continue with its questionable effects.
    b) As local communities become part of these supply chains, their dependence on continuing to be a part of the supply chain increases, and a balanced investment in their own

communities often decreases. As a result, local and hence regional development at multiple-levels is compromised and then all must become part of the global business machinery in order to survive. There are, hence, huge costs at the community and regional levels.

c) The culture and the society journeys are also compromised, and instead of growing to express their own uniqueness and possibilities, outcomes of journeying to the mental phase in their own trajectories, they continually circle at a standardized level because the basis of creativity has been marginalized by assimilation into a strong global machinery.

3. By the nature of the unrefined vital consciousness, the costs to humanity of remaining at that level increase much faster than if corresponding shifts were made to the mental levels of the respective journeys. Mental-level dynamics are by their very nature more inclusive of a wider set of issues and, hence, more balanced in resulting action. Consideration of such balance has a longer-term positive effect that lowers hidden costs to humanity. By failing to shift to this level, there are rapidly escalating opportunity costs.

These same costs that propagate out across the world are also easily experienced locally at the site of the incoming Walmart.

On the flip side, the incoming of a highly organized force such as Walmart, albeit of a stagnated vital level, that has in fact succeeded in spreading its often welcome vital way of being in many parts of the world, can as per the reality of intersecting journeys, cause a corresponding counter *organization* at the point of its presence so that all potential journeys have the chance to alter by progressing along their respective trajectories. It is to be hoped that this is the case and that such a reality may be proactively stimulated through thoughtful policy administered at the local level.

If so, then rather than Walmart displacing local producers and suppliers, there is the possibility of local producers and suppliers becoming part of a hybrid Walmart-local *ecosystem*. Such a development pushes the vital boundaries of the business journey to operate in another way that becomes more cognizant of the long-term benefits of strengthening localities for the sake of localities rather than for the sake of business alone or for Walmart alone. This development also pushes possible stagnation in the local community journey so that there is the acceptance of a new energy in the rearrangement of local activity.

Further, this and other such expanded *ecosystems* can now feed into the global supply chain, to alter the very nature of the global supply chain itself. Rather than the usual vital-level heuristic of minimizing one-sided or manager-viewed cost–in this case Walmart's as in managing the supply chain, a new mental-level heuristic of maximizing unique and local development could become the arbitrating factor in management of global supply chains, thereby pushing the supply chain journey to the next level in its own P-V-M trajectory. Companies that develop localities along their global supply chains, based on respective uniqueness should be the ones rewarded, because in reality such development strengthens the long-term wealth of the world.

As Walmart enters India, there is a chance to cause several potentially stagnated journeys to progress. This can be facilitated by substituting old ways of being and old measures of success by new measures that cause new behavior in the long term.

As a measure of such real positive development, the following should be tracked over the next couple of years:

1. Shift from vital to mental-level consumer behavior manifest in a shift from impulse- and desire-based to more thoughtful buying.
2. Increase in price of products as real social and environmental costs are factored into cost of products.
3. Increase in local community, cultural, social capital with comprehensive development of local *ecosystems*.
4. Change in nature of supply chains so that they morph into robust development chains through acceptance and assimilation of local business/cultural/spiritual ways of being.
5. Change in reward to companies that cause true development along supply chains rather than compromise supply chains.
6. Change in the nature of development so that expectations of continued short-term financial growth is replaced by expectations of balanced long-term holistic growth.

In many respects what happens in India in the retail sector over the next few years is crucial to the overall development of the world. This is so for a number of reasons:

1. Retail in India is predominantly unorganized. Greater degree of organization that will accompany the incoming of the likes of Walmart will make it a far more serious, globally integrated industry with much more substantial effects on society and the environment.
2. Such organized retail will integrate a huge middle class, by some estimates twice the size of the USA, into the global market.
3. An unchecked retail sector at the head of what could currently be considered cancerous global supply chains, and driven by continued and unrefined vital-level consumer demand is a recipe for global disaster. On the environmental side, greenhouse gas (GHG) emissions will increase by a huge factor, global temperatures will continue to rise, and the rest could be history. On the social side, more of the same will reinforce a self-destructive paradigm of business-as-usual, and the rest could be history.

On the other hand, a more well-thought out Indian retail environment, where the emphasis is to consciously shift the intersecting consumer, supply chain, business, culture, and society journeys to the mental level in their respective journeys, will usher in a whole different and far-more balanced era in global development.

Addressing the Antibiotic *Apocalypse* through the Fractal for Progress

Weakness at any scale can be traced to a fundamental inability to move out of a condition of complacency. This is true of a faltering global economy, of a failing market, of an outdated culture, of a team that is stuck at a level of dysfunction, of an individual who insists on meeting others with hostility and irritation, or at the micro-level, of the inability to address the rise in drug-resistant infections.

When the UK Chief Medical Officer sounds that the antibiotic *apocalypse* is nigh,[2] and that one can die from a routine infection because we have run out of antibiotics, it is perhaps time to look for a solution that moves away from the obvious inadequacy of current accepted trends of research, and strike a new path of thought.

One such path is offered by the ubiquitous fractal for progress. In this approach, there is a fundamental pattern of progress that is true regardless of scale. Hence, it is true regardless of the type of organization. An organization may be the human body, a complex market, a multi-geography business unit, the World Wide Web, or an academic theory, among others, for instance.

In this approach, an organization is subject to a certain orientation, such as the physical, the vital, or the mental, which will determine entirely the characteristics, dynamics, and possibility of the organization. The *physical* refers to experiencing reality primarily through what the eyes can see, the *vital* through the medium of often self-assertive energy, and the *mental* through the vehicle of thought, curiosity, questioning, or idea. An organization that is arrested at any one level will of necessity experience problems, which are the means by which it is forced to move to another orientation. Weakness, hence, arises when a system or organization has become complacent and is stuck at a certain level, when in reality it should constantly be progressing.

The *antibiotic apocalypse that is nigh* is the desperate call from a system that is transfixed only by what the eye can see. Infection is not the problem. In reality, the problem is the weakness of the system or body, and infection exists to remind that it has to move away from its current beliefs and moorings that continue to enforce such weakness.

Research that continues to separate the agent of disease or infection from the rest of the system is representative of the physical level because it sees everything as separated and different, and falsely attributes power to something that in reality has none. Introducing poison, whether antibiotics or some other such *medicine*, into the body can only increase the weakness of the body. Obviously then infection

[2] James Gallagher, "Antibiotic 'apocalypse' warning," http://www.bbc.co.uk/news/health-21178718, 2013 (downloaded July 11, 2013).

will appear as drug-resistant because the poison has only functioned to further weaken any natural defense.

Shifting orientation to a vital or more energy-oriented paradigm, one begins to see that strength and weakness are a function of the play of energies and in a reality where infection seems to have the upper-hand, points to the necessity of changing the energetic relationship to strengthen the real fulcrum of control, the body, rather than attribute false power to something that is only a response.

Shifting orientation even further to the realm of thought or idea, the real focus of research needs to be on the inherent power of healing that we know exists in every human body and have viscerally experienced at some stage or another in our lives. Indeed that must become the focus of all future health approaches and research efforts.

If this journey of progress is pursued, not only will the *antibiotic apocalypse that is nigh* prove to be incorrect, but even the incredible threat of burgeoning medical expense of an ageing population felt now in the USA and also in other parts of the world be more directly addressed. The Health and Human Services Department expectation that the health share of GDP will continue its historical upward trend, reaching 19.5 percent of GDP by 2017, for instance,[3] will be reversed, and the budget will be forever balanced allowing future Presidents to truly embark on a path of building strength from within.

Facebook: David or Goliath?

Analyzing what could be next for Facebook is to a large extent going to depend on the context of analysis. If one were to go by the recently released Facebook movie *The Social Network*, the context comes across as a run-of-the-mill story of the past rather than a defining driver of the future. It is not the possibility of global shift, of Facebook being a key stimulus in accelerating the much needed and in fact inevitable shift from the current *vital* milieu to a more meaningful *mental* milieu that comes across in the movie, but rather the

[3] HealthAffairs, "Health spending projections through 2017: The Baby-boom generation is coming to Medicare," http://content.healthaffairs.org/content/early/2008/02/26/hlthaff.27.2.w145.full.pdf+html (2008; downloaded July 11, 2013).

success of a venture that has been intricately woven with the all too known small human themes that represent a humanity of the past, rather than a humanity of the future.

It is lengthy litigations, intellectual property struggles, power struggles, and frustrated or un-flourishing love that are key scenes and themes, all the etchings and motives of a vital world, that are propped up as the drivers of the Facebook phenomenon. In my mind, this is a gross misinterpretation and misrepresentation of the promise of Facebook. And the gravity of this misinterpretation is clear from a few summary signs, such as the unanimous *A* rating by Yahoo Movies critics, *A–* rating by over 800 users a few days after the movie screened, and the movie's topping the box office on opening weekend.[4]

But then again, if it is a vital world we live in, then it is the vital dynamics so well portrayed in the movie that the majority is going to find attractive. And yet, Mark Zuckerburg on his Facebook profile states "I'm trying to make the world a more open place by helping people connect and share."[5] This aspiration is clearly representative of a key movement that must occur for the vital to shift to the mental at the macro or global level.

At a micro-level, the dysfunction or common characteristics of the vital are represented by movements such as fear, greed, and selfish desire that in a fractal scheme of things (where a fractal is a pattern that repeats itself on different scales) manifests on a larger scale in such things as lengthy litigations, power struggles, and frustrated love that are the very stuff of the movie about Facebook. On a still larger scale, this pattern manifests in the macro-level dysfunction we see playing itself at the global level today—unsustainable business practices, large corporate Goliath-like monopolies seeking only to exercise their self-perceived right to appropriate all resources for their own use and profit, with all human beings being relegated to the status of *asset* or *liability*, among others—the all too common stories

[4] The Hollywood Reporter, "'Social's' $23 mil solid start tops box office," http://www.hollywoodreporter.com/news/socials-23-mil-solid-start-28668 (2010; downloaded July 11, 2013).

[5] Mark Zuckerburg, https://www.facebook.com/zuck (2010; downloaded July 11, 2013).

most large entities almost unconsciously play out because that is the implicit nature of monopoly alive today.

It is amidst this backdrop, this context, where unnatural monopolies intend on prolonging their devastating grip on humanity—the macro-level vital milieu—that phenomenon such as Facebook becomes immensely important. For not only does Facebook potentially "make the world a more open place by helping people connect and share", but more importantly it allows collectivities and communities that can challenge the status quo to more easily come into being. It is such communities that can challenge Monopoly, that allow David to overcome Goliath. The movement from the vital to the mental also needs the emergence of identity—of individual identity—this is critical, and Facebook allows an audience to gather around instances and expression of identity, thereby strengthening that identity.

In its own trajectory, Facebook must embrace the possibilities that allow the shift from the vital to the mental. It must move away from the gravitation of its Facematch beginnings and the trappings of the themes that have made *The Social Network* apparently so popular, to its David overcoming Goliath promise.

"Here Is the Future": My Interaction with Lars Dalgaard, CEO of Success Factors

I was a speaker representing Stanford University Medical Center (SUMC) at the SuccessFactors 2010 Conference. While I presented SUMC's recent developments in the performance management area, I want to focus on an interaction I had with Lars Dalgaard, CEO of SuccessFactors.

Lars launched the conference and passionately spoke about SuccessFactors' growth and product plans. It is interesting to see an organization grow as rapidly as his in the course of only 10 years. In 2010 SuccessFactors had about 80,00,000 users worldwide. No doubt such rapid growth is itself a sign of effectively promising to move the needle on established practices from the status quo (seed/physical) and the irrationally assertive (vital) to the more rational or mental possibilities in the HR field, which is sorely in need of progressive thinking on many different fronts.

After his address, I walked to the stage and introduced myself to Lars. I had a copy of my book *Connecting Inner Power with Global Change*, and presented this to him saying, *Here is the future.* He replied saying, "I can see the conviction in your eyes. I will read it."

Perhaps Lars quickly grasped or will grasp why I approached him. But nonetheless, I will elaborate:

1. SuccessFactors continues to create some powerful tools that are now focused on Business Execution through mobilizing human resources. Goal management, performance management, compensation management, succession planning, and work-based collaboration are key elements of this approach.
2. Effective use of these tools will definitely help an organization more effectively execute on business goals.
3. This does not though necessarily equate to continued business success. If a business is headed in the wrong direction to begin with, then all that the application of SuccessFactors Business Execution tools will do is expedite the failure of the business. This will be the case because now a set of goals, measurements, and actions will be organized much more effectively around the misdirection to accelerate failure rather than success.
4. The choice of such business direction is in fact the critical issue, precisely because in today's uncertain times, many base assumptions that global business has grown up with are being severely challenged.
5. In my opinion, these challenges are in fact the result/reaction of a purposeful, conscious, fractal-based world system, that is insisting that economy, business, and person cut to the chase and realize that big issues out there have their origin in small patterns in here at the level of the person.
6. Paradoxically, the choice of business direction is more than anything else a function of the consciousness a decision-maker lives in, the result of small patterns of perception, awareness, and assumptions that define that consciousness.
7. Human resource focused software has to get to this level of granularity of helping people and organizations more effectively

manage the base patterns that create much of the dysfunction we continue to see at every level of organizational complexity.

8. Further, there is a direction to the development of the world system, and hence economies, markets, and industries that is revealed by the fractal for progress synonymous with progress at each of these levels.
9. In my opinion, the real winners in the ERP/HR software space are not necessarily the SuccessFactors, SAPs, Oracles, and PeopleSofts of the world, but those software organizations that are able to bring the pattern-based reality of organizational and market dynamics with their underlying links to human-based seed-patterns into focus. It is these patterns that need to be altered for true progress, regardless of level, to take place.

Google vs China

Who are we? Are we cogs in a machine whose very movements and thoughts are to be programed and controlled by a State? Can what benefits the larger business playing field be taken as law in determining how the individual should conduct herself or himself in life? Is that the meaning of this fantastic world journey that we are all on together?

Let us assume that, on one hand, there is a journey of progress that China is currently on. Hence, it is self-impelled to traverse the physical, vital, and mental phases of its journey. In its current state, the world is primarily viewed from a command-and-control perspective. Citizens are assets to be mobilized by central state machinery for the benefit of the State, which both the central machinery and the citizens exist for, solely. Obviously, freedom of expression is curtailed. And obviously, there is nothing wrong with invasion of privacy so long as what the State believes to be true is not compromised. This is a deeply physical view of things in which all is subdued and held in tight control like a seed, and in this view any dynamic that disturbs this equation is to be shunned. Hence, it is perhaps fair to say that China in its journey is currently at the physical level. Now, there has of course been a lot of progress on the business front, but we can make the case that this vital-type progress has served the essentially physical orientation.

This orientation is also out of sync with what we are proposing to be the fundamental urge of the integrated world system. The urge is an implicit movement, embedded in the DNA of life, to successfully traverse the journey from the physical to the vital to the mental. This means that such views as has created the operative reality in China does need to, in one way or another, be transcended.

Enter the possibility that the Internet has bought forward and the recent interactions between Google and China. These events challenge the physical-phase world view held by China and, if successful, would cause the China journey to progress to the vital phase. Remember that in the physical phase, humans are assets to be mobilized by machinery – they are cogs in a wheel. In the vital phase, there is experimentation and freedom to express. This is a critical phase; for only in completing it can the truer identity resident in each human breast even begin to come to the surface.

Hence, from the larger perspective of closing the gap or aligning the implicit urge resident in the integrated world system with China's journey, intervention and boldness by companies such as Google is perhaps warranted, and arguably gives them the moral right to lift Internet-based censorship. For China to recognize this would be a big step forward.

Introducing another aspect into this analysis, the question, then, is what side of the struggle should one land on? Is it surprising that companies such as Microsoft and Hewlett-Packard, who have supposedly built themselves by and stood for human freedom should now refuse to comment on censorship[6] and instead placate the issue by stressing the importance of China as a market? In one way of looking at it, it should be surprising. In another, not at all—because both Microsoft and Hewlett-Packard, and many, many other companies the world over are part of a Business journey which is itself only at the vital level, where each often seeks for irrational growth, likely regardless of true cost to humanity.

[6] Richard Waters, "Silicon Valley questions Google stance," http://www.ft.com/intl/cms/s/0/c0eb89e4-0207-11df-8b56-00144feabdc0.html#axzz2YIQFcCUR (2010; downloaded July 11, 2013).

So now, we have a play of the China journey, The business journey, that is both stagnated, and the boldness of a company like Google that is perhaps an instrument leveraged to help fulfill the implicit urge for progress in nature.

The questions are as to can China win in a struggle that is fundamentally opposed to the urge implicit in the movement of a world system? If it is to maintain its current view of things, then at what cost? How much human possibility will be suppressed? How much human blood will be shed? Will it have to collapse and splinter as a country so that some of it has a chance to fulfill this fundamental urge of nature? On the other hand, can businesses, such as Microsoft, Hewlett-Packard, among many other businesses, continue to operate with such bottom-line business orientation only, in a world that is an integrated, intelligent, and purposeful world that implicitly seeks for true, harmonious, and sustainable growth? If they do so, then at what cost?

Both these stagnated journeys will find themselves continuing on their ultimately irresistible journeys. The protagonists of these journeys can do so consciously and pay a lower price for doing that now, or they will be forced to do so unconsciously and in such case, they will pay a much higher price than they ever imagined. This is inevitable in a world that seeks for its own progress.

In another way of looking at it, we are saying that there is an overriding world journey that will progress at any cost. When it is opposed in its movement, by stagnated journeys like those of China or Business, then instruments are leveraged to intersect with the stagnated entities to cause their progress. Progress can be accelerated by such opposition; but ultimately, sustainable shift comes about by shifting the base pattern at the root of the fractal. The root is none other than the person and the embodied attitudes, perceptions, and behaviors that animate a person.

The Future of Consulting

Like oxygen, money should be thought of as an impersonal force flowing to facilitate activity. Oxygen is available to all without charge, and the more one maintains the health of their body, the more oxygen can freely flow through it to create a reinforcing loop of health. If one engages in activities that diminish the health of the body, whether through ingestion of toxins of various kinds or through lack of sleep or exercise, the pathways in the body get obstructed and gradually the ability to draw oxygen diminishes. This is like a reinforcing loop that accelerates the deterioration of the body. That same amount of oxygen that was being drawn by one person now flows elsewhere. In this manner, nature optimizes the maintenance of her constructs so that those constructs that are in harmony with a progressive and sustainable way of being continue in this state.

Similarly, if there is positive organizational activity, money should automatically flow to that organization to sustain it. In the case of the oxygen flow, there is a natural set of checks and balances that alters the flow of oxygen; hence, when an organization, be it a human, animal, or plant, has ceased from sustainable existence, the oxygen flow is reduced. In the case of more complex human-made organizations, be they corporations, not-for-profits, or societies, the automaticity is obfuscated because of the interference of a common orientation particular to human beings—the physical–vital orientation (physical component—viewing tomorrow's world as the same as yesterday's world; vital component—viewing the world as a field of exploitation).

The physical–vital orientation is like a node that draws activity to it. Only, it cannot be sustained because it tends to be inherently out of sync with the larger system. It conducts activity for its own sake rather than for the good of the system, and for a larger balance to be restored, the orientation of organizations has to move toward a mental—intuitional orientation (mental component—viewing the world as a play of ideas; intuitional component—syncing activities with a purposeful, contextual world system). In such an orientation, the right relationship between self and the larger system more easily comes into focus, and the dynamics so initiated are more naturally aligned with the purpose and sustainability of the larger system. Even the fractal nature of life may then be more clearly perceived and the ripple effects of a feeling, thought, or act on larger and larger organizations more easily comprehended.

Yet, the larger and containing system has its own purpose, logic, and way of being, and ultimately all physical–vital orientations are forced to complete journeys to yield to the mental–intuitional orientation, failing which the stagnated organizations face extinction. When today we are faced with challenges as fundamental as climate change, which threaten to alter our very material bases, this is nothing other than a defense mechanism set in motion by the containing system to ensure its own sustainability. Either the stagnated organizations change their mode of being, that is, make the transition from a physical–vital orientation to a mental–intuitional orientation, or they face extinction.

Organizations with physical–vital orientations exist with their small self as reference, and seek to fulfill their existence in small ways that they think will enrich their existence. Hence, they may act to fulfill desire, or short-sighted ambition, or to conquer other organizations. In the final analysis, though, such orientation is self-defeating since it blocks or veils possible symbiosis with the larger, contextual system. In the mental–intuitional orientation, the need for symbiosis becomes clearer at the outset, and the possibility and purpose inherent in the contextual system finds easier expression through the strivings of the constructs anchored in such mental–intuitional orientation. The flow of money, resource, idea, and capability becomes a relatively seamless exchange between the seemingly isolated organization—be it a person or a corporation, and as in the interchange of oxygen, all proceed in an optimized way so long as such mental–intuitional orientation is the cornerstone of its operation. In other words, the cost of money is reduced.

Over the last few centuries, most organizations have existed in the physical–vital state to aggrandize their conception of themselves, that is, their isolated self. Business principles that epitomize competition and victory over other corporations have been promoted. All resources, including human resources, are viewed as assets or liabilities. This approach has left a long and seemingly unending trail of debris and destruction behind it. The time for such orientation is now ending. What is most needed now is a transition from the essentially physical–vital to the essentially mental–intuitional way of being. This is true for all organizations regardless of scale. Hence, it is true of an idea, of a person, a team, a department, a corporation, a market, and a society. After all, each of these organizations draws its way of being from the essential combination of physical, vital, mental, and intuitional building blocks that then define its existence. Further, the combination of building blocks that define a society's way of being can only be changed when there is a parallel seed change at the level of the person. Hence, there is a fractal reality that animates organization. For a pattern once in existence at the base level tends to reinforce itself on larger and larger scale.

Most organizations have reinforced yesterday's patterns in today's operations. They have learned how to reinforce their essential physical–vital orientation even by appropriating mental elements to do so. The mental capacities and capabilities are in service of a physical–vital outlook so that at the far-end, it seems that even possibilities like sustainability and CSR, that are generally themes one associates with the larger system and hence naturally to be more mental–intuitional in nature, are not really that possibility, but appendages that make the essential physical–vital reality look more compelling. The point is that the essential reality remains the same, and therefore its impact on society, through fractal pressure is also of almost the same nature as a physical–vital construct without this mental appendage. Nothing really changes then, and confrontational walls like climate change that challenge and destroy have to be erected by the conscious, purposeful world system.

What organizations need the most, whether they realize it or not, is this transition from the essentially physical–vital to the essentially mental–intuitional, starting at the root—the level of the person. It is only so that global recessions, climate change, and other massive debilitating dynamics will seize to be, because it is only then that the conscious and purposeful world system will be assured of its own comprehensive sustainability in which more and more organizational constructs are expressing both uniqueness and diversity by seizing on game-changing mental and intuitional dynamics that push these possibilities to the surface.

Fractal system's architecture is about seeing the deeper relationship between individual organizations and the contextual world system that we are all a part of. It is about becoming aware of the fractal links that bind one layer of organization with the next, from the micro to the macro. It is about becoming aware of the fundamental building blocks that determine the active dynamics of a layer of organization—the physical, the vital, and the mental building blocks. It is about rearranging these fundamental building blocks so that the mental–intuitional leads and the physical–vital follows, thereby forever and sustainably altering the dynamics of society and environment. This is the future that organizational operation has to move toward. Obviously, this is also the future that consulting has to move toward.

Yet today, there are consulting companies that continue to assist corporations in maintaining and winning the short-sighted, self-defeating physical–vital game. The Big Four—Pricewaterhouse Coopers, Deloitte Touche Tohmatsu, Ernst & Young, and Cap Gemini—fall into this category. So, do other consulting companies such as McKinsey, BCG, A.T. Kearney, Booz, and Bain, even though they charge a higher price for it. It is imperative that the world views of these consulting companies change radically so that they can become agents in bringing about fractal system's architecture type consulting that can alone truly help longer term and sustainable existence of any scale of organization. Even the younger and more sustainably oriented consulting companies, of the likes of Business for Social responsibility, SustainAbility, and BluSkye, while tending to appropriate more of the mental–intuitional elements still seem to continue to reinforce the essential physical–vital reality of corporations. Hence, the fractal-based analytics and foundation being created by organizations such as Aurosoorya become very important because it is focused on assisting organizations make the transition from an essentially physical–vital to an essentially mental–intuitional way of being. An approach of this nature will alone create lasting and secure sustainability because it addresses the issues of unsustainability at its absolute core.

A New Bases and Standard of Financial and Economic Activity

The support stone of the old stable arch of financial operation was removed in 1971, when the gold standard was exited. According to the World Gold Council, only 20-cubic meters of gold has been mined through human history. This is the consummate symbol of the physical or seed phase of financial evolution. Physical implying that the world and its laws are fixed, determined by what the eye can see. Under the Bretton Woods system, the gold price was fixed in dollars at US$35 per ounce, and other currencies' exchange rates were fixed to the dollar. Hence, gold anchored all currencies. This meant that the money supply was limited. This also meant that it was hard for inflation to rise and that bubbles of all kinds would largely be avoided.

As John Authers, in his insightful book *The Fearful Rise of Markets*[7] points out, by removing the gold standard the rules of world trade changed overnight. The price of gold rose, which meant that governments and traders who had been accumulating surpluses of dollars, found that their dollars purchased substantially less gold. This caused currencies to float (as opposed to being anchored to the dollar) and exchange rates to diverge. But most significantly, oil exporters, represented by OPEC now received far less gold for oil. This caused OPEC to raise the price of oil. This further triggered inflation in the US and a weakening of the dollar, which led to a further increase in oil prices. The US, hence, and the rest of the world, thus found itself tied to a new global standard—the oil standard. Irrational monopolies of all kinds, to hold on to limited interpretations of power were reinforced and the world economic activity continued feverishly and unsustainably into the vital phase.

Oil is a flowing source of energy and a representative of the vital phase. And this is what the shift from gold to oil signifies. However, it is not openly and easily available energy, such as exists in the Sun, but the result of dead and crushed plants and animals existing now as fluid in the depths of the Earth. The energetic possibility contained in this crushed material is in the first place obtained from solar energy. Hence, oil is a derivative energy obtained from the past, made from essentially physical–vital beings that once existed on the surface of the Earth. Given this, its utility has to be finite, and this is borne out by the phenomena of peak oil, which suggests that once the

[7] John Authers, *The Fearful Rise of Markets: Global Bubbles, Synchronized Meltdowns, and How to Prevent them in the Future* (Upper Saddle River: FT Press, 2010).

extraction of oil has peaked, there is less of it available in the Earth. Estimates suggest that we have already passed that point in time. In other words, oil as a medium of energy, and even as a symbol of financial operation, has only a finite life. But during that life, symbolically speaking, being of the essence of the physical–vital, we can expect its era to be characteristically physical–vital. That is an increasing energy driven by myopia, rather than order, driven by selfishness rather than selflessness, driven by destruction, rather than creation.

This trend also has an implication for what kind of standard will be created next. Following the notion of the ubiquitous fractal journey, with base orientation shifting from the physical to the vital to the mental, it is clear that an attempt to create a *mental* standard needs to be next, that is, for progress to happen. The physical standard was handed down to us through centuries of habit. The vital standard was driven by a perception of exploiting limitation – the oil standard emerged, not through holistic thought, but through limited vital-bound thought. With the reality of peak oil, the next standard could very well be some other limited resource like water. But that would mean entering another round of perhaps even heightened global irrationality. The standard must therefore become something that should shift us away from the control and rigidity of the physical, embodied in the gold standard, and the recklessness and irrational monopolies of the vital, embodied in the oil standard, to the encouragement of bottom-up and globally distributed innovation, perhaps embodied in a solar-like energy standard.

Solar-like energy is by definition globally distributed and available forever. Money flow and creation of wealth needs to be tied to the ability to harness this type of energy, which in effect is infinite, which means that progress and development can in effect become infinite. Solar energy, for instance, in its passive action already fosters many ecosystem services, and therefore foundation of commerce whether we realize. If it or something like it, solar-like energy, could also more consciously, thoughtfully, and actively be harnessed, way beyond everything that is currently being done today by all the futurists around the world, then a new standard of wealth, that is non-monopolistic and available to all through *acts of creativity*, would come into being. This creativity, measured in how such solar-like energy is being harnessed, stored, used, and leveraged, could be the basis of new money creation, and in effect become a new standard for ordering global commerce.

When we ask the question as to "Who controls the gold that money will buy?", it is clear that because of its relative scarcity, there will always be only a few in power. When the gold standard existed, it was clear that the USA was the sole power in the world. When we ask the question as to "Who controls the oil that money will buy?" today's reality of cartels, government–corporate–military oligopolies, corporate monopolies with all their attendant ugliness becomes real. When we ask the question as to "Who controls the solar-like energy that money will buy?" the possibility of the shift from monopolistic to democratic systems of power becomes real.

That solar-like energy will be used as the standard to anchor all commerce is inevitable. The sooner we realize this and take steps to reorient our systems of business and economy around this, the sooner will truer sustainability come into being.

Reflections on Financial Crises

The Flash Crash of May 6, 2010: How Out of Touch with Reality Are We?

What the flash crash of May 6, 2010, really affirmed was how out of touch we are with the reality we have created. In a few minutes, the hard-work of hundreds of thousands of people toiling day-after-day to earn an honest living was by some estimates negated because of automated sell orders. In a few minutes, the ideals that many hold, high ideals of democracy, equality, fraternity where all citizens are treated equally and have a say in how life should develop came crashing to the ground as the surge of sell-orders, not motivated by a balanced perspective seeking the greater good, but motivated by that same physical–vital consciousness seeking its own selfish gain, played itself out yet once again.

In a few minutes, the absurdity of what we continue to create smashed into our fragile order with its massive face of chaos. In a few minutes, we reinforced the tremendous price we are willing to pay for a continued physical–vital way of being. Our karma boomerangs at us with tidal-wave-like disaster and like the increasingly powerful storm systems of climate change confront us with the poor choices of our own doings.

Instead of facing the question of the absurdity of our global financial system, where we have effectively given up control to an absolute casino mentality, we seem to be more concerned with creating circuit breakers to avoid future flash crashes.[1] This is no doubt of some practical importance, but unfortunately pushes back the dealing with the real issue confronting the very survival of the ideals we believe to be true and self-evident—democracy, liberty, and equality—and that of ensuring a reasoned and sustainable progress of our global civilization.

For, in reality, the continually increasing sophistication of technology further increases the power of monopolized flows of money, that are not monopolized by reason, but by an unfortunate and uncaring short-sighted mentality of speculation. The risks are now too large, and the price we will pay for not taking action to reverse the global monopolization of money power that we have inadvertently allowed to arise out of continuing to live in a physical–vital consciousness, will be the continued economic and even cultural and ideological weakening of larger and larger regions of the world—Greece, Spain, Ireland, Iceland, Japan, the USA, and the EU (European Union)—as is already evident.

The signs are clear and action to reverse the inadvertent monopolization of the very power—money power—that has come to drive our progress needs to be taken now.

The Common Response to Crises

Every time an economy threatens to fail, it results in upheaval in the global economy, and the same inadequate responses from the financial and political communities.

I believe that the underlying cause is continued adherence to a simple linear view of things, when in fact the world we live in is an integrated, purposeful, conscious, and fractal-based world system. Within this system, there is a special class of journeys—the physical–vital–mental journey that is the key to aligning with the underlying system to therefore allow the system to work its magic in our lives.

[1] Michael Mackenzie, "Breaking circuit to halt repeat of 'flash crash'," http://www.ft.com/intl/cms/s/0/673b7bae-6e6b-11df-ad16-00144feabdc0.html#axzz2YIQFcCUR (2010; downloaded July 11, 2013).

From time-to-time, there are more system-based theories of this nature that find their way into the mainstream press. I remember pausing when in the *Financial Times* I read an opinion on the Greek Crisis coming to the USA.[2] The author Niall Ferguson, also the author of *Ascent of Money*,[3] referred to the *fractal geometry of debt* in suggesting that the Greek crises, Iceland crises, and Ireland crises were all similar, just on different scales. This is the first time I have seen an analysis of this nature in the *Financial Times*, and to me it illustrates how the mainstream is beginning to move away from linear to even fractal-based system thinking. I will also quickly mention that what the author, Niall Ferguson, was pointing out, is in fact an illustration of a contrary journey—a journey that is led by the physical or vital component, rather than the mental component. If we were to replace this contrary journey with the physical–vital–mental journey, in effect the financial crises will begin to be more effectively solved.

Why such tremendous power has been given to only one dimension of life, the unrefined economic aim when life is quite evidently multidimensional, is the underlying question. This dogma of economic growth often at any cost, and the demand that all in an economy exist as assets to further the one-dimensional goals of the economy is quite frankly an outmoded way of being quite simply rooted in a physical–vital orientation.

Its time is fast drawing to a close, and if we listen carefully enough in the silence behind the actions we see that this physical–vital orientation is seeking for completion of its journey, to tend toward the mental orientation. Hints of what this may look like flash into the inner mind: the meaning of wealth expanded; money de-monopolized so that numerous communities, rather than Central Banks, have power over their respective destinies; creative activity democratized—themes I will continue to return to in these chapters.

Every time an economy falls, the same rote actions are followed: austerity measures proclaimed, watchful eyes cast on debt repayments,

[2] Niall Ferguson, "A Greek crisis is coming to America," http://www.ft.com/intl/cms/s/0/f90bca10-1679-11df-bf44-00144feab49a.html#axzz2YIQFcCUR (2010; downloaded July 11, 2013).

[3] Niall Ferguson, *The Ascent of Money: A Financial History of the World* (New York: Penguin Books, 2009).

stress levels among the common people escalated, potential fire walls set up, and vultures on the side lines waiting to swoop in for the kill. It is interesting to note that in a staff paper from the IMF[4] where thinking on financial crises has been fixed for 30 years, it is being proposed that Central Bankers expand their portfolio of tools, beyond interest rate adjustment. This is a huge change, clearly moving from the physical to the vital. But it cannot or will not be enough.

It is time to examine the system behind the system and enter into the deeper logic that is beginning to surface.

Making Sense of Market Crises

Established wisdom suggests that one crisis is the same as the next. Hence, each of the following crises tends to be addressed in similar ways.

1. The 1973–1974 Bear Market
2. The 1987 Synchronized Global Crash
3. The 1990s Japanese Asset Bubble and the South East Asian Crises
4. The 2000 Dot-Com Crisis
5. The 2004 Housing Crisis
6. The 2010 Greek Debt Crisis

However, I propose a contextual framework against which each of these crises has to be assessed. This framework is based on a universal pattern of sustainable progress that is very commonly visible and is summarized by the physical–vital–mental journey.

I start from the 1973–1974 crises because that was a result of a major shift in global economic reality when the Gold Standard was abandoned. For a good three decades, the global economy had functioned in a relatively predictable, stable way, always maintaining the status quo because all currencies were pegged to the US dollar. This

[4] Chris Giles, "IMF floats plan to raise targets for inflation," http://www.ft.com/intl/cms/s/0/46c20458-1775-11df-87f6-00144feab49a.html#axzz2YIQFcCUR (2010; downloaded July 11, 2013).

state of affairs was more like the inert seed of a plant, the physical state where the world is what the eye can see. Little inflation exists, the money supply is fixed, and what happens is the result of stable recycling of possibilities. This state can be thought of as the starting point in the physical–vital–mental trajectory.

When the Gold Standard was abandoned though, currencies deanchored from the US dollar and began to float, and there was a lot more volatility that was introduced into the global situation. What had been known and what we had relied on for decades was abandoned, and no nation could anymore be assured of the wealth in its possession. Hence, another standard was sought and the transition from the physical to the vital stage was securely put into place.

The oil embargo of 1973 precipitated the emergence of the Oil Standard, giving OPEC far more power on the global economic stage. Prices all over the world began to escalate and dynamics of inflation reentered the global economic situation with force. This resulted in the 1973–1974 bear market in the USA and elsewhere and accelerated the destructive vital dynamics that has had relatively free reign over the last four decades.

By 1987, there was the first global economic synchronized crash. All major stock markets around the world lost significant value at the same time. From a rational perspective, this makes no sense. Different regions around the world and different markets should be subject to different market conditions and a more local cyclicality in investment rhythm. For markets and regions around the world to divert from this implies that dynamics have become irrational. Such irrationality is a sure sign that the vital level has become far more active since is now aggressive self-seeking that drives things.

Subsequent crises of the 1990s, such as the Japanese Asset Crises, the Asian Crises, and the Russian financial crises quickly came into being as money unleashed from rationality and reason sought a home where it could make quick returns regardless of larger issues of sustainability.

Rationality, reason, purpose, and sustainability are the dynamics that are more prevalent when the mental stage is reached. That must be the aim of any policy maker and regulator. The good news is that impelled by the ubiquitous journey in circumstance, the first decade of the 2000s has seen this urge coming more to the forefront.

Hence, in 2000, the Dot-Com Crisis was of a very different nature. This signified the possibility of the mental stage where a whole new infrastructure allowing power to shift from monopoly to democracy more practically came into being.

The US Housing Crisis of 2004 and on, powerfully brought to the surface some of the perversities in a Finance led solely by the vital level. This is the shadow that emerges to remind us of where never to go again. The 2007–2009 Bear Market was more of a tug-of-war between the past and the future, with the past, represented by the dynamics inherent in industries such as pharmaceutics, oil and gas, retail, food and agriculture vying for further attention and investment to continue their self-serving patterns of the past, against the new dynamics represented by the Internet that we all know has begun to arise at the same time.

The Greek Debt Crisis and the European Union Sovereign Debt Crises and the Occupy Movement bring into relief the whole question of wealth. What is it? Is it the one-dimensional metric that has driven the whole one-sided vital development of the last four decades to its current state of obvious instability or is it something else that is multidimensional and factors in culture, spirit, and human possibility.

When viewed in this manner, we can more clearly see what must be done to usher in a period of global financial and business sustainability.

What the *Occupy* Movement Represents

On September 17, 2011, the Occupy Movement started with an estimated 1,000 people gathering to Occupy Wall Street. By October 15, 2011, this movement spread to 951 cities in 82 countries to form a single global protest. This single global protest is a unique phenomenon and represents the visceral urge to move the global business machinery to a more sustainable way of operating so that all layers of society and environment are figured in and balanced in the reconfigured *business* equation that must result.

Government and Central Bank action the world over, following the financial crises of 2008–2010, has obviously been focused on the short term. But let us look at the nature of their short-term interventions.

They have done much to allow the flow of money to continue as per vital-level growth models. Therefore, they have sucked up junk assets, lowered interest rates, and forgiven parasitic corporations. This intervention is perhaps warranted, because in the absence of this, the world as we know it, would have changed too rapidly and social unrest risen meteorically. Rebellion, *a la* the French Revolution would have become the norm and Bastille Days the common nature of day. This may still happen if a longer-term mental outlook is not quickly worked out. That is why the seed of response has to change.

The Occupy Wall Street Movement reflected this inability to truly move things to the mental level.

The fundamental problem has been that value has been equated with vital level as opposed to mental-level value. This is a form of Nazism. It is a bastardization of all that is sacred, in which standards of excellence are equated to contours on the surface or on the face of things, as opposed to the uniqueness inherent in development and culture and civilization. When value of assets sync up so that investment in India and investment in Brazil are not related anymore to the unique need in India and the unique need in Brazil, but simply to an investor's overall level of fear or greed, then we know that this bastardization has become the way of life. It is imperative that this be reversed in its tracks. The financial system as a whole has to be overhauled for this to happen.

Our current global crisis is unique. It has never happened before in recorded history. This is evident from some simple observations. First, the very playing field of all businesses is uniquely challenged by the phenomenon of climate change; it is not negative local effects from local action any more, but negative global effects from local action now—a dangerous situation. Ecosystems get destroyed as temperatures rise, and the very resource base of any modern-day business is permanently crippled. The perception that it is an exploitable resource base is flawed at its root, and it is the fundamental perception that has to change to right this. This base pattern, decidedly vital in nature, creates many contrary or stagnated journeys in its wake. Climate change is the ultimate macro wake-up call pointing to the absolute urgency of shifting the base pattern at its very root.

If we are at the boundary between the vital and mental way of being, then that has to become the context of truly addressing the current crises. This is not a one-time crisis. We have been living in this overarching vital-level arc since at least the birth of the Amsterdam Stock Exchange, if not even before that. Crises have occurred because of the bubbles that keep bursting. And this will continue until we make the needed shift into the mental way of operating. All crises have been opportunities to shift away from dysfunction. Instead as a result of the crises, we have quickly always tried to put things back to the way they were. The Crash of 1929, preceding the Great Depression, has been likened as being similar to today's global crisis. Some important measures were taken then to reverse the bastardization of value. But little was done to democratize markets to really move to the creativity, uniqueness, and sustainability more inherent at the mental level.

This is at the crux. We need to democratize markets so that truer local and sustainable innovation is unleashed. Instead we began a much longer arc that integrated more and more of the world into the unstable equation of bubbled business and markets. The integration, synchronization, and bastardization have reached the limit of its playing field. We are at the inevitable end of a dysfunctional way of being. In some respects, if we assume that we live in a purposeful world, then we can see that such an integration may have its purpose in which it ensures that there can be no havens that will not finally want to change.

I think this is borne out by the developments of October 15, where 951 cities in 82 countries have joined in a single global protest.

Summary

Market crises can be better understood and addressed if we understand the context within which they occur. In this chapter, context has been positioned as related to development along the ubiquitous flower model. Knowing at what stage of the growth from seed to flower a crisis is synonymous with, allows a far more intelligent response to the crisis. The nature, for example that of the Dot-Com crises, is fundamentally different from the nature of the US Housing Crisis. The former, for example, is a definite push into the future. The latter is a dampening pull from the past. The former helps us cross the threshold into the realm of the flower. The latter is a gravitation back to some level driven by the physical–vital. At stake is the whole question of progressive civilization versus prolonged stagnation, and hence being able to recognize the difference between crises is critical.

Reflections from the 2012 US Presidential Elections

Many very pertinent issues relevant to true and sustainable global development surfaced in the recent 2012 US Presidential Debates. To place these in context, we first consider a chapter from earlier US political development in the life of the 33rd president of the USA, Harry Truman. We also consider a general philosophical view offered from the summit of a hill or mountain that provides insight into political party development. These considerations lead us into some of the issues and lessons for global leaders that surfaced in the recent 2012 US Presidential Elections.

The Offices of the Small Are Dead. Long Live the Office of the Future!

Recently, I watched Truman, the movie. In contrast to the prevalent dynamics of our times, it was refreshing to see the story of a person who becomes the US President without trying to or without the desire to do so.

And yet, there were incredibly significant decisions that Truman made – the containment of Communism by supporting South Korea against North Korea, the use of atomic weapons to defeat Japan, the rebuilding of Europe using US funds after World War II, the recognition of Israel, the ending of racial discrimination in the armed forces, and the instinct to veto an act that monitored the activities and powers of labor unions in a time when Business was strongly incarnating the unrefined vital dynamic – among others.

Many of these are historic decisions that have altered the course of the world, and to even debate if these were the right decisions, one has at the very least to not be bound by the dynamics of the small self. In terms of the ubiquitous fractal journey, this means beginning to move away from the physical–vital (P-V) orientation toward the mental–intuitional orientation. Further this movement toward the menntal–intuitional orientation is seen as necessary and inevitable for any progressive or sustainable organization, regardless of scale.

The P-V orientation is dictated by a sense of small boundedness (physical) and animated by the need of constantly fulfilling desires to satisfy that smallness (vital). In today's world, we see this dynamic alive everywhere.

Truman, because he was arguably less motivated by the P-V orientation, could more easily open to the M-I orientation. To consistently choose the M-I orientation over the P-V orientation becomes a rite of passage, an initiation, in which one progressively opens to dynamics of a different order. This means Truman conceivably became an instrument for something more progressive than perhaps he or others around him could imagine.

Perhaps his insistence that it was the Office of the President and not Truman who was more important, and his deliberate putting of himself into that state in his interactions with those around him, hints at this orientation that drove him, and to the initiation that had seized him.

In this day and age, the issues we are faced with are no less in magnitude than those the world had faced between 1940 and 1950. What manifested then as the struggle between freedom and small boundedness, the struggle between race equality and race superiority, the struggle between peace and war, the struggle toward a more holistic orientation of business as opposed to the continuance of business-as-usual, and the struggle for the use of money for selfless as opposed to selfish aims, has vastly amplified itself today. It is, therefore, the requirement of today to invite mental–intuitoinal initiation on a much larger scale. The P-V dynamics so alive in the institution of Business and Finance, and in the running of countries around the world, has to be replaced by the dynamics of M-I so that it is this possibility that leads the bounded, selfish P-V orientation.

But whereas in the 1950s, it was the few who led the many, the big difference today is that the many now have the chance to lead. The Arab Spring, the Occupy Movement, the EU Sovereign Debt Crises manifest in the Greek Rebellion, the Indian Anti-Corruption movement, the uprise in South America, among others, hang in balance waiting the incarnation of this greater dynamic.

It is the Office of the Future that must become alive, and that every individual and collectivity must help ground through initiation into M-I. Verily, the Office of the President must replicate and replace itself in fractal fashion by the similar yet different Office of the Future so that all presidents, all corporations, all organizations, all institutions, and all countries will be accountable solely to it.

The offices of the small are dead. Long live the Office of the Future!

The Way of the Summit: Some Insights for Election and Re-election

If you were to look down from the summit of a peak, you would perhaps see different paths etched into the ascending terrain. These paths of course all meet at the summit, and in fact merge at that plateau to become one. In their ascent though these paths may have started at different places, travelled through different conditions, and may or may not intersect, depending on what is encountered on their journeys.

The structure and dynamics of these paths shed insight into party politics and governance of a country, and understanding of these will benefit the presidential candidate or party that can so learn from them.

Imagine the summit as being the goal, the haloed destination of an intense pilgrimage a country may be undertaking to arrive finally at a foundation from which new journeys and possibilities can be envisioned. The starting point and articulated raison d'être of these paths may be democratic or republican, capitalist or socialist, or any other set of dichotomies or uniquenesses depending on the country one belongs to.

The field of fractal system architecture sheds insight into the dynamics of these ascending paths:

- A path that remains unique to itself represents a possibility needing to be worked out on its own. Clearly as far as governance of a country is concerned, it will be rare for proponents of such a unique path to remain in power indefinitely. This is simply because the foundation at the summit demands that different possibilities be integrated.
- A path that intersects with another may have stagnated before such an intersection takes place. If so, the shock of the intersection can cause both paths to re-examine their stagnation, address it, and move on wiser, through the next phase in their respective journeys.
- A path that intersects with another and merges with that so that neither is the same, but now is the synthesis of both paths, represents a coming together and a prelude to the pattern of the plateau at the summit. This is rare, but will likely signify a victory, and the increasing of that party's electorate.
- The spiral path that circles slowly upward is the path of nature. This is the default path that is activated again and again should the independent paths streaming up the peak never want to objectively consider the others it may encounter. Hence, it must exist so that each independent possibility can be given a turn in working itself out. Imagine the time taken for the spiral path to cross over the independent path as being one presidential term, or perhaps two, if there is more to be gained from that path at that time, in the scheme of things.

Any candidate would, therefore, be wise to ask:

- Is the path I am on wide enough to warrant another term? If not, the spiral path will ensure that power cedes to the other possibility.
- Is the path I am on ready to learn from the path I am now head-to-head with and create a synthesis that is greater than

either of the independent paths? If so, then power will likely remain here.

- Is the path I am on going to alter because it has truly learned from the intersection with another path? If so, then power will likely remain here.

Since all paths must merge at the top, that is, must create a whole that loses nothing of the best of each possibility, the repeating and ever-present question is, will the pilgrimage the country is on be broad enough to encompass many distinct possibilities?

If not, then nature may reveal the active volcano under the summit, and through the consequent outpouring of fresh lava, create materials and the terrain for the re-embarking on new journeys.

Living Other Lives: A Critique of the US 2012 Presidential Debates

In listening to both presidential candidates during the US 2012 presidential debates, it seemed that they were riddled with contradictions.

President Obama's general groundedness was a far cry from the 2008 presidential debates. It seemed that his trademark self-composure, self-confidence, and idealistic view of the world had all but evaporated. There were moments where that other self came forward, but in general, it was another Obama that stood in front of us on both evenings in October.

It was almost as though there were a great struggle in the being of the president. That voice of idealism and authenticity was still there, but it was subdued and overtaken by another voice. What was this other voice? Was this the voice of the reality of office? The voice perhaps, of the reality of all the politicking and of the endless compromise that an idealist needs to make to govern?

It seemed that President Obama is *living another life*, a life not quite in tune with the authenticity of who he is, and this lack of alignment was manifesting in the aloofness and lack of confidence we saw in general on the evenings in October. As per fractal system's architecture point of view, it may be that his voice and stance were being driven by a contrary journey led by the physical–vital rather than the mental–intuitional possibility.

On the other hand, Presidential Candidate and Governor Mitt Romney's voice seemed to carry more confidence, at least on the surface. But his voice too was riddled with contradiction. It did not carry the stamp of authenticity. It seemed more a party voice, trained to give the illusion of an effective commander-in-chief and representative of the republican dream.

For instance, he confidently spoke of how China has not been playing by the rules of the world, and that were he to become president, he would on day one label them as a currency manipulator. He also spoke of how Obamacare has essentially disadvantaged small- and medium-sized businesses by making the cost to hire employees too high. The problem is that his approach on China is going to do the very same thing – that is, severely disadvantage business. Assume he labels China as currency manipulators, and as a result they are forced to let the Yuan float freely. This will substantially escalate the cost of doing business for every single American enterprise This is because China has become the world's manufacturing base and is integrated into every supply chain of just about every company in the world. China is the top trading partner of the USA. YTD 18 percent of total US imports come from China—the highest proportion of any of its import partners. Further, after Canada and Mexico, China is the top export partner of US companies.[1]

So, the reality is that US business will be hit harder if Romney comes to office, because it will likely take more than four years to truly change ground conditions so that US manufacturers are integrated into every supply chain of even US companies.

Romney's real voice, his authentic self came forward in his closing remarks on the evening of October 16, 2012. Particularly what felt very authentic were his statements: "My-my passion probably flows from the fact that I believe in God. And I believe we're all children of the same God. I believe we have a responsibility to care for one another. I-I served as a missionary for my church. I served as a pastor

[1] US Census Bureau, "Top trading partners," http://www.census.gov/foreign-trade/statistics/highlights/top/top1208yr.html (2012; downloaded July 11, 2013).

in my congregation for about 10 years. I've sat across the table from people who were out of work and worked with them to try and find new work or to help them through tough times".[2]

So, Romney too, is really *living another life*. The general lack of authenticity, though veiled by apparent confidence, is probably due to this. Were he to become the president and were he to reappear for the debates four years hence, there are three possible stances he would take.

If he were riddled with contradiction, as we saw Obama so riddled, we may conclude that perhaps here is an idealist, and the pressure of office has caused infighting between separate voices in his self, as in the case of President Obama. If he were confident, we may be left to conclude one of the two things. First, here is someone who is perhaps a seasoned and habitual liar and has lost his soul in some deal made along the way. Second, and certainly the more difficult of the two, here is someone who really walks his truth and has made a difference in the affairs of the country and the world.

Clearly, what we want is a president who exhibits the last of these possibilities. We know though, that this is the most difficult and will require the President to truly become a creative force, and new root pattern of a brave and bold repeating journey set to sweep the world stage.

Whether an Obama or a Romney, let us hope that this—a creative force putting into effect brave and needed root patterns—is what we always get, not just in the USA but in all the countries of the world.

Foreign Policy for a Peaceful World

Presidential Candidate and Governor Mitt Romney concluded his remarks[3] in the Foreign Policy section of the US 2012 Presidential Election debate with the thought that the USA is the hope of the

[2] CBS News, "Presidential Debate Part 2," http://www.cbsnews.com/8301-250_162-57533848/transcript-second-2012-presidential-debate-part-2/?pageNum=7&tag=page (2012; downloaded July 11, 2013).

[3] Politico Presidential Debate Transcript, http://www.politico.com/news/stories/1012/82712.html (2012; downloaded July 11, 2013).

Earth. What we need though is a global environment in which it is not just the USA that is the hope of the Earth, but in fact each country is clearly a hope for the Earth. This will require a mix of stabilization, conflict reframing and resolution, and a different vision of the value of global diversity.

The following are some thoughts to be considered in achieving this:

1. While there is value in the effort being made now to contain Iran's nuclear ambitions, this has to be put in perspective. When according to Romney, Pakistan already has 100 nuclear warheads and is critically close to becoming a failed state, it seems that the real effort has to be to stabilize the situation in Pakistan.
2. The situation with China is more complex than has been portrayed by either presidential candidate. China is often aggressive in its interaction with the world on both a business and a military front. Romney already pointed out some instances of business aggressiveness such as piracy, counterfeiting, and currency manipulation. But further:

    - China's human rights records and treatment of workers are in question
    - It has converted huge tracts of productive land into desert, polluted running and still bodies of water, and continues to massively compromise biodiversity.
    - It has reinforced the notion that people exist for State, not only in China, but in Africa too, thereby relegating humans to the stature of assets.

    On the military front:

    - Pakistan has received help in advancing its nuclear weapon technology from China.
    - China occupied Tibet for its strategic position and has reportedly placed missiles aimed at many key cities around the world. It is further reported that there is a massive build up of infrastructure to convert it into a future war zone.[4]

[4] Gurmeet Kanwal, "China preparing Tibet as future war zone," http://www.deccanherald.com/content/165996/china-preparing-tibet-future-war.html (2012; downloaded July 11, 2013).

- China has also claimed Taiwan as its own and continues to make border incursions into Kashmir and Arunachal Pradesh.

3. To a large extent, the conversion of China into the world's manufacturing center has further enabled this aggressiveness. China's becoming the world's manufacturing center has been driven by vital-level desire, in no small measure led by the consumers of the USA itself. This is a short-sighted deal in which USA progressively loses control of its future, and funds China to potentially begin a systematic exploitation of the areas around it to begin with, and other areas of the world in time. Already its reach is firmly established in Africa. The solution is not just to reverse this, though that is part of the solution. In addition, the business journey in general has to be elevated to the mental level so that short-term solutions simply become a thing of the past. When Obama refers to nation building, and especially the need to build the USA, this is what must be done: the basic business-as-usual mentality has to be converted to a business-as-sacred mentality. In itself, this will require investment in many supporting institutions and into the notion of truly democratizing markets.
4. Stabilization in the Indo–Pak–China region will require that the USA choose its strategic partners more carefully in the future. The USA needs to build an exceptional alliance with India, already the largest democracy on the planet and an absolutely needed counter-weight in the region. This alliance should span many different areas: business relationships, educational relationships at many different levels, military partnership, and most importantly, increased cultural and spiritual exchange. Two countries at opposite poles of the world, with originally completely diverse view of the world, cannot but learn from each other and greatly benefit each other in the bargain. This of course has already been going on at some level for decades. But to make this more clear and overt would be a good thing – perhaps more sister cities, many more exchanges, not driven by the need for personal gain, but by the need for building a genuine cultural relationship, and culminating in a freer program

for double citizenship between the two countries. The need for such an approach is further borne out by the current EU Crises. Mere economic union has manifested in the European Sovereign Debt Crises and the possible destabilization of the whole region, and is simply an inadequate foundation on which to build a future.

5. Conflict the world over has to be recognized as the intersection of stagnated fractal journeys. The conflict exists to get each independent nation journey to move to the next stage in its journey. Seen from this point of view, there is a freeing reason, engineered as it were by a higher power, by which nations involved can truly move to the next stage in their own development. In the next section of this chapter, I look at this in more detail as it has manifested in the Indo–Pak–China region. Similar analyses will yield as to how conflict the world over can be thought of and potentially resolved. Peace talks will be accelerated as a result of such analyses and the resulting mindset of all involved.
6. We have to go beyond the economic growth military might formula for world peace that Romney proposes. This is ultimately a no-win scenario and, as Obama points out, takes us back a few decades to the era of the Cold War. What the world needs most is the recognition of the diversity of each country and the reinterpretation of global interaction based on inherent values that each country embodies. True global stability will only be arrived at if there are no doctrines, including the western business doctrine that is being artificially thrust upon many parts of the world. It has to be recognized that each country is unique and has its own trajectory of development that needs to be traversed. Here, the field of fractal system's architecture can play a key part. Each country and/or region has to traverse its own fractal journey. A case in point is the Arab Spring, which really is a movement of the region away from the decades old physical phase it has been locked in, primarily through the device of rebellion. The question is as to how can this region be assisted to move to the vital, and then on to the mental level where it will begin to more securely leverage that which makes

it unique. To support uniqueness, much has to change in the world, including the make up of the UN Security Council.

Fractal system's architects will recognize that the very approaches summarized in the points above – stabilization, conflict resolution and reframing, and a different vision of the value of global diversity – are none other than the physical, vital, and mental orientations, respectively. The implication of this is that if vision of the value of global diversity (the mental orientation) were to become the anchor around which other approaches were organized, this would yield the most progressive foreign policy, more in tune with sustainable development of the world.

Summary

One of the advantages of a presidential election is that it brings to the surface much of what can perhaps be considered as both *good* and *bad* that is happening in the world. The 2012 US presidential election was no exception. In the presidential debates, the underlying struggle between authenticity and playing out a role in office was brought strongly to the forefront.

This of course sheds light on the basic struggle that an Idealist will likely have to experience in trying to keep on top of the current-day realities of governance. But to put this struggle that we witnessed in the debates in context, we first considered the life of a presidential legend, in terms of Harry Truman the 33rd president of the USA. We further considered the broader wisdom inherent in paths that move upwards toward the summit of a peak. Such considerations allow us to weigh current presidential terms and parties in terms of ideals that it is no doubt more difficult to uphold.

Such an analysis allows us not to get too deeply embedded in the compromising practicalities of global leadership and allows us to remain more focused on the right thing to be done. Some of the particulars bought up in the presidential debates and, particularly foreign policy, have been viewed from this perspective.

Reflections on Various Global Political Developments

Development of the EU

"A day will come when all the nations of this continent, without losing their distinct qualities or their glorious individuality, will fuse together in a higher unity and form the European brotherhood. A day will come when the only battlefield will be the marketplace for competing ideas. A day will come when bullets and bombs will be replaced by votes." These words were spoken by Victor Hugo in 1849.

Yet today, in the continuing turmoil precipitated by the EU Sovereign Debt Crises, one must ask what is to be done to move the EU securely forward to the vision voiced by Victor Hugo almost two centuries ago.

Certainly, a problem is that financial investment is a global dynamic that in its current incarnation could not care for anything other than an immediate financial return. If there is a perceived hot spot, then money will flow to it. If there is a perceived problem, then money will flow away from it. But as history tells us, every bubble is followed by a burst. The bubble enriches the few. The burst impoverishes the many. Culture, civilization, brotherhood, and individuality are tossed aside, in the fervor of speculation

Global financial investment, hence, appears to be at odds with the very values espoused by the EU. Here is an extract from the official website of the EU:[1]

[1] Europa.Eu, http://europa.eu/abouteuropa/index_en.htm (2013; downloaded July 11, 2013).

"The EU wishes to promote humanitarian and progressive values, and ensure that mankind is the beneficiary, rather than the victim, of the great global changes that are taking place. People's needs cannot be met simply by market forces or imposed by unilateral action."

But as the continuing riots in Europe, through Greece, Sweden,[2] and most recently Spain,[3] point out, this is not really the case. Humanity is unfortunately the victim of the global changes that are taking place. And yes, people's needs *cannot* be met simply by market forces. But what is to be done about this?

In *Redesigning the Stock Market*,[4] I have suggested an approach to begin to manage the vicissitudes of markets and also suggested revisions to the body of financial theory responsible for these in the first place. While these suggestions will help in disentangling the forces that currently compromise the goal the EU has set for itself, and put into focus the financial aspect responsible for the turmoil, more needs to be done.

The financial complications have been intensified by the EU rushing ahead with the creation of a single European currency, the Euro, which has replaced the local currencies in 12 of its 27 member states. But the upkeep of this currency requires some stringent conditions at the member state level. This includes criteria such as keeping the rate of inflation within a 1.5 percent band of the average inflation, and long-term interest rates within 2 percent variance of the average interest rates, of the three member states with the lowest inflation. Further, national budget deficits must be below 3 percent of GDP, public debt may not exceed 60 percent of GDP, and exchange rates must have remained within the authorized margin of fluctuation for the previous 2 years.

But how are member states to manage this if they do not even have control of the money that flows into and out of their countries?

[2] Bob Taylor, "Swedish riots could represent Europe's future," http://communities.washingtontimes.com/neighborhood/what-world/2013/may/29/swedish-riots-could-represent-europes-future/ (2013; downloaded July 11, 2013).

[3] Daily Mail, "Demonstrators riot in Spain," http://www.dailymail.co.uk/news/article-105333/Demonstrators-riot-Spain.html (2013; downloaded July 11, 2013).

[4] Pravir Malik, *Redesigning the Stock Market: A Fractal Approach* (New Delhi: Sage, 2011).

I am not saying that they should have an absolute and rigid control – that is not even possible. What I do suggest, however, is that the emphasis on money as it is currently defined and understood has to be enhanced so that there is more subtlety and sensitivity inherent in it. But how is that to be done when a single currency replaces many diverse ones that arguably were a better reflection of local ground conditions?

Here a key principle in the formation the EU is at stake. This is the principle of subsidiarity that can be thought of as a key organizing principle of decentralization. The idea is that a matter ought to be handled by the smallest, lowest, or least centralized authority capable of addressing that matter effectively. But the opposite is happening as living standards are slashed because taxes are used to bail out governments, and austerity is forced on local populations by an ever remote governing body.

It is no wonder that David Cameron in his speech earlier this year[5] clearly states that Britain will never be part of the single currency. How can she, when doing so will undermine her very independence and national sovereignty? And that is the question that each of the member states really needs to ask themselves.

Has the development of the EU proceeded so that she can really call herself a Union? Referring to the ubiquitous fractal model, where the first stage is the physical and the status quo tends to be maintained, the second stage is the vital and energy asserts itself often irrationally, and the third stage is the mental where intent resident in the seed expresses itself, that perhaps is the blueprint of all sustainable development, the question is what are the stages that the EU has really traversed? The values of the EU, no doubt inspired by visionaries such as Victor Hugo, suggest the great goal before it. It is clearly not at that mental level yet.

As a politician from a member state has stated, Europe has been able to reconcile its geography and its history. But has it really? The reconciliation is not at the end point that perhaps many feel it is at, but only the starting point. Initial conditions have been put in

[5] David Cameron, "David Cameron's Europe speech in full, "http://www.telegraph.co.uk/news/newsvideo/uk-politics-video/9820375/David-Camerons-Europe-speech-in-full.html (2013; downloaded July 11, 2013).

place—the promise conceptualized, the geography outlined. But now the real journey is to begin. And there are many pitfalls along the way that at any moment may even force it to go back to the drawing board. How can the rich diversity of each of its member states be kept intact, and yet become the bridge to a single union?

The notion of union itself has to be examined. If one thinks of union as the coming together of nations in a common declaration of purpose without achieving that, then yes, that could be a union. But as we know more and more marriages end in annulment. So it is definitely not a sustainable union. This appears to be the model that the EU has adopted in imagining itself to be a union. But by its very definition, it is fraught with instability.

Of necessity it has to move to the next working definition of Union in fractal for progress gradient.

If we think of union as member states sticking it out through thick and thin as per their initial vision to finally arrive at some common and workable approach to manage union in real time, then yes that could be a union. But as many reports indicate, even the ability of the governing body to arrive at that status is in question. One recent article from June 10, 2013, in the *Financial Times*[6] suggests it has ways to go in doing this. And Britain's stance exemplifies this. So, clearly if the EU is to remain a union, it has to move to this definition in the gradient. As a result of this part of the journey, hopefully the diversity inherent in each member state becomes a real difference that is cherished without compromise.

If the second stage is successfully traversed, then there is the real promise that Europe's incredible diversity will become the engine by which unity is achieved. And this means that a new equation will be worked out for investments and finance that replaces our current caricature of the promise, that the laziness is valued equally with the precision, and that equality, fraternity, and liberty in all fields become the cornerstone of progress.

Then perhaps, the vision voiced by Victor Hugo will someday be realized, and the great EU Odyssey fulfilled.

[6] Marcel Fratzscher, "The ECB must open itself up," http://www.ft.com/intl/cms/s/0/7e58a3ea-d1bc-11e2-9336-00144feab7de.html#axzz2YIQFcCUR (2013; downloaded July 11, 2013).

Leadership in Global Finance and Market Thinking

Recent global market events have so easily created a series of negative effects. The two events that I start with are the fed indicating that it is going to reverse quantitative easing (QE;[7] and the Chinese Central Bank similarly allowing interest rates to rise.[8] They are doing so for different reasons, but when layered on top of the already volatile financial situation in the EU,[9] a suggestive picture appears.

Here we have three major centers of global financial activity, each slowing down on injecting cheap money into regional markets. The last few years have seen each of these centers continuing to inject cheap money and suck up junk assets. Doing so has pushed back the examination of what is really happening globally.

But what is it that is really happening. Unfortunately, finance as it is currently configured paints an incomplete picture partly because it has failed effectively to integrate its two sides of behavioral with mainstream finance. As a result, its grand market and portfolio theories are hardly practiced, even though there is a belief that they are, and some ineffective hybrid under the name of established wisdom takes its place.

Established wisdom suggests that the out-of-date companies, industries, and models of business and trading have to be supported at any cost, and that is exactly what has been done. Working people around the world have contributed to the continued bailout of that which arguably should be left to die, with their hard-earned tax dollars. Established wisdom suggests that if large regional centers do not support inefficient banks, industry, and companies, then that is going to

[7] Robin Harding, "Bernanke sees 2014 end for QE3," http://www.ft.com/intl/cms/s/0/17078b02-d905-11e2-84fa-00144feab7de.html#axzz2YIQFcCUR (2013; downloaded July 11, 2013).

[8] Simon Rabinovitch, "PBoC dashes hopes of China liquidity boost," http://www.ft.com/intl/cms/s/0/d244210c-d8ae-11e2-a6cf-00144feab7de.html#axzz2YIQFcCUR (2013; downloaded July 11, 2013).

[9] Martin Sandbu, "Forget the Fed—It's the ECB that should worry investors," http://www.ft.com/intl/cms/s/0/03858014-d993-11e2-98fa-00144feab7de.html#axzz2YIQFcCUR (2013; downloaded July 11, 2013).

have a ripple effect and cause an irreversible weakening in the global economic system. It is not that what has to happen, but because some partial financial model says that this is what will happen, that fear and anxiety kicks in, and then of course it tends to happen. So really, the arrestation of potential QE by the US, China, and possibly the EU, only has its effects because like Pavlov's dog, we have been conditioned to believe that this is the case.

There has been continued lack of insight when it comes to the integration of the sides of finance, which quite simply can be effectively brought together under the aegis of the fractal for progress model that I continue to propose as the ubiquitous model of all sustainable growth. The three stages—physical that reflects the status quo, the vital that reflects assertive and even aggressive growth, the mental that reflects purpose and truer curiosity resident in the seed—suggest psychological or behavioral orientations (as in behavioral finance) that can become the axis around which different mainstream financial models kick-in. Models such as efficient market hypothesis and portfolio theory are relevant only when the underlying psychological orientation is at the mental stage, and different models need to be used prior to that stage. I have suggested a number of alternative models and discussed the integration of the two side of finance in *Redesigning the Stock Market*.[10]

The fact is that the often irrational injection of cheap money over the last few years, following the supposed global financial crises, as already mentioned, has pushed back the examination of what is really happening. And what is really happening is that there has been a continued shift in the democratization of markets as already suggested earlier in the book. Power is inevitably moving away from the elite to the rest of the people, and all the hue and cry about the continued global financial crises is perhaps nothing other than a Pavlovian response or even a Machiavellian play by those who want to maintain outdated monopolistic power invoking the crutch of, as suggested, blinded and partial financial and market models.

Because the bluff has not been called, these defunct financial and market models have successfully been able to cause panic and have

[10] Pravir Malik, *Redesigning the Stock Market*, 2011.

caused governments such as Greece, Italy, Ireland, Iceland, Spain, and Cyprus, to mention some recent ones, to arrest their own rhythm of indigenous development by siphoning development funds through the channels of interest, debt, and other payments, and accepting irrational and curious fiscal conditions that limit ability to respond to real-time societal reactions.

Seems like a short-sighted deal, and it is surely time to wake up. And that is exactly what has been happening. The events of the last few weeks in Brazil and Turkey point again to what is really happening—the inevitable democratization of markets. A million took to the streets in Brazil last week in an outcry against the obvious inequity between layers in society.[11] The continued unrest in Turkey too is a demand for more democracy and prosperity,[12] and only reinforces the movement that began with the Greek rebellions and the Occupy Movement, and continued with the Arab Spring two years ago.

Leaders around the world have to begin to see the forest through the trees. The grip that outdated financial thinking has on governments has to be removed. Central banks have to work to democratize local markets. Leaders have to do more to complete their own fractal journeys. There is an urgent reinterpretation of markets, finance, and leadership itself, which needs to take place. A process of systematic desensitization to the status quo orientation that continues to plague us has to take place and a systematic resensitization as envisioned by Pavlov needs to take place about the possibilities of the ubiquitous fractal journey.

Of course all of this is inevitable. The fractal for progress will ensure it. The only question is does it happen through a lot of reluctant kicking and screaming or will it happen more consciously and easily.

Let us hope that it is the latter.

[11] Joe Leahy, "Brazil: The power of the streets," http://www.ft.com/intl/cms/s/0/5e79204e-da5a-11e2-a237-00144feab7de.html#axzz2YIQFcCUR (2013; downloaded June 6, 2013).

[12] Daniel Dombey, "Erdogan woos Turks with promises of more prosperity," http://www.ft.com/intl/cms/s/0/21fa50e4-d8fb-11e2-a6cf-00144feab7de.html#axzz2YIQFcCUR (2013; downloaded July 11, 2013).

Espionage and Political Development

At some point in the future, it will perhaps be true to say that the individual, a country, and the world will stand as equal powers in the scheme of things. From a fractal perspective, this has to be true since the micro is as equal as the macro, and even, the micro and the macro are meaningful reflections of each other. But what might such a reality mean?

There would be an utter recognition that each of these incredible organizations is a valid and necessary reality endowed by a deep and original creative source that gives it right to be.

The individual will be the result of an eon-long process of the development of consciousness in which it is not the habitual and often meaningless patterns that we see playing themselves out in us but something truly unique and creative that derives its inspiration from a source that we perhaps rarely glimpse now. Such individuals will be naturally in tune with all individuals around them, expressing their unique score in the music of creation. Equally, countries will be seen as organized around a theme, a deep theme, absolutely necessary to the wholeness of the world. And the world will continue to be that incredibly nurturing matrix in whose womb all other developments and compositions are forever taking place.

In such a scenario, there would be no secrets, and even no need for secrets. For individuals are world citizens, belonging to but not bound by unique areas or countries of the world. All may roam around freely and contribute to the development of the world by virtue of who they are, no matter where they are. The questions of espionage and of privacy do not even arise. How can they if for instance the consciousness of another individual, a country, or the world may even be experienced in one's own consciousness as part of oneself.

This is in the future. But what it implies is that there is a journey with that as goal that we are on now. In that journey whatever else may be, one thing is for sure: at no point can the existence of any of the incredible three-fold organizational constructs be compromised to the point of disappearance. Progress of the individual has to continue, as does the progress of the country and the world.

The recent spotlight on US espionage in Europe[13] bought to the surface by the Snowden disclosures, and any individual privacy concerns[14] about activity on the Internet should be considered in light of the larger context of the journey and the ultimate equality of the three-fold powers of individual, country, and world.

Let us begin with boundary conditions derived from some obvious threats to the world from its past. Perhaps the most recent is World War II and the prolonged confrontation between the allied and axis powers. The resolution of this confrontation in favor of the allied powers was critical to continued development of civilization. Had the axis powers won, Hitler's destructive vision would have reigned and the world been set back by centuries.

In such a circumstance, it is understood that whatever needs to be done to protect the sacred institution of the world, even if at a very high cost, is worth it. In such a circumstance, any kind of espionage is perhaps warranted and upholding the individual and even country become secondary in the balance of things. But this is only if the situation is so out of balance that great sacrifice has to be made to ensure the progressive continuance of the world. Similarly, it can be argued that if the institution of country is at stake, or the institution of individual, then similar sacrifice needs to be made by the other two in order to ensure the progressive continuance of the third.

So, the question now is as to is there a similar threat that perhaps any of the three-fold constructs face that may warrant special consideration to uphold it in the scheme of things? It is perhaps true that on a global scale, the three largest known threats we face are those of climate change, terrorism, and the global financial crises. Barring arguments, let us suppose that this is true.

So, if climate change were a threat as great as the allied–axis confrontation, what rights would that give the world over country and individual? Certainly this may be the right to enforce GHG regulation,

[13] Richard McGregor, "For US spies, Europe is both partner and fair game," http://www.ft.com/intl/cms/s/0/20d985f2-e3f7-11e2-91a3-00144feabdc0.html#axzz2YIQFcCUR (2013; downloaded July 11, 2013).

[14] Geoff Dyer, "US intelligence denies 'unilateral' internet data collection," http://www.ft.com/intl/cms/s/0/87532b6a-d085-11e2-a050-00144feab7de.html#axzz2YIQFcCUR (2013; downloaded July 11, 2013).

the right to ensure that the range of valuable ecosystem services are not compromised, the right to police countries whose business and foreign policy may compromise sustainable development, leading to the right to put in place a framework by which decisions made, at any scale, do not exasperate the problem of climate change. Assuming terrorism today is as great a threat as the allied–axis confrontation, what rights would that give the world over country and individual? In such a case, the Five Eyes agreement[15] among the USA, the UK, Canada, New Zealand, and Australia is even not enough and should be assertively expanded to include more countries and even means. Further, surveillance of individuals focused on terrorist threats would also have more credibility. Assuming the global financial crisis is as great a threat as the allied–axis confrontation then forced regulation on a larger scale, than even the 1933 Glass-Steagall Act[16] following the Great Depression of 1929 would also be warranted.

But these are all boundary conditions and should kick in only if we have reached a situation as desperate as when Hitler threatened to successfully impose a standard to the meaning of the *perfect* individual and race. Similarly, it is easy for the powerful to impose their belief and consequence on innocent others, and in the three-fold developing scheme of things unless it is clear that the situation has become allied–axis like, it is ideally the balance of the three-fold anchor points of individual, country, and world that would arbitrate the development of things, whether this be the management of climate change, terrorism, or the global financial crises. But for this to be the political structure of the world will have to change.

This may mean that it is not just the *rich* and *elite* nations, by our current definitions of rich and elite that arbitrate the development of the world. The meaning of wealth will need to expand to become multidimensional so that even *poorer* nations, be they the Democratic Republic of the Congo, Mozambique, or Senegal, are recognized for their richness and given a seat at the table. This may mean that all individuals, not just those with a Harvard or Imperial College degree,

[15] Wikipedia, "UKUSA Agreement," http://en.wikipedia.org/wiki/UKUSA_Agreement (2013b; downloaded July 11, 2013).
[16] Wikipedia, "Glass-Steagall Act," http://en.wikipedia.org/wiki/Glass%E2%80%93 Steagall_Act (2013c; downloaded July 11, 2013).

are given the right to work and to create a proud and meaningful existence for themselves regardless of the socioeconomic strata they may originate from. This may mean that work itself is not constructed to enrich just the few established paths of development, but expands out to express all the deep, creative possibility inherent in the human soul. This may mean that the very symbol of wealth be expanded beyond its current equivalence to cash, to include a range of different currencies—be it joy, peace, silence, beauty, knowledge, or industry.

But our handling of the underlying condition of which espionage is a symptom, is going to be a function of the consciousness with which we approach it. From a fractal system's architecture perspective, this consciousness is a function of the stage of development the journey is in. Hence, if it is in the physical state, there will be a drive to maintain the status quo, just as the seed will continue as a seed forever unless external conditions change it. Reality will be perceived as what the eye can see, and hence the problems of climate change, terrorism, and financial crises will continue to be handled independently, and the rationale for elaborate espionage programs, be they on one's own citizens or on other countries of the world, will continue forcefully in their own right, rather than espionage being seen as a symptom of a deeper condition, that ultimately is in process of evolving. In such a scenario, Snowden will be brought to justice for a problem much larger than what he was implicated in, Morales' and other president's flights will continue to be diverted on the order of a threatened nation,[17] and the world will continue as a very reactive place.

If it is the vital state, there will be a drive toward experimentation and even assertive experimentation. Not all experiments are equal nor fruitful, but it could be that released from the shadow of yesteryear thinking some experiments may truly set a path toward the mental stage. Such possibilities may include terrorism being viewed as a side effect of the global financial crises. Financial crises itself could perhaps be thought of as being the condition in which development funds circle only among a favored elite, and its resolution, as causing

[17] Andres Schipani, "Brazil condemns Europe for Bolivian aircraft diversion," http://www.ft.com/intl/cms/s/0/c97c044e-e3db-11e2-91a3-00144feabdc0.html#axzz2YIQFcCUR (2013; downloaded July 11, 2013).

it to flow wherever it is truly needed, so that even the Sierra Leones and the Sudans of the world receive funds to develop along lines that are consistent with the deep theme that animates them. If the poorest nations of the world develop, then the incentive for disenfranchised youth to join terrorist organizations is minimized, and terrorism itself diminishes in possibility. Further, if funds are distributed to a variety of groups to pursue development along their own lines of possibility, then the problem of replicating the American Dream in China will not be repeated in every country that tastes progress, and the slowdown in exaggerations of consumer conspicuousness will halt the engines of climate change, as other developmental paradigms are pursued instead.

In this scenario, espionage also becomes something different as the threat of targeting symbols, such as the World Trade Center, loses meaning. It is not then espionage driven by the instinct for survival, which is perhaps what is driving the USA's supposed ramp up in this area, but espionage to learn what other possibilities beyond one's own narrow view of world development exist. Already a spin-off of this, alluded to as the *Snowden effect* by Markus Kerber, chief executive of Federation of German Industries, is one in which cyber security creates a huge number of jobs, enhances the possibilities for growth, and helps create a more digital industry model in the EU.[18]

In the mental stage, ideas and purpose resident in the seed come to the forefront and begin to organize events. This is perhaps where the political structure of the world changes along the lines already outlined, and we are more securely propelled to that inevitable reality where individual, country, and world stand as fully free and equal powers. As a continuation of this scenario, espionage perhaps becomes that willed glimpse by which a part of oneself is revealed in its truer beauty and abundance and causes the uniting power of love to flow more freely than ever before.

[18] Markus Kerber, "Europe should turn itself into a cyber war fortress," http://www.ft.com/intl/cms/s/0/71a9eb00-e3d1-11e2-91a3-00144feabdc0.html#axzz2YIQFcCUR (2013; downloaded July 11, 2013).

Multipolarity Is the Answer

In her address to the Senate Foreign Relations Committee on March 1, 2011, Secretary of State Hillary Clinton stated: "We are in a competition for influence with China; let's put aside the moral, humanitarian, do-good side of what we believe in, and let's just talk straight realpolitik."[19] This statement gets to the crux of our current paradigm on international relations where the world playing field is led by might, and to maintain it and its balance is the primary consideration in a nation's foreign policy. While there is obviously truth to this, that truth is a function of where we are at in the global fractal journey for development. While we currently stand more in the vital level, the growing acuteness of our global problems signals that the vital level is hitting against its boundaries, and that we are potentially at the transition to a relatively more fruitful mental phase.

Power does not belong to the few nor to the mighty. It belongs to all. But each and every one must realize this and act as if they each are empowered ambassadors of the world. Vital consciousness at the individual level has to transition to a truer mental consciousness. The continuing spate of revolution in North Africa and the Middle East perhaps puts this dynamic into focus, as citizens seek to seize back the power that truly always belonged to them. This pattern of rebellion must generalize itself on a much deeper and larger scale and become a driver of accelerating the transition from the vital to the mental.

The current bases of global power, whether American, or in Clinton's concern, Chinese, has as its heart the dysfunctional and short-sighted contract that every citizen of the world has implicitly agreed to—that their happiness and well-being will be determined by the acquisition of often meaningless product, for which they will pay a self-serving third party a sum of money that in reality does not begin to cover the costs of creating the product. In the bargain each will inadvertently pay for the product with a price much higher than they have imagined. For assuming that acquisition of meaningless

[19] Daniel Dombey, "US struggling to hold role as global leader Clinton says," http://www.ft.com/intl/cms/s/0/5ff5669c-4508-11e0-80e7-00144feab49a.html#axzz2YIQFcCUR (2011; downloaded July 11, 2013).

product is the aim of existence, implies that the models, engines, and supply chains that enable this transaction will be upheld and supported by each and all, one way or another regardless of what it takes. This practice has been reinforced by any nation in power over the last few centuries. But its time is fast coming to an end.

This global economic and social model is seriously flawed, starting with the issuance and power over currency by a few elite institutions at one end, and ending with the continued destruction of environment and society at the other. No wonder, Ban Ki-moon, the Secretary General to the UN, in his address to the World Economic Forum on Jan 28, 2011, has called for a new world economic model.[20]

The current economic model has implicitly propped up the flawed model of scarce polarity. The rich grow richer at the expense of the poor and this is true regardless of scale of observation. The world for the last few decades has been decidedly unipolar, with the USA being the reference of all *meaningful* dynamics, and only now is transitioning to possible bipolarity with China in the ascendant,[21] as per past definitions of power. But one way or another, all past definitions have to end, and that is what transitioning from the vital to the mental means. Clinton's recommendation to put aside the moral, humanitarian, do-good side, and practice realpolitik instead is the quintessential summary of the vital level, and quite frankly of all that has to disappear, rather than be reinforced through the bipolar world we are fast entering into. Bipolarity means that we just accelerate the rat race we have been a part of. So does tri-polarity or quadri-polarity, for that matter. We do not want to simply practice a foolishness on larger and larger scale. Demand then fast outpaces supply and in the accelerating battle for scarcer resources, the very basis of the world economic and social order comes undone, blow by painful blow. This is not a scenario worth supporting.

[20] Ban Ki-moon, "Secretary-General's remarks to the World Economic Forum Session on Redefining Sustainable Development," http://www.un.org/sg/statements/?nid=5056 (2011; downloaded July 11, 2013).

[21] James Kynge, "The China Syndrome," http://www.ft.com/intl/cms/s/0/2ab8c5a8-45e1-11e0-acd8-00144feab49a.html#axzz2YIQFcCUR (2011; downloaded July 11, 2013).

Instead, people all over the world have to continue to rise, continue to take back that power, and establish true multipolarity as the bases of the world economic and social model. While national currencies may remain, locally issued currency, down to the smallest scale has to become reality. Self-organization and increasing self-reliance at the community level has to become the bases of a world society and economy. People have to exercise their power to not allow destructive resource and market exploitation in the areas and regions they live in. This means increasingly saying *no* to the established and ascendant poles and to cronies that support them that may wish to continue to reinforce their short-sighted ways of being on the world. If the transaction of buying meaningless and ill-conceived product ends, established money power gets destabilized.

Clinton would be much better advised, therefore, to do what it takes to end the rat race, by changing the current means and very definition of establishing global power. Then, there will not be a Chinese threat to worry about.

Multipolarity practiced at every scale is the answer.

Summary

Developmental problems such as being experienced by the EU today can also be seen as the stagnation of a fractal journey, where the notion of Union has itself to evolve to become more complete and holistic. The pursuit of Ideals of union such as voiced by Victor Hugo in the 19th century have to be examined more carefully and forces disentangled and understood more completely for such union to indeed take place. In particular is the force of global finance, a way of thinking that has woven itself so intricately with everything else that it is hardly recognized that in its current incarnation, it is contrary to the notion of true union because it compromises the true founts of stability, that of diversity. Symptoms have to be separated from their causes, and the focus on espionage and its possible destabilizing effects put in balance in light of the underlying political development that needs to occur.